Quizlet 사용법

스마트폰, 태블릿, 컴퓨터에서 재미있고 효과적인 어휘 공
Flash Card와 Spell Check, 게임 등의 서비스를 제공하며, 미국에서는 이미 수요 교육 수단으로
자리잡은 학습 시스템

01 Quizlet 사용방법

Step 1. 네이버 QR 인식기 또는 별도의 QR 인식기를 실행시켜
페이지 상단의 QR코드를 인식합니다.

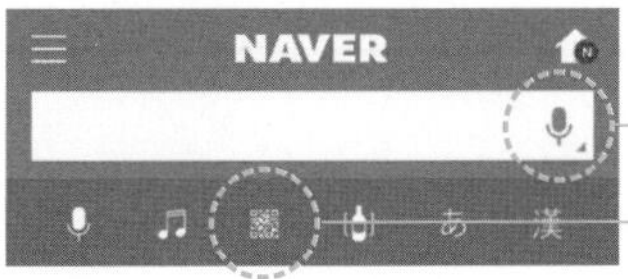

ⓐ 네이버 앱에서 마이크 아이콘 클릭합니다.
ⓑ QR 코드 인식기를 클릭합니다.

Step 2. 원하는 학습 일차를 선택합니다.

Step 3. 원하는 어휘의 MP3 음원을 선택하여 듣습니다.

02 Quizlet의 다양한 학습기능

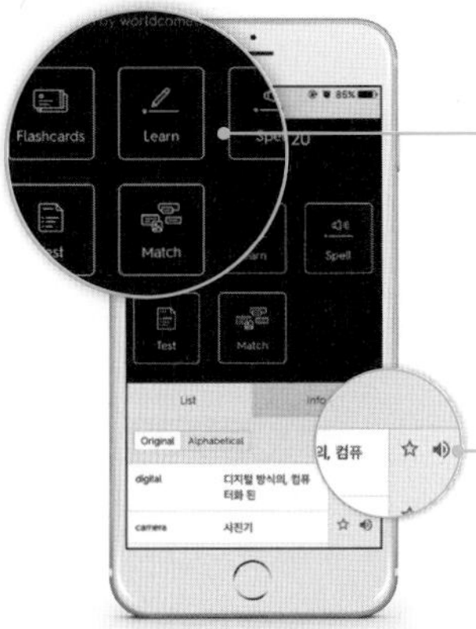

STUDY와 PLAY를 통해 다양한 방식으로
재밌게 학습할 수 있습니다.

- STUDY : Flashcard, Learn, Spell, Test
- PLAY : Match

단어 혹은 스피커 버튼을 누르면
음성을 들을 수 있습니다.

* Google Play에서 Quizlet 어플리케이션 다운로드 및 이용이 가능합니다.

QR 코드 사용법

보다 쉽고 간편하게 접근할 수 있는 학습 방법!
QR코드 인식을 통한 Word Max 6단계 시리즈 음원 바로 듣고 학습하기

01 네이버 앱을 통해 QR코드 사용하기

Step 1. 네이버 QR 인식기 또는 별도의 QR 인식기를 실행시킵니다.

Step 2. 내지의 QR 코드를 인식합니다.

Step 3. MP3 음원이 유튜브를 통해 다운로드 없이 이용 가능합니다.

WORD MAX 5 5300

WorldCom Edu

WORD MAX 5300 5

초판	2016년 10월 31일
지은이	김 지 훈, 김 채 원
영문검수	Kenneth Drenen
책임편집	신 은 진
편집팀	월드컴 에듀 편집팀
펴낸이	임 병 업
디자인	임 예 슬, 김 지 현, 차 지 원
펴낸곳	(주)월드컴 에듀
등록	2016년 10월 31일
주소	서울시 강남구 남부순환로 2706, 5층 (도곡동, 차우빌딩)
전화	02)3273-4300 (대표)
팩스	02)3273-4303
홈페이지	www.wcbooks.co.kr
이메일	wc4300@wcbooks.co.kr

WORD MAX 5300 여는 글

언어를 배울 때 어휘 학습은 모든 언어 학습자가 가장 먼저 시작하는 분야이면서 동시에 가장 숙달하기 어려운 분야입니다. 이는 문법이나 읽기, 듣기와는 다른 어휘 학습의 독특한 측면이며 다른 학습 방식이 필요한 이유이기도 합니다. 수능을 비롯한 최근의 영어 시험 경향은 결국 어휘사용능력이 전반적인 문제 해결의 핵심 요소가 되고 있습니다.
WORD MAX 5300은 최신 경향에 맞추어 가장 효율적인 어휘 학습 방식을 제공하고자 합니다.

WORD MAX 5300시리즈는 과학적인 방법으로 최대의 효과를 얻을 수 있도록 어휘를 엄선했습니다.

WORD MAX 5300시리즈는 총 6권의 수준별 구성으로 최신 출제 경향과 엄선된 예문 및 다양하고 풍부한 리뷰 테스트를 통해 어휘 활용 능력을 최대화 할 수 있도록 구성했습니다.
최근 12년의 수능 및 각종 시험 기출 문제와 교과서 자료를 중심으로 자체 데이터베이스를 통해 학습 대상 어휘를 엄선했습니다. 특히 기출 빈도와 출제 예상도를 고려하여 선정한 어휘들은 효율적인 어휘 학습을 도와 줄 것입니다.

단계별로 세분화되고 실용성 있는 어휘 학습 환경을 제공합니다.

Level 1~3은 핵심적인 어휘를 풍부한 예문과 리뷰 테스트를 통해 예비중학 과정부터 중등 내신 대비까지 학생들의 기본적 영어 능력 향상에 도움이 되도록 구성했습니다.
Level 4~6은 최근 12년간의 수학능력시험, 모의고사, 학력평가의 기출문제를 토대로 어휘를 선정하였습니다. 더불어 각 어휘의 출제 맥락을 연구하고 수준별 분류 및 보정과정을 통해 단순 어휘 학습을 넘어 전반적인 영어 활용 능력을 향상 시킬 수 있게 구성했습니다.

다양한 어휘 활용 연습 기회를 제공하여 전반적인 영어 실력의 향상을 목표로 합니다.

WORD MAX 5300시리즈는 일일 테스트를 비롯한 Review Test의 총 8개 섹션의 다양한 테스트를 통해 학습한 어휘를 완전히 이해하고 활용할 수 있도록 했습니다. 쓰임에 따라 다양한 뜻을 가진 어휘들과 이에 대한 실용성 높은 예문들은 영어 사용 능력 향상에 확실한 도움이 될 것입니다.

어휘 학습 방법에 대한 이견은 많지만 어휘 학습 대상 선정의 중요성에 대해서는 연구자와 일선 교육자 모두 공감하고 있습니다. WORD MAX 5300시리즈를 충실히 학습한다면 어휘를 학습하는 재미 뿐만 아니라 영어 전반에서 실력 향상을 성취 할 수 있을 것이라 자부합니다.

WORD MAX 5300시리즈와 함께 어휘 학습에 최고의 결과를 얻을 수 있기를 기원합니다.

- 월드컴 에듀 편집팀 일동

구성 및 활용

1 단계별 30일 구성의 계획적 어휘 학습!

'단어 → 어구 → 예문' 순으로 자연스럽게 확장되는 학습을 통해 어휘력을 향상합니다.

하루 30개
단계별 30일 구성

유의어, 반의어, 연관 단어 등의
제시를 통해 어휘력을 확장합니다.

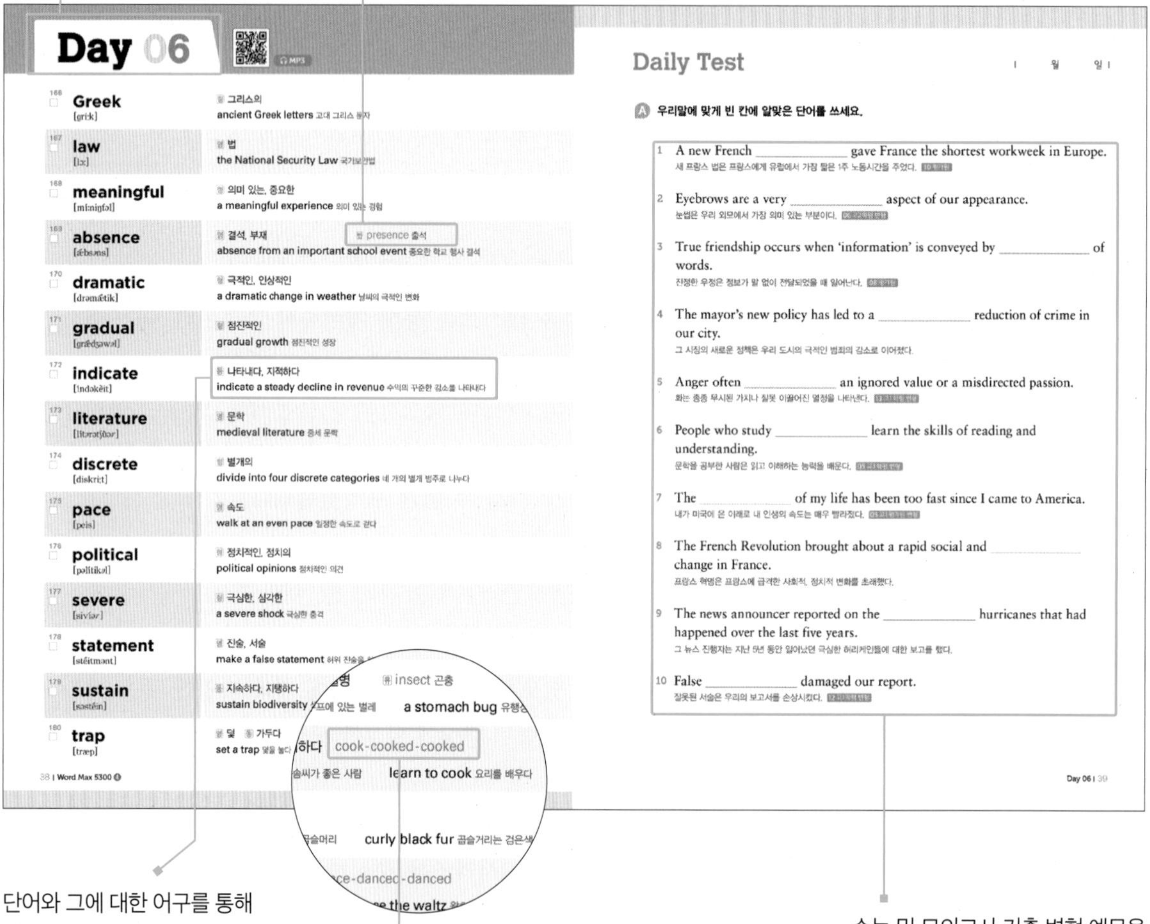

단어와 그에 대한 어구를 통해
다양한 어휘 학습을 가능하게 합니다.

동사의 3단 변화형과 비교형 제시를 통해
시제별 동사 형태를 연습합니다.

수능 및 모의고사 기출 변형 예문을
통해 표제어를 응용 학습합니다.

2 Review Test 7가지 유형으로 학습 점검하기!

2일마다 학습한 어휘를 다양한 유형의 문제를 통해 반복 학습합니다.

한영 빈칸 채우기
우리말 해석에 따라 어구를 완성합니다.

영한 빈칸 채우기
영어 문장에 알맞은 단어를 찾아 빈 칸에 씁니다.

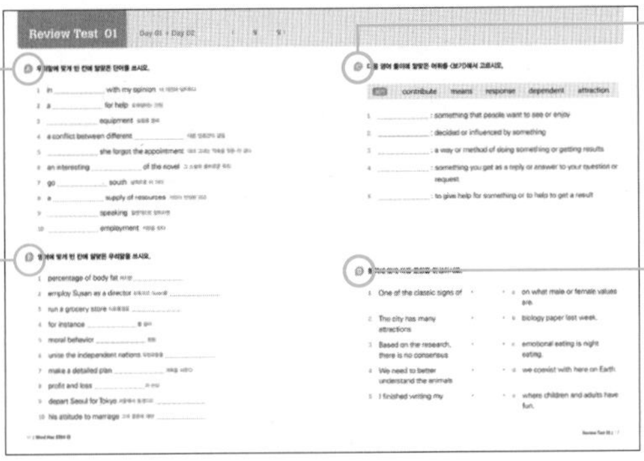

영영 풀이
보기에서 영영 풀이에 해당하는 단어를 찾아봅니다.

문장 완성
문맥상 알맞은 문장끼리 연결하여 완성된 문장을 학습합니다.

영영 어휘활용
문장에서 문맥상 알맞은 단어를 선택합니다.

문장 완성
우리말에 따라 보기에서 알맞은 단어를 골라 문장을 완성합니다.

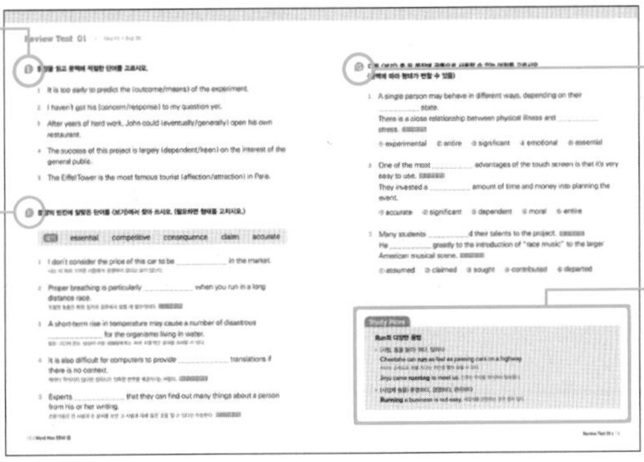

공통 어휘 찾기
두 문장에 공통으로 들어가는 다양한 형태의 어휘를 찾아봅니다.

Study More
표제어에 대한 확장된 개념을 제시함으로써 다양한 관점에서 어휘력을 향상 시킬 수 있습니다.

3 Work Book

워크북을 활용하여 단어의 철자와 뜻을 한번 더 반복 학습합니다.

쓰기 노트

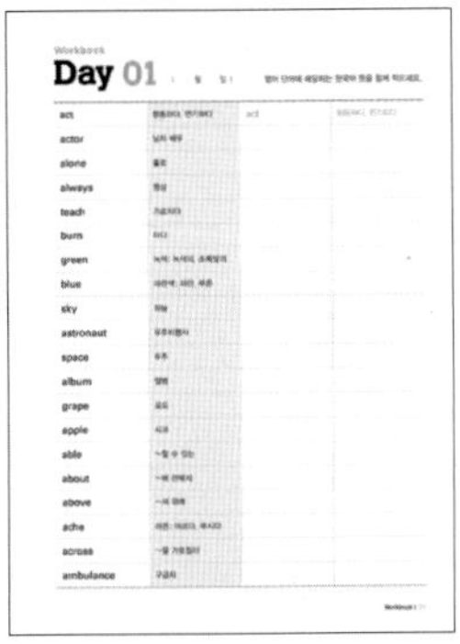

일일 테스트

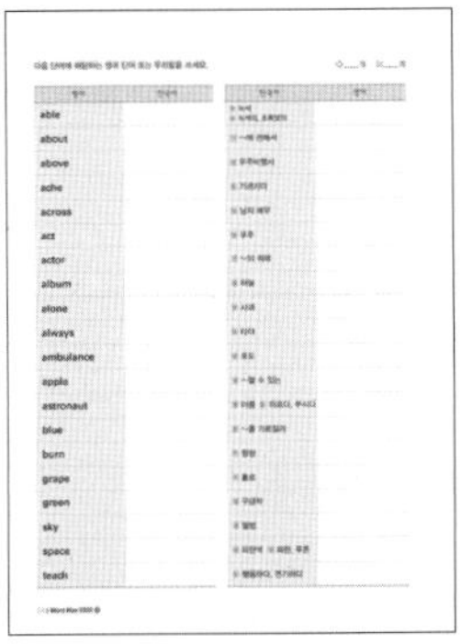

목차

★ 책 속의 책 Workbook 제공

WORD MAX 5 5300

Day 01

MP3

001 **consumption** [kənsʌ́mpʃən]
명 소비(량)
annual consumption of water 연간 물 소비량

002 **experienced** [ikspí(:)əriənst]
형 경력이 있는, 능숙한
recruit experienced staff 경력이 있는 직원들을 모집하다

003 **immediate** [imí:diət]
형 즉각적인, 직접적인, 당면한, 가장 가까운
an immediate response 즉각적 반응

004 **remains** [rimeinz]
명 유적, 유해
the remains of ancient Rome 고대 로마의 유적

005 **majority** [mədʒɔ́(:)rəti]
명 대다수, 과반수 형 다수의, 과반수의
the majority of foreign athletes 외국 운동선수의 대다수

006 **previous** [prí:viəs]
형 이전의, 앞선
discover a previous record 이전 기록을 발견하다

007 **alternative** [ɔ:ltə́:rnətiv]
명 대안 형 대체의
develop new alternative energy 새로운 대체 에너지를 개발하다

008 **definition** [dèfəníʃən]
명 정의
the definition of a planet 행성에 대한 정의

009 **determined** [ditə́:rmind]
형 단호한, 결심한
her determined resolution 그녀의 단호한 결심

010 **annual** [ǽnjuəl]
형 연간의
an annual report about natural disasters 자연 재해에 관한 연간 보고서

011 **context** [kántekst]
명 문맥, 맥락, 전후 사정
in context 문맥상으로

012 **shift** [ʃift]
동 이동하다, (견해, 태도 등을)바꾸다 명 이동
shift from LA to Jeju LA에서 제주도로 이동하다

013 **contrary** [kántreri]
형 반대되는
contrary to her expectation 그녀의 기대와는 반대로

014 **evolution** [èvəlú:ʃən]
명 진화
the theory of evolution 진화론

015 **besides** [bisáidz]
부 ~외에도, 게다가
He can speak English besides French. 그는 영어 외에도 불어를 말 할 수 있다.

Daily Test

| 월 일 |

A 우리말에 맞게 빈 칸에 알맞은 단어를 쓰세요.

1 In mordern world, people expect ______________ results and satisfation.
현대에는 사람들이 즉각적인 결과와 만족을 예상한다. 2010 수능 변형

2 Fossils are the ______________ or imprints of dead plants and animals.
화석들은 죽은 식물과 동물의 유해 또는 자국이다.

3 The vast ______________ of people spend their entire lives close to home.
대다수의 사람들은 자신들의 온 생애를 집 가까이에서 보낸다. 09 고1학평 변형

4 In the face of rising oil prices and few energy ______________, consumers are left powerless.
유가의 상승과 그에 대한 대체 에너지가 없는 상황 앞에서, 소비자들은 무기력하게 남겨진다.

5 Scientists argued for days about the ______________ of a planet.
과학자들은 며칠 동안 행성의 정의에 대해서 토론했다.

6 The ______________ young boy kept singing and singing.
단단히 결심한 어린 소년은 계속해서 노래하고 또 노래했다. 15 고3학평 변형

7 The US has an ______________ award ceremony, the Vendy Awards, for the best sidewalk chefs.
미국은 매년 최고의 길거리 요리사를 위한 Vendy Awards라는 시상식을 개최한다. 13 고3평가원 변형

8 When you read a new word in ______________, there is a very good chance that you will be able to guess its meaning.
당신이 문맥에서 새로운 단어를 읽을 때, 그 단어의 의미를 추측 할 수 있는 매우 좋은 기회가 있다. 07 고1학평 변형

9 As the continental plates began to ______________, Pangaea broke into seven continents.
대륙판이 움직이기 시작하면서, Pangaea는 7개의 대륙으로 조각나기 시작했다.

10 Through ______________, animals and plants have been able to adapt to the environment.
진화를 통해서, 동물과 식물들은 환경에 적응할 수 있게 되었다. 09 고2평가원 변형

Day 01

MP3

016 **junk** [dʒʌŋk]
명 쓰레기, 쓸모없는 물건
get rid of junk 쓰레기를 제거하다　junk food 인스턴트 음식, 정크푸드

017 **client** [kláiənt]
명 의뢰인, 고객
protect their client 그들의 의뢰인을 보호하다

018 **device** [diváis]
명 장치, 기기
a safety device 안전 장치

019 **vast** [væst]
형 광대한, 방대한
a vast area of rainforest 방대한 열대우림 지역

020 **numerous** [njúːmərəs]
형 수많은
numerous popular songs 수많은 인기 있는 노래들

021 **ensure** [inʃúər]
동 보장하다, 반드시 ~하게 하다, 확보하다
ensure happiness in your life 당신의 인생에 행복을 보장하다

022 **monitor** [mánitər]
동 감시하다, 관찰하다　유 observe 감시하다
monitor his every movement 그의 일거수 일투족을 감시하다

023 **intense** [inténs]
형 격렬한, 극심한
cause intense pain 격렬한 고통을 야기하다

024 **fellow** [félou]
명 동료　유 colleague 동료, companion 동료, 동반자
a good fellow 좋은 동료　fellow entrepreneurs 동료 기업가들

025 **agricultural** [æ̀grəkʌ́ltʃərəl]
형 농업의, 농사의
agricultural implements 농기구

026 **massive** [mǽsiv]
형 엄청난, 거대한, 극심한　유 huge 거대한, 막대한
massive earthquakes 엄청난 지진　a massive sandstorm 극심한 황사

027 **interact** [ìntərǽkt]
동 소통하다, 상호작용하다
interact well with friends 친구들과 소통을 잘 하다

028 **occasionally** [əkéiʒənəli]
부 가끔
get up early occasionally 가끔 일찍 일어나다

029 **primitive** [prímitiv]
형 원시의, 초기의
the most primitive form of art 가장 원시적인 형태의 예술

030 **vocabulary** [voukǽbjəlèri]
명 어휘, 용어
extensive vocabulary 풍부한 어휘

Daily Test

| 월 일 |

A 우리말에 맞게 빈 칸에 알맞은 단어를 쓰세요.

1 I scheduled a meeting with a ______________ for Saturday 2 P.M.
나는 토요일 오후 2시에 고객과 미팅 일정을 잡았다. 07 고3평가원 변형

2 Magnets are critical in many electronic ______________.
자석은 많은 전자 기기에서 대단히 중요하다.

3 There are ______________ deserts in the Arab World, and in parts of those deserts nomads live.
아랍 세계에는 방대한 사막들이 있고 그 사막들 곳곳에서 유목민들이 살고 있다. 13 고3학평 변형

4 The streets of New York are home to ______________ trucks and vans, all selling food.
뉴욕의 거리들은 음식을 파는 수많은 트럭과 밴들의 터전이다. 13 고3평가원 변형

5 Do you want to ______________ you are recruiting the right people for your company?
당신은 회사를 위해서 적합한 사람을 채용하고 있는지 확실히 하고 싶습니까? 09 고2평가원 변형

6 Researchers ______________ students taking part in a program to improve their skills at studying.
연구원들은 그들의 학업 능력을 향상시키기 위해 프로그램에 참여한 학생들을 관찰했다. 14 고3학평 변형

7 The ______________ products picked up from Hawaiian farms in the morning are on dinner tables in Californian homes by evening.
아침에 하와이 농장에서 공수된 농산품들은 밤에는 캘리포니아 가정의 저녁 식사 위에 오른다. 13 고3평가원 변형

8 Good people are ______________ able to do bad things, and bad people can sometimes behave like angels.
선한 사람들은 때때로 나쁜 짓을 할 수 있고 나쁜 사람들은 때때로 천사같이 행동할 수 있다. 14 고3학평 변형

9 Unlike the modern society, the ______________ society had less specialized knowledge to transmit.
현대 사회와 달리 원시 사회는 전달할 전문 지식이 더 적었다. 2011 수능 변형

10 If students read various books, they will be able to build up their ______________.
만약 학생들이 다양한 책을 읽는다면, 그들은 풍부한 어휘를 기를 수 있게 될 것이다.

Day 02

MP3

031 **account for** [əkáunt fər]
동 차지하다, 설명하다
account for a quarter 4분의 1을 차지하다

032 **capable** [kéipəbl]
형 유능한, ~할 수 있는
a capable engineer 유능한 기술자

033 **influence** [ínfluəns]
명 영향 동 영향을 미치다
have a strong influence on adolescents 청소년에게 강한 영향을 미치다

034 **domestic** [dəméstik]
형 국내의, 가정 내의
domestic spending 국내 소비

035 **trend** [trend]
명 추세, 경향
recent social trend 최근의 사회적 추세

036 **council** [káunsəl]
명 의회, 이사회, 협의회
UN Security Council UN 안전 보장 이사회

037 **definitely** [défənitli]
부 분명히, 틀림없이
definitely remember 분명히 기억하다

038 **endangered** [indéindʒərd]
형 멸종 위기에 처한, 위험에 처한
protect endangered animals 멸종 위기에 처한 동물을 보호하다

039 **fiber** [fáibər]
명 섬유(질)
carbon fiber 탄소 섬유 high in fiber 섬유질이 풍부한

040 **isolated** [áisəlèitid]
형 고립된, 외딴, 격리된 동 isolate 격리하다, 고립시키다
an isolated island 고립된 섬

041 **mere** [miər]
형 단순한, (한낱) ~에 불과한
mere flattery 단순한 아부 a mere assumption 단순한 가정

042 **density** [dénsəti]
명 밀도, 농도 형 dense 빽빽한, 밀집한, 밀도가 높은
the population density in Paris 파리의 인구 밀도

043 **regard** [rigá:rd]
동 ~으로 여기다, 간주하다 명 관심, 고려, 존경
regard herself as a princess 그녀 스스로 공주처럼 여기다

044 **burden** [bə́:rdən]
명 짐, 부담
burden to society 사회의 부담

045 **ecosystem** [ékousìstəm]
명 생태계
destroy the ecosystem 생태계를 파괴하다

Daily Test

| 월 일 |

A 우리말에 맞게 빈 칸에 알맞은 단어를 쓰세요.

1 The currents in the world's major oceans have a great ______________ on climate and marine life.
세계 주요 해양들의 해류는 우리의 기후와 해양 생활에 있어 많은 영향을 미친다.

2 The most common measure of the value of production is Gross ______________ Product (GDP).
가장 일반적인 생산의 가치 측정은 국내 총 소득(GDP)이다. 15 고2학평 변형

3 Some scientists say that if global warming ______________ continue, we will see stronger hurricanes and typhoons.
일부 과학자들은 만약 지구 온난화의 추세가 계속 된다면, 우리는 더 강한 허리케인과 태풍을 볼 것이라고 한다.

4 The city ______________ passed a bill that bans charity groups from providing food to homeless people in downtown parks.
시의회는 자선 단체가 시내 공원에 있는 노숙자들에게 음식을 제공하는 것을 금지하는 법안을 통과시켰다. 08 고3학평 변형

5 Mathematics ______________ influenced Renaissance arts.
수학은 명백하게 르네상스 예술에 영향을 주었다. 2005 수능 변형

6 If you are ______________ in your private life, your success will not last long.
만약 당신이 당신의 사생활 속에 고립된다면, 당신의 성공은 그리 오래가지 못할 것이다. 09 고3평가원 변형

7 Many disciplines are better learned by entering into the doing than by ______________ abstract study.
많은 학과목이 단순한 추상적 학습보다는 실제로 행동에 옮김으로써 더 잘 학습된다. 10 고3평가원 변형

8 Salt water has a higher ______________ than fresh water.
소금물은 맑은 물보다 농도가 더 높다.

9 If we ______________ animal welfare as the most important thing, we should start to ban all sports in which animals are treated cruelly.
만약 우리가 동물 복지를 가장 중요한 것으로 여긴다면, 우리는 동물들이 잔인하게 다루어지는 모든 운동 경기들을 금지하기 시작해야 한다. 06 고1학평 변형

10 The role of humans in today's ______________ differs from that of early human primitive society.
오늘 날의 생태계에서 인간의 역할은 초기 인간 원시사회 때와는 다르다. 13 고1학평 변형

Day 02

MP3

046 motivation [mòutəvéiʃən]
명 자극, 유도, 동기(부여)
prime motivation 주된 동기 the proper motivation 적절한 동기부여

047 executive [igzékjətiv]
명 (기업, 조직의) 경영 간부(이사, 중역) 형 경영의, 운영의
an executive in a computer company 컴퓨터 회사에 대표로 있다

048 philosophy [filásəfi]
명 철학, 인생관
grant a degree in philosophy 철학 학위를 수여하다

049 strict [strikt]
형 엄격한, 엄밀한
stick to a strict diet 엄격한 식단을 고수하다

050 initial [iníʃəl]
형 처음의, 초기의 명 첫글자, 머리글자
the initial symptoms of flu 감기의 초기 증상 an initial fee 입회비

051 observation [àbzə:rvéiʃən]
명 관찰, 관측
his powers of scientific observation 그의 과학적 관찰력

052 permanent [pə́:rmənənt]
형 영구적인, 종신의 유 perpetual 영속하는, 영구의
make a permanent plan 영구적인 계획을 만들다

053 solid [sálid]
명 고체 형 고체의, 단단한, 튼튼한, 건실한
liquids and solids 액체와 고체 solid partnership 탄탄한 동반자 관계

054 civilization [sìvəlizéiʃən]
명 문명, 문명사회
the civilization of ancient Greece 고대 그리스 문명

055 distinct [distíŋkt]
형 뚜렷한, 분명한, 별개의 유 noticeable 눈에 띄는, 현저한
four distinct seasons 뚜렷한 사계절

056 distribution [dìstrəbjú:ʃən]
명 분배, 분포, 배급
the distribution of planets 행성의 분포

057 core [kɔ:r]
명 핵심, 핵 형 핵심적인, 가장중요한
the core of the argument 주장의 핵심

058 protein [próuti:n]
명 단백질
essential protein 필수 단백질 high in protein 단백질이 풍부한

059 refrigerator [rifrídʒərèitər]
명 냉장고 유 fridge (줄임말) 냉장고
purchase a new refrigerator 새 냉장고를 구매하다

060 relevant [réləvənt]
형 관련 있는 유 related 관계가 있는
a relevant question 관련 있는 질문

Daily Test

| 월 일 |

Ⓐ 우리말에 맞게 빈 칸에 알맞은 단어를 쓰세요.

1 The book gave me the confidence, determination and _______________ to succeed.
그 책은 내게 자신감과 단호함, 그리고 성공하고자 하는 동기를 주었다. 11 고3 평가원 변형

2 Matthew was dedicated to the prosperity of the nation in terms of politics and _______________.
Matthew는 정치와 철학적인 측면에서 국가 발전에 헌신했다. 09 고3 평가원 변형

3 Some reptiles direct their _______________ attack at the head of their prey.
일부 파충류는 먹이를 처음 공격 할 때 그들의 머리를 겨냥한다. 13 고2 학평 변형

4 We learned that the first _______________ photograph was invented in 1825.
우리는 최초의 영구적 사진이 1825년에 발명되었다고 배웠다.

5 Sound waves can travel through _______________ and liquids.
소리의 파장은 고체와 액체를 통해서 이동 할 수 있다.

6 To explain how the ancient Egyptians developed a successful _______________, you should first look at the geography of Egypt.
어떻게 고대 이집트인들이 성공적인 문명을 이룩했는가를 설명하기 위해서 당신은 반드시 이집트의 지리학을 봐야 합니다. 2009 수능 변형

7 The bandages were wrapped very tightly to keep the _______________ figure of the mummy intact.
미라의 뚜렷한 모습을 유지하기 위해서 붕대는 매우 단단하게 둘러졌다.

8 Selling is tied no longer to production but to _______________.
판매는 더 이상 생산과 연결되어 있지 않고 분배와 연결되어 있다. 09 고2 학평 변형

9 Deep inside the Earth's center is the _______________.
지구 중심의 깊은 내부는 중심핵이다.

10 Please, keep your comments _______________ to the issue at hand.
여러분의 의견을 당면한 문제에 관련있는 것으로 제한해 주세요.

Review Test 01

A 우리말에 맞게 빈 칸에 알맞은 단어를 쓰시오.

1 recruit ______________ staff 경력이 있는 직원들을 모집하다

2 the ______________ of a planet 행성에 대한 정의

3 get rid of ______________ 쓰레기를 제거하다

4 cause ______________ pain 격렬한 고통을 야기하다

5 ______________ implements 농기구

6 have a strong ______________ on adolescents 청소년에게 강한 영향을 미치다

7 carbon ______________ 탄소 섬유

8 the population ______________ in Paris 파리의 인구 밀도

9 the ______________ symptoms of flu 감기의 초기 증상

10 the ______________ of ancient Greece 고대 그리스 문명

B 영어에 맞게 빈 칸에 알맞은 우리말을 쓰시오.

1 an immediate response ______________ 반응

2 discover a previous record ______________ 기록을 발견하다

3 protect their client 그들의 ______________을 보호하다

4 numerous popular songs ______________ 인기 있는 노래들

5 a massive sandstorm ______________ 황사

6 the UN Security Council UN 안전 보장 ______________

7 a mere assumption ______________ 가정

8 prime motivation 주된 ______________

9 a solid partnership ______________ 동반자 관계

10 the core of the argument 주장의 ______________

C 다음 영어 풀이에 알맞은 어휘를 <보기>에서 고르시오.

보기	previous	massive	initial	domestic	permanent

1 ______________ : before or earlier in time or order

2 ______________ : lasting forever or for a long time

3 ______________ : related to local, home, or own country

4 ______________ : happening first or at the beginning

5 ______________ : very large in size or quantity; very strong or heavy

D 문맥에 맞게 다음 문장을 완성하시오.

1 Fossils are the remains or imprints •	• a many electronic devices.
2 Magnets are critical in •	• b influenced Renaissance arts.
3 Mathematics definitely •	• c but to distribution.
4 If you are isolated in your private life, •	• d of dead plants and animals.
5 Selling is tied no longer to production •	• e your success will not last long.

E 문장을 읽고 문맥에 적절한 단어를 고르시오.

1 The (majority/fiber) of the residents in the region voted for Kevin.

2 There are many (trend/domestic) flights from Seoul to Jeju Island.

3 John likes Italian food. Eric, (on the contrary/in other words), prefers French food.

4 You need to (account/ensure) for your absence from the meeting yesterday.

5 We (regard/interact) the current situation as a second opportunity.

F 문장의 빈칸에 알맞은 단어를 〈보기〉에서 찾아 쓰시오. (필요하면 형태를 고치시오.)

보기 consumption endangered permanent annual monitor

1 Do you know the ______________ of broccoli has risen almost ten times in the last 25 years?
지난 25년 사이에 브로콜리 소비가 거의 10배가 증가한 것을 아십니까? 11 고2학평

2 The bank offered me a 2 percent ______________ interest rate.
그 은행은 내게 연간 2퍼센트의 이자율을 제시했다. 15 고2학평 변형

3 My task in this laboratory is to ______________ the remote telescope in Hawaii.
이 연구실에서 내 업무는 하와이에 있는 원격 망원경을 관찰하는 것이다. 11 고2학평 변형

4 At Air Pacific, we know that earning the trust of our clients is a ______________ and ongoing endeavor.
Air Pacific에서는 고객과 직원들의 신뢰를 얻는 것은 영구적이며 지속적인 노력이라는 것을 알고 있습니다. 11 고2학평

5 Many species of tree are now ______________, including mahogany and teak.
마호가니와 티크를 포함한 많은 종의 나무들이 멸종 위기에 처해있다. 14 고3평가원

G 다음 <보기> 중 두 문장에 공통으로 사용할 수 있는 어휘를 고르시오.

1 Sometimes children may want to do more than they are __________ of doing. 15 고2학평

In the 1960's it was held that only humans were __________ of rational thought. 15 고2학평 변형

① burden ② distinct ③ besides ④ mere ⑤ capable

2 Beavers exert their __________ by physically altering the landscape. 12 고3평가원

Another factor that __________s perception is the context. 08 고2학평

① ensure ② influence ③ isolate ④ alert ⑤ interact

3 With that one crucial __________ in thinking, my whole attitude changed. 15 고3평가원

Unlike last year, there seems to be a slight __________ in public opinion this year.

① context ② observation ③ shift ④ definition ⑤ evolution

Study More

'en-' : [동사에서] '~한 상황에 처하게 하다' 또는 '~이 되게 하다'의 뜻을 나타낸다.

- [endanger] 동 위태롭게 하다
  Sam's serious mistake **endangered** the future of his company.
  Sam의 심각한 실수가 그의 회사의 미래를 위태롭게 하였다.

- [enlarge] 동 확대하다, 확장하다
  Extensive reading will help to **enlarge** your vocabulary. 다독은 당신의 어휘가 확장하는 것을 도울 것이다.

Day 03

MP3

061 alert [əlɔ́ːrt]
형 경계하는, 조심하는, 기민한, 빈틈 없는 동 (위험 등을)알리다
an alert leader 기민한 지도자 be alert to ~을 경계하다

062 extraordinary [ikstrɔ́ːrdənèri]
형 뛰어난, 비상한, 기이한
people with extraordinary talents 비상한 재능을 지닌 사람들

063 isolation [àisəléiʃən]
명 고립, 분리, 격리 동 isolate 고립시키다, 격리하다
reduce fear and isolation 두려움과 고립을 감소시키다

064 prior [práiər]
형 이전의, 사전의
prior knowledge of biology 생물학에 대한 사전지식

065 subtle [sʌ́tl]
형 미묘한
his subtle emotion 그의 미묘한 감정

066 temporary [témpərèri]
형 일시적인, 임시의
temporary equilibrium 일시적인 평형

067 estimate [éstəmit]
명 추정(치), 견적 동 추산하다
a realistic estimate 실질적인 추정

068 welfare [wélfɛ̀ər]
명 복지, 후생
welfare without growth 성장 없는 복지

069 accuracy [ǽkjərəsi]
명 정확도, 정확 형 accurate 정확한, 정밀한
incredible accuracy 놀라울 만한 정확도 with accuracy 정확하게

070 avalanche [ǽvəlæ̀ntʃ]
명 눈사태
cause a massive avalanche 대규모 눈사태를 일으키다

071 countless [káuntlis]
형 무수한, 수많은
the death of countless sheep 수많은 양들의 죽음

072 debt [det]
명 빚, 부채
get out of debt 빚을 갚다 a debt of 3000 dollars 3000달러의 빚

073 excess [ékses]
명 지나침, 초과
an excess of stress 지나친 스트레스

074 tune [tjuːn]
명 곡조, 선율, 가락 동 조율하다, 조화시키다
love tunes 사랑의 곡조 tune a piano 피아노를 조율하다

075 fatigue [fətíːg]
명 피로, 피곤
chronic fatigue 만성 피로 be faint with fatigue 피로해서 어질어질하다

Daily Test

| 월 일 |

A 우리말에 맞게 빈 칸에 알맞은 단어를 쓰세요.

1 When one ground squirrel sees a predator under a tree, it sounds an alarm call that ______________ other squirrels to run.
땅다람쥐 한마리가 나무 아래에서 천적을 발견했을 때, 그는 주변의 다람쥐들에게 뛰라는 경고음을 보낸다. 15 고3 평가원 변형

2 Scientists call the ______________ event the 'Big Bang,' and they believe this is the reason our universe was born.
과학자들은 이 기이한 현상을 'Big Bang'이라 불렀고 이것이 우리 우주가 탄생한 이유라 믿었다.

3 ______________ feels like being in a room with no exit.
고립 상태는 출구가 없는 방 안에 있는 것과 같다. 2008 수능 변형

4 It was ______________ that four out of every five people watched the World Cup in 2002.
2002년에 5명 중 4명의 사람이 월드컵을 시청했다고 측정되었다.

5 It is time for the government to try to increase ______________ spending for the elderly.
정부가 노인들을 위한 복지 소비를 늘려야 할 시점이다. 11 고3 학평 변형

6 I doubted the ______________ of the information in the report.
나는 그 보고서 속 정보의 정확성을 의심했다.

7 Basically, an ______________ occurs when there is more stress on the top layer of snow than on the bottom layer.
기본적으로, 눈사태는 눈의 바닥 층보다 위층이 더 많은 압박을 받을 때 발생한다.

8 ______________ animals died in a mountain fire.
수 많은 동물들이 산불로 인해 죽었다.

9 Whistling a ______________, Victor walked over to his house.
휘파람을 한 곡조 부르면서, Victor는 그의 집으로 걸어갔다. 12 고3 학평 변형

10 ______________ and pain are your body's ways of saying that it is in danger.
피로와 고통은 당신에게 당신의 몸이 위험에 처해 있음을 말해주는 것이다. 12 고1 학평 변형

Day 03

MP3

076 **statistics** [stətístiks]
명 통계(학)
release new statistics 새로운 통계를 발표하다

077 **relief** [rilíːf]
명 안도, 경감, 구호품, 위안
temporary relief 일시적 안도 a sense of relief 안심

078 **via** [váiə]
전 ~을 경유하여, 거쳐
fly home via London 비행기를 타고 런던을 경유하여 집에 가다

079 **astronomy** [əstrάnəmi]
명 천문학 형 astronomical 천문의, 천문학의
devote her life to astronomy 천문학에 그녀의 삶을 헌신하다

080 **circular** [sə́ːrkjələr]
형 원형의, 순환적인, 에둘러 말하는
a circular table 원형 탁자 operate a circular route 순환로를 운영하다

081 **defend** [difénd]
동 방어하다, 지키다, 변호하다 유 protect 보호하다, 지키다
defend themselves 그들 스스로를 방어하다

082 **enhance** [inhǽns]
동 ~을 높이다, 향상시키다 유 improve 개선하다, 증진하다
enhance my English proficiency 나의 영어 숙련도를 높이다

083 **grasp** [græsp]
동 꽉 잡다, 이해하다 명 꽉 쥐기, 이해, 파악
grasp her hand tightly 그녀의 손을 꽉 잡다

084 **interpret** [intə́ːrprit]
동 해석하다
interpret the ancient Greek poem 고대 그리스 시를 해석하다

085 **contemporary** [kəntémpərèri]
형 현대의, 동시대의
contemporary American society 현대의 미국사회

086 **phase** [feiz]
명 단계
the last phase of the experiment 실험의 마지막 단계

087 **predator** [prédətər]
명 포식자, 천적
predators in the sea 바다의 포식자들

088 **confirm** [kənfə́ːrm]
동 확인하다, 확정하다
confirm a reservation 예약을 확인하다

089 **recognition** [rèkəgníʃən]
명 인식, 인정, 승인 동 recognize 알아보다, 인식하다
automatic recognition 자동 인식 get recognition 인정 받다

090 **bias** [báiəs]
명 편견, 치우침 형 biased 편향된, 선입견이 있는
have a strong political bias 강한 정치적 편견을 갖고 있다

Daily Test

| 월 일 |

A 우리말에 맞게 빈 칸에 알맞은 단어를 쓰세요.

1 I wanted to tell Mrs. Park that the financial ______________ will make a great difference in my life.
나는 Mrs. Park에게 재정상의 (부담) 완화가 제 인생에서 커다란 차이를 만들어 줄 것이라고 말씀드리고 싶었다. 16 고3평가원 변형

2 In the experiment, one group listened to the story ______________ radio, while the other group watched it on a television.
이 실험에서, 한 그룹은 라디오를 통해 이야기를 들었고 다른 그룹은 텔레비전을 통해 이야기를 시청했다. 15 고3평가원 변형

3 Thanks to his new novel, I began to pay attention to ______________.
그의 새 소설 덕분에, 나는 천문학에 관심을 갖게 되었다.

4 Your skin is connected to every system in the body-from your ______________ and digestive systems to your nervous systems.
피부는 순환계와 소화계 부터 면역계와 신경계에 이르는 신체의 모든 체계와 연결되어 있다. 11 고3학평 변형

5 Some animals rely on their own senses to ______________ themselves.
몇몇 동물들은 그들 스스로를 지키기 위해 자신의 감각에 의존한다. 14 고3평가원 변형

6 The English teacher asked Tom to ______________ the last sentence.
영어 선생님은 Tom에게 마지막 문장을 해석하라고 시켰다.

7 Some ______________ artists share their feeling, but they are also caught up in the system of art exhibition.
어떤 현대 예술가들은 그들의 감정을 공유하지만, 그들은 또한 예술 전시회 시스템에 말려들게 된다. 2010 수능 변형

8 Her sketch was the first major ______________ of the tower design.
그녀의 스케치는 그 탑 디자인에 첫 주요 단계였다.

9 A school of fish will split in two to avoid a ______________ and then quickly regroup.
물고기 떼는 천적을 피하기 위해 두 무리로 나뉘었다가 다시 빠르게 하나로 합쳐졌다. 14 고3평가원 변형

10 Scientists should be careful to reduce ______________ in their experiments.
과학자는 그들의 실험에 대한 편견을 줄이기 위해 주의를 기울여야 한다. 2013 수능

Day 04

MP3

091 **be derived from** [bi diráivd frəm]
~에서 유래되다
be derived from ancient languages 고대 언어에서 유래되다

092 **dilemma** [dilémə]
명 딜레마
be in a dilemma 딜레마에 빠지다 a moral dilemma 도덕적 딜레마

093 **extensive** [iksténsiv]
형 광범위한, 대규모의
an extensive area 광대한 지역

094 **reference** [réfərəns]
명 참조, 언급, 추천서
find reference materials 참조 자료를 찾다

095 **cliff** [klif]
명 낭떠러지, 절벽
stand at the edge of the cliff 절벽 끝에 서 있다

096 **glance** [glæns]
동 힐끗 보다 명 흘끗 봄, 번득임
glance around 주위를 힐끗 보다 glance up 힐끗 올려다보다

097 **somewhat** [sʌ́mhwʌ̀t]
부 다소, 어느 정도
somewhat irrelevant 다소 무관한

098 **component** [kəmpóunənt]
명 요소, 부품
key components of the report 그 보고서의 핵심 요소

099 **diminish** [dimíniʃ]
동 줄어들다, 감소하다
diminish in speed 속도를 줄이다 diminish gradually 점차 감소하다

100 **abound** [əbáund]
동 풍부하다, 많이 있다
abound with ~로 풍부하다 abound with fish 물고기가 풍부하다

101 **assignment** [əsáinmənt]
명 숙제, 임무, 배정, 배치
do a math assignment 수학 숙제를 하다

102 **confusion** [kənfjú:ʒən]
명 혼란
identity confusion 정체성의 혼란 create confusion 혼란을 야기시키다

103 **corporation** [kɔ̀:rpəréiʃən]
명 기업, 회사
multinational corporation 다국적 기업

104 **eliminate** [ilímənèit]
동 제거하다, 삭제하다, 탈락시키다
eliminate the dangerous virus 위험한 바이러스를 제거하다

105 **self-esteem** [istí:m]
명 자존감, 자부심
have low self-esteem 자존감이 낮다

Daily Test

| 월 일 |

Ⓐ 우리말에 맞게 빈 칸에 알맞은 단어를 쓰세요.

1 One of the best ways to resolve a ______________ is simply to start writing.
딜레마를 극복하는 가장 좋은 방법 중 하나는 간단히 글쓰기를 시작하는 것이다. 2010 수능 변형

2 Logic has an ______________ and well-defined set of rules and guidelines.
논리는 광범위하고 잘 정의된 일련의 규칙과 지침이다. 10 고2학평 변형

3 I was pleased to receive your email requesting a letter of ______________ for a scholarship.
나는 당신의 장학금을 요청하는 이메일을 받아서 매우 기뻤습니다. 11 고3평가원 변형

4 Bats live in caves, ______________ and even in tree hollows.
박쥐는 동굴, 절벽 그리고 심지어 나무 속 꺼진 곳에서도 산다.

5 Wendy found her thumb to be ______________ more swollen.
Wendy는 그녀의 엄지가 다소 더 부어 올랐음을 알았다. 12 고3평가원 변형

6 Learning and memorizing facts was an important ______________ of the mathematics instructional program.
사실을 학습하고 암기하는 것은 수학 교육 프로그램의 중요한 요소이다. 14 고3평가원 변형

7 Cliches in writing ultimately ______________ the interest and effectiveness of the subject.
글짓기 속 클리셰는 궁극적으로 주제의 흥미와 효율성을 감소 시킨다. 15 고1학평 변형

8 Judy struggled with the endless ______________ and exams.
Judy는 끝없는 과제와 시험과 씨름했다. 2016 수능 변형

9 A group of animals fleeing from a predator can create ______________.
적을 피하는 한 무리의 동물들은 혼란을 야기할 수 있습니다. 14 고3평가원 변형

10 The doctor came up with a vaccine to ______________ malaria and yellow fever during the Spanish-American war.
그 의사는 스페인과 미국간의 전쟁 동안 말라리아와 황열병을 제거할 백신을 찾아냈다.

Day 04

MP3

106 **admission** [ədmíʃən]
명 입학, 입장
change the admission policy 입학 정책을 바꾸다

107 **slang** [slæŋ]
명 속어, 은어
limit the use of slang 속어 사용을 제한하다

108 **sophisticated** [səfístəkèitid]
형 세련된, 정교한, 복잡한
sophisticated consumers 세련된 소비자

109 **trigger** [trigər]
동 유발하다, 촉발시키다 명 방아쇠
trigger asthma 천식을 유발하다 squeeze the trigger 방아쇠를 당기다

110 **certificate** [sərtífəkit]
명 증서, 수료증
receive a teacher's certificate 교직 이수증을 받다

111 **disorder** [disɔ́:rdər]
명 혼란, 무질서, 장애
a state of disorder 무질서의 상태 neurological disorders 신경 장애

112 **innocent** [ínəsənt]
형 무고한, 순수한
innocent civilians 무고한 시민들

113 **mechanism** [mékənìzəm]
명 기계 장치, 구조, 체계
the mechanism of a computer 컴퓨터의 구조

114 **passive** [pǽsiv]
형 수동적인
play a passive role 소극적 역할을 하다

115 **pottery** [pɑ́təri]
명 도자기
make pottery 도자기를 만들다

116 **precise** [prisáis]
형 정확한, 정밀한
the precise measurement 정확한 측정

117 **prehistoric** [prì:histɔ́(:)rik]
형 선사 시대의
prehistoric remains 선사시대 유물

118 **split** [split]
동 나누다, 쪼개다, 분열시키다 명 분열, 분할, 틈
split a cake into three pieces 케이크를 세 조각으로 나누다

119 **breed** [bri:d]
동 새끼를 낳다, 사육하다 명 가축의 품종
breed horses 말을 사육하다

120 **mature** [mətjúər]
형 성숙한, 숙성된 동 어른이 되다, 성숙해지다
mature teenagers 성숙한 10대 his mature attitude 그의 성숙한 태도

Daily Test

| 월 일 |

A 우리말에 맞게 빈 칸에 알맞은 단어를 쓰세요.

1 ______________ and parking are free until next Saturday.
다음 주 토요일까지 입장과 주차는 무료입니다. 14 고3 평가원 변형

2 The company uses ______________ computer programs to analyze customer feedback.
그 회사는 고객의 의견을 분석하기 위해 정교한 컴퓨터 프로그램을 사용한다.

3 Food allergies can ______________ certain reactions in your body that may range from extreme sneezing to a swollen tongue.
음식 알레르기는 심한 재채기에서부터 혀가 부어오르는 것에 이르는 신체 반응들을 유발할 수 있다. 09 고3 학평 변형

4 The boy's full name, as recorded on his birth ______________, was Henry Albert David.
그의 출생 기록에 따르면 그 소년의 이름은 Henry Albert David였다. 14 고2 학평 변형

5 During the war, 2 million ______________ people died.
전쟁 동안에 2백만 명의 무고한 사람들이 죽었다. 13 고3 평가원 변형

6 Employers should consider how to limit ______________ smoking at work.
고용주들은 직장 간접흡연을 제한할 수 있는 방법에 대해 숙고해야 한다. 08 고3 학평 변형

7 Ann went to the ______________ shop and bought some clay plates as a gift for her grandmother.
Ann은 도자기 가게에 가서 그녀의 할머니를 위한 선물로 몇 개의 도자기 접시를 구입했다.

8 Susan's explanation on the matter was simple and ______________.
그 문제에 대한 Susan의 설명은 간단하고 정확했다.

9 Our ______________ ancestors would surely have taken advantage of caves.
우리의 선사시대 조상들은 확실히 동굴의 이점을 사용해 왔을 것이다.

10 Researchers in France have come up with an ultrasonic sensor that will listen to cheese as it ______________.
프랑스의 연구가들은 숙성될 때 치즈의 소리를 들을 수 있는 초음파 센서를 생각해냈다. 10 고3 평가원 변형

Review Test 02

Day 03 + Day 04

A 우리말에 맞게 빈 칸에 알맞은 단어를 쓰시오.

1 an ________________ leader 기민한 지도자

2 people with ________________ talents 비상한 재능을 지닌 사람들

3 with ________________ 정확하게

4 ________________ her hand tightly 그녀의 손을 꽉 잡다

5 the last ________________ of the experiment 실험의 마지막 단계

6 stand at the edge of the ________________ 절벽 끝에 서 있다

7 ________________ gradually 점차 감소하다

8 change the ________________ policy 입학 정책을 바꾸다

9 receive a teacher's ________________ 교직 이수증을 받다

10 ________________ remains 선사시대 유물

B 영어에 맞게 빈 칸에 알맞은 우리말을 쓰시오.

1 a realistic estimate 실질적인 ________________

2 the death of countless sheep ________________ 양들의 죽음

3 interpret the ancient Greek poem 고대 그리스 시를 ________________

4 predators in the sea 바다의 ________________

5 confirm a reservation 예약을 ________________

6 a moral dilemma 도덕적 ________________

7 create confusion ________________을 야기시키다

8 eliminate the dangerous virus 위험한 바이러스를 ________________

9 squeeze the trigger ________________를 당기다

10 innocent civilians ________________ 시민들

C 다음 영어 풀이에 알맞은 어휘를 〈보기〉에서 고르시오.

보기 estimate eliminate alert prior innocent

1 ______________ : to give someone important information such as a warning

2 ______________ : existing or occurring before something else; former

3 ______________ : to guess the size, amount, distance, etc., of something

4 ______________ : to get rid of something or to remove something

5 ______________ : free from guilt; not harmful

D 문맥에 맞게 다음 문장을 완성하시오.

1	Isolation feels like being •	• a	and exams.
2	Whistling a tune •	• b	in a room with no exit.
3	Some animals rely on their own senses •	• c	to defend themselves.
4	Judy struggled with the endless assignments •	• d	limit passive smoking at work.
5	Employers should consider how to •	• e	Victor walked over to his house.

E 문장을 읽고 문맥에 적절한 단어를 고르시오.

1 I can't exactly say what they are but there are (subtle/circular) differences between the two pictures.

2 (Owing/Prior) to going home we need to clean the classroom.

3 I think the price of this watch is (somewhat/hopefully) expensive.

4 Because we had only one apple, I (eliminated/split) it into two pieces.

5 The human body is made up of a (circular/countless) number of cells.

F 문장의 빈칸에 알맞은 단어를 〈보기〉에서 찾아 쓰시오. (필요하면 형태를 고치시오.)

보기 temporary abound contemporary sophisticated extensive

1 That's a smart thing to do, but it's only a ______________ remedy.
그건 현명하기는 하지만 일시적인 치료일 뿐이야. 2011 수능

2 The company uses ______________ computer programs to analyze customer's feedback.
그 회사는 고객들의 피드백을 분석하기 위해 정교한 컴퓨터 프로그램을 사용한다.

3 Juan's essay ______________ with poetic descriptions of his hometown.
Juan의 에세이는 자신의 고향에 대한 시적인 묘사가 풍부하다.

4 In the recent past glaciers were far more ______________ than they are today.
얼마 전까지 빙하는 오늘 날보다 훨씬 더 광범위했다. 08 고3평가원

5 To me, someone who only reads books by ______________ authors looks near-sighted.
내게는 동시대의 작가들 책만 읽는 사람은 근시안적으로 보인다. 2006 수능

G 다음 <보기> 중 두 문장에 공통으로 사용할 수 있는 어휘를 고르시오.

1 Women, contrary to men, want to find ___________ by talking about the problems of their day. 04 고3학평 변형
The guard breathed a sigh of ___________. 09 고3학평

① astronomy ② accuracy ③ pottery ④ relief ⑤ confusion

2 The special airplane has a powerful telescope for ___________ observations of the galaxy. 11 고2학평 변형
The ___________ location of the restaurant can be found on the map.

① precise ② fatigue ③ passive ④ innocent ⑤ prehistoric

3 Regular reading of newspapers can also ___________ your general knowledge. 15 고3평가원 변형
Music works on our emotions. For example, it can create or ___________ our mood. 2008 수능 변형

① diminish ② enhance ③ defend ④ estimate ⑤ glance

Study More

혼동하기 쉬운 단어 conform vs. confirm

- [conform] 동 순응하다, 따르다
  It is very important to **conform** to the safety rules of the swimming pool.
  수영장에서 안전 규칙을 따르는 것은 매우 중요하다.
- [confirm] 동 확인하다, 입증하다
  Scientists **confirmed** that taking a nap is useful to increase work efficiency.
  과학자는 낮잠을 자는 것이 일의 효율을 증대시키는 데 유용하다는 것을 확인했다.

Day 05

MP3

121 **correlation** [kɔ̀(:)rəléiʃən]
명 연관성, 상관관계
a correlation between age and height 나이와 키의 상관관계

122 **induce** [indjú:s]
동 유도하다, 유발하다
induce investment 투자를 유도하다

123 **substance** [sʌ́bstəns]
명 물질, 실체, 요지 형 substantial (양, 가치 등이) 상당한
avoid harmful substances 유해한 물질을 피하다

124 **diversity** [divə́:rsəti]
명 다양성
protect the cultural diversity 문화 다양성을 보호하다

125 **stable** [stéibl]
형 안정적인 반 unstable 급변하는, 불안정한
a stable recovery 안정적인 회복

126 **strain** [strein]
명 부담, 압박, (근육 등의) 접질림, 삠 동 잡아당기다, 긴장시키다
stress and strain of public life 공적 생활의 스트레스와 부담감

127 **prominent** [prámənənt]
형 유명한, 두드러진 유 notable 주목할만한
a prominent movie director 유명한 영화 감독

128 **bond** [bɑnd]
명 유대, 끈
a bond of friendship 우정 어린 유대

129 **noticeable** [nóutisəbl]
형 뚜렷한, 현저한
noticeable improvement 뚜렷한 향상

130 **satisfy** [sǽtisfài]
동 만족시키다, 충족시키다
satisfy the condition 조건을 충족시키다

131 **dislike** [disláik]
동 싫어하다 명 반감, 싫음
dislike carrots 당근을 싫어하다 a hearty dislike 심한 반감

132 **anthropologist** [ænθrəpa:lədʒist]
명 인류학자
a cultural anthropologist 문화 인류학자

133 **tuition** [tju:íʃən]
명 수업, 교습
receive private tuition in English 영어 개인 교습을 받다

134 **intent** [intént]
명 의도, 의향 형 몰두하는, ~에 전념하는
conceal strategic intent 전략적인 의도를 감추다

135 **circulation** [sə̀:rkjəléiʃən]
명 순환, 유통, 판매부수
have good circulation 순환이 좋다

Daily Test

| 월 일 |

A 우리말에 맞게 빈 칸에 알맞은 단어를 쓰세요.

1 As we all know, there is no ______________ between hoping for rain and the appearance of clouds.
우리가 모두 알다시피, 비가 오길 바라는 것과 구름이 나타나는 것과는 어떠한 연관성도 없다.

2 The researcher found that the lavender is the best smell to ______________ sleep.
그 연구원은 라벤더 향이 잠을 유발하는데 최고의 향인 것을 알아냈다. 10 고3 평가원 변형

3 In the United States, 30% of all prescriptions from pharmacies contain ______________ derived from plants.
미국에서는 약국에서 조제되는 모든 처방약의 30%가 식물에서 얻은 물질을 포함하고 있다. 13 고3 평가원

4 We can guess that habitat ______________ refers to the variety of places where life exists.
우리는 서식지 다양성이란 생물이 존재하는 장소들의 다양성을 말하는 것임을 추측할 수 있다. 2011 수능 변형

5 We are relieved to hear that Helen's blood pressure is now ______________.
우리는 Helen의 혈압이 이제는 안정적임을 듣고 안심했다.

6 In search of our identity, we form ______________ or social groups with people whom we want to be like.
정체성을 탐구할 때, 우리는 닮고 싶은 사람들과 유대하고 사회적 집단을 형성한다. 2012 수능 변형

7 ______________ attempted to tell the classic story of Hamlet to Tiv elders.
인류학자들은 티브족 성인들에게 고전 작품 햄릿을 이야기해주는 것을 시도했다. 2012 수능 변형

8 When I was in twenty, I worked part-time to pay my ______________.
내가 스무살 때, 나는 학비를 충당하기 위해 아르바이트를 했다.

9 Restoration assumes that one can recreate an artist's original ______________.
복원은 예술가의 본래 의도를 재창조할 수 있다고 가정한다. 13 고3 평가원 변형

10 Some viruses affect muscles needed for respiration and ______________.
일부 바이러스는 소화하고 순환하는 데 필요한 근육에 영향을 미친다.

Day 05

MP3

136 readily [rédəli]
부 손쉽게, 순조롭게
blush readily 쉽게 얼굴이 빨개지다 readily available 쉽게 이용할 수 있는

137 apparent [əpǽrənt]
형 분명한, 명백한
for no apparent reason 분명한 이유 없이

138 assist [əsíst]
동 돕다, 지원하다 명 조력, 원조
assist a person financially ~에게 재정적으로 지원하다

139 era [í(:)rə]
명 시대, 연대
the romantic era 낭만주의 시대 the end of an era 한 시대의 끝

140 sake [seik]
명 이익, 동기
for the sake of ~을 위해서

141 abundant [əbʌ́ndənt]
형 풍부한, 넘쳐나는
an abundant harvest 풍작 abundant material 넘쳐나는 재료

142 evaluate [ivǽljuèit]
동 평가하다, 검토하다 유 assess 재다, 평가하다
evaluate his English proficiency 그의 영어 숙련도를 평가하다

143 adequate [ǽdəkwit]
형 적당한, 충분한
adequate methods 적당한 방법

144 draft [dræft]
명 초안, 밑그림, 선발, 징집 동 밑그림을 그리다, 초고를 쓰다
the final draft 최종 원고 the first draft of the report 보고서의 초고

145 expedition [èkspidíʃən]
명 탐험(대), 원정, 짧은 여행
go on an expedition 탐험을 떠나다

146 commerce [kámə(:)rs]
명 상업, 무역
foreign commerce 외국 무역 electronic commerce 전자 상거래

147 stack [stæk]
명 더미 동 쌓다, 포개다
a stack of clothes 옷 한 더미 stack books 책을 쌓다

148 entry [éntri]
명 입장, 가입, 참가, (사전 동의) 개별 항목
no entry 출입 금지 gain entry to the golf club 골프 클럽에 가입하다

149 earning [ə́:rniŋ]
명 소득, 획득 동 earn (일하며)벌다, 얻다
his average earnings 그의 평균 소득 earning gap 소득 격차

150 enthusiastic [inθjù:ziǽstik]
형 열렬한, 열광적인 유 passionate 열렬한, 정열적인
enthusiastic about her work 그녀의 일에 열정적인

Daily Test

| 월 일 |

A **우리말에 맞게 빈 칸에 알맞은 단어를 쓰세요.**

1 The ______________ complexity of a man's behavior overtime is largely a reflection of the environment in which he finds himself.
시간이 흐르면서 복잡한 것 같아 보이는 인간의 행동은 주로 인간이 처한 환경의 복잡성을 반영하는 것이다. 15 고3평가원

2 Compasses ______________ people hiking in the mountains, sailors navigating the sea or pilots flying in the air.
나침반은 사람들이 산에서 하이킹하고 선원들이 바다를 항해하거나 또는 조종사들이 상공에서 비행할 수 있도록 도와준다.

3 I think that music for motion pictures often serves to authenticate the ______________ or provide a sense of nostalgia.
난 영화 음악이 종종 그 시대를 증명하거나 향수를 일으키는 역할을 한다고 생각한다. 15 고3평가원 변형

4 At one point in time the world's oceans were ______________ with fish species.
어느 한 시점에서 세계 해양은 어종이 풍부해졌다.

5 The time available was not ______________ for Lina's needs.
이용가능한 시간은 Lina가 필요한 만큼 충분하지 않았다.

6 I can send you a first ______________ of our plan and the estimate within two days.
이틀 내로 우리의 계획에 대한 첫 번째 초안과 견적을 보내드릴 수 있습니다 2008 수능 변형

7 When Napoleon invaded Egypt in 1798, some scholars accompanied the ______________.
나폴레옹이 1798년에 이집트를 침공했을 때, 몇몇 철학자들은 그 원정에 함께했다. 2014 수능 변형

8 Mobile ______________ is favored more by women than by men.
휴대전화 상거래는 여성들이 남성보다 더 선호한다. 09 고2평가원 변형

9 Failure to comply with any of the club rules will result in ______________ being revoked.
모임 규칙을 따르지 않는다면 입장 자격이 박탈될 것입니다.

10 The risk associated with an investment can be defined as the probability of ______________ an expected profit.
투자와 관련된 위험은 기대 수익을 얻을 가능성으로 규정될 수 있다. 15 고2학평 변형

Day 06

MP3

151 ambiguous [æmbígjuəs]
형 애매모호한, 여러 가지로 해석되는 유 vague 막연한, 애매한
dislike his ambiguous attitude 그의 애매모호한 태도를 싫어하다

152 crude [kru:d]
형 대충의, 미가공의 명 원유, 미정제품
a crude drawing of the vase 대충 그린 꽃병 그림

153 guilty [gílti]
형 유죄의, 죄책감을 느끼는
be found guilty 유죄로 판명 나다 guilty conscience 죄책감

154 Celsius [sélsiəs]
형 섭씨의
Celsius thermometer 섭씨 온도계

155 stun [stʌn]
동 기절시키다, 망연자실하게 만들다 +stunning 형 깜짝 놀랄, 굉장히 멋진
be stunned for a moment 잠시 동안 기절하다

156 offspring [ɔ́(:)fsprìŋ]
명 자식, 자손
offspring of primitive man 원시시대의 후손

157 compensation [kàmpənséiʃən]
명 보상, 보상금
make compensation for the accident 사고의 보상을 요구하다

158 diabetes [dàiəbí:ti:z]
명 당뇨병
suffer from diabetes 당뇨병에 걸리다

159 medication [mèdəkéiʃən]
명 약(물)
take medication 약물을 복용하다 effective medication 효과적인 약

160 polish [páliʃ]
동 닦다, 광을 내다 명 광택제, 윤내기, 윤, 광택
polish the glasses with a handkerchief 안경을 손수건으로 닦다

161 devastating [dévəstèitiŋ]
형 파괴적인, 충격적인, 치명적인 동 devastate 완전히 파괴하다
a devastating earthquake 파괴적인 지진

162 magnetic [mægnétik]
형 자기의, 자석같은, 매력있는
magnetic polarity 자기적 양극성 magnetic forces 자력

163 bargain [bá:rgin]
동 흥정하다 명 흥정
bargain with a vendor 상인과 흥정하다

164 asthma [ǽzmə]
명 천식
cause asthma 천식을 일으키다 an asthma attack 천식 발작

165 genuine [dʒénjuin]
형 진짜의, 진품의 유 authentic 진정한, 진짜의
a genuine diamond ring 진짜 다이아몬드 반지

Daily Test

| 월 일 |

A 우리말에 맞게 빈 칸에 알맞은 단어를 쓰세요.

1 In any form of writing, you should avoid ______________ expressions where possible as you can.
어떠한 형태의 글에서도, 당신은 가능한 한 모호한 표현은 피해야 한다.

2 Many of us are ______________ of passing on information we hear without knowing for whether it is true.
우리들 중에는 사실인지 확실히 알지도 못하면서 정보를 전하는 잘못을 저지르는 사람이 많다. 12 고1학평 변형

3 Seeds contain the plant's ______________ and a small supply of food to get the young plant started.
씨앗은 식물의 자손과 어린 식물들이 싹을 틔울 수 있도록 소량의 영양소를 함유하고 있다.

4 If one of the parties fails to keep the promise, the other has a right to receive ______________.
만약 한쪽 편이 약속을 지키지 못하게 되면, 상대편은 배상을 요구 할 권리를 가진다. 2010 수능 변형

5 Patients with ______________ use insulin to help their bodies process sugars normally.
당뇨병이 있는 환자들은 혈당을 정상적으로 조절하기 위해 인슐린을 이용하고 있다. 04 고2평가원 변형

6 Sue is given ______________ to reduce her anxiety of spiders.
Sue는 거미에 대한 두려움을 줄이기 위해 약을 처방받았다.

7 The 2004 Indonesian tsunami was the most ______________ in modern history.
2004년 인도네시아의 쓰나미는 현대 역사상 가장 파괴적이었다.

8 Magnets are objects made from metals with a ______________ field.
자석은 자기장을 지니고 있는 금속으로 만들어진 물체이다.

9 During the annual sale, people paid half of what the grocery store normally charged and felt lucky about the ______________.
정기 세일 기간 동안 사람들은 식료품점에서 부르는 값의 절반을 지불하고 그 거래에 대해 운이 좋다고 느꼈다. 2010 수능 변형

10 Astronomers now believe that Pluto is not a ______________ planet.
천문학자는 이제 명왕성이 더 이상 진짜 행성이 아니라고 믿는다.

Day 06

MP3

166 **lever** [lévər]
명 지레, 지렛대
the principle of the lever 지렛대의 원리

167 **biodiversity** [baioʊdaiv3:rsəti]
명 생물의 다양성
biodiversity conservation 생물의 다양성 유지

168 **dominate** [dámənèit]
동 ~을 지배하다, (경기에서) 우위를 차지하다 형 dominant 우세한, 지배적인
dominate public opinion 여론을 지배하다

169 **enterprise** [éntərpràiz]
명 기업, 회사, 사업(운영)
public enterprises 공공 기업들

170 **expressive** [iksprésiv]
형 (생각, 표정을) 나타내는, ~을 나타내는
expressive with your feelings 당신의 감정을 나타내는

171 **horizontal** [hɔ̀(:)rəzántəl]
형 수평의, 가로의 반 vertical 수직의, 세로의
draw a horizontal line 수평선을 긋다

172 **ultimate** [ʌ́ltəmit]
형 궁극적인, 최후의, 근본적인 명 ~의 궁극, 극치, 최후점
find ultimate solutions 궁극적인 해결책을 찾다

173 **real estate** [rí:əl istéit]
명 부동산, 토지, 팔 집 형 real-estate 부동산의
a real estate agent 부동산 중개업자

174 **assistance** [əsístəns]
명 도움, 지원, 원조 유 aid 도움, 조력, 원조
offer practical assistance 실질적 도움을 제공하다

175 **substitute** [sʌ́bstitjù:t]
동 대체하다 명 대체품, 교체선수
employ substitute teachers 대리 교사를 고용하다

176 **cereal** [síriəl]
명 곡물, 시리얼
cereal crops 곡물 eat a bowl of cereal 시리얼 한 그릇을 먹다

177 **recess** [risés]
명 휴식, (의회 등의) 휴회 기간, 구석진 곳
a short recess 짧은 휴식 call a recess 휴식을 선언하다

178 **inefficient** [ìnifíʃənt]
형 비효율적인, 비능률적인 유 ineffectual 효과가 없는, 무익한
inefficient use of resource 자원의 비효율적 사용

179 **spectacular** [spektǽkjələr]
형 장관을 이루는, 멋진, 극적인 유 impressive 강한 인상을 주는
spectacular sunrise 장관을 이루는 일출

180 **equilibrium** [ì:kwəlíbriəm]
명 균형, 평정
equilibrium of force 힘의 균형

Daily Test

| 월 일 |

Ⓐ 우리말에 맞게 빈 칸에 알맞은 단어를 쓰세요.

1 It is shortsighted to rely solely on protected areas to preserve ______________.
생물의 다양성을 보존하기 위해 오직 보호구역에만 의지하는 것은 근시안적이다. 16 고3학평 변형

2 For decades, American automobiles ______________ world markets.
수십년 동안, 미국 자동차업계는 세계 시장을 지배했다.

3 Would you like to become part of an enjoyable and rewarding ______________ experience?
여러분은 즐겁고 보람된 기업 경험에 참여해보고 싶습니까? 09 고2평가원 변형

4 I think one of the toughest parts of isolation is a lack of an ______________ outlet.
난 고립 상태가 주는 가장 힘든 면 중 하나는 표현의 출구가 없다는 것이라 생각한다. 2008 수능 변형

5 Our ______________ goal is to get three gold medals at the Olympics.
우리의 궁극적인 목표는 올림픽에서 세 개의 금메달을 따는 것이다.

6 Because ______________ prices rose, many of our neighbors sold their homes and lots.
부동산 가격이 오르면서, 많은 이웃들이 자신들의 집과 땅을 팔아버렸다. 2014 수능 변형

7 As the Internet is a familiar resource for young people, it is logical that they would seek ______________ from this source.
인터넷이 젊은 사람들에게 친숙한 수단이기 때문에, 그들이 이 정보원에서 도움을 구할 것이라는 것은 논리적이다.
16 고3평가원 변형

8 I bought baby ______________ and two bottles of orange juice.
나는 아기용 시리얼과 오렌지 쥬스 두 병을 샀다.

9 Applying a single plan to everything can be ______________ and sometimes contradictory.
모든 일에 한 가지 계획을 적용하는 것은 비효율적이고 때로는 모순적일 수 있다. 15 고2학평 변형

10 Homeostasis is the word we use to describe the ability of an organism to maintain internal ______________.
항상성은 내적인 평형상태를 유지하는 생명체의 능력을 묘사하기 위해서 우리가 사용하는 단어이다. 2012 수능 변형

A 우리말에 맞게 빈 칸에 알맞은 단어를 쓰시오.

1 a ______________ between age and height 나이와 키의 상관관계

2 protect the cultural ______________ 문화 다양성을 보호하다

3 a ______________ of friendship 우정 어린 유대

4 for no ______________ reason 분명한 이유 없이

5 the first ______________ of the report 보고서의 초고

6 ______________ conscience 죄책감

7 suffer from ______________ 당뇨병에 걸리다

8 ______________ with a vendor 상인과 흥정하다

9 ______________ with your feelings 당신의 감정을 나타내는

10 offer practical ______________ 실질적 도움을 제공하다

B 영어에 맞게 빈 칸에 알맞은 우리말을 쓰시오.

1 induce investment 투자를 ______________

2 noticeable improvement ______________ 향상

3 readily available ______________ 이용할 수 있는

4 go on an expedition ______________ 을 떠나다

5 gain entry to the golf club 골프 클럽에 ______________ 하다

6 offspring of primitive man 원시시대의 ______________

7 a devastating earthquake ______________ 지진

8 an asthma attack ______________ 발작

9 biodiversity conservation ______________ 유지

10 draw a horizontal line ______________ 선을 긋다

C 다음 영어 풀이에 알맞은 어휘를 〈보기〉에서 고르시오.

보기	adequate	prominent	abundant	bond	stable

1 ______________ : fixed in position or state and does not change easily

2 ______________ : very well-known, famous, or important

3 ______________ : a close connection joining two or more

4 ______________ : enough or suitable for something

5 ______________ : existing in a large amount or number

D 문맥에 맞게 다음 문장을 완성하시오.

1 Mobile commerce is favored •		• a metals with a magnetic field.
2 Sue is given medication •		• b more by women than by men.
3 Magnets are objects made from •		• c to reduce her anxiety of spiders.
4 Astronomers now believe that •		• d two bottles of orange juice.
5 I bought baby cereal and •		• e Pluto is not a genuine planet.

E 문장을 읽고 문맥에 적절한 단어를 고르시오.

1 We need a (stable/noticeable) supply of water to grow fruits and rice.

2 He does not listen to other people. It is why I (assist/dislike) him.

3 Justin changed his eating habits for the (bond/sake) of his health.

4 The football manager (substituted/polished) a fresh player for an injured player.

5 Many (crude/prominent) people, including famous politicians and artists, attended the meeting.

F 문장의 빈칸에 알맞은 단어를 〈보기〉에서 찾아 쓰시오. (필요하면 형태를 고치시오.)

보기 enthusiastic circulation dominate abundant adequate

1 Mosquitoes can live in cold temperatures. They are ______________ in Antarctica.
모기는 추운 기후에서도 살 수 있으며 남극에도 넘쳐난다. 08 고2 학평

2 We're looking for new members who are ______________ about improving the environment of our city.
우리는 시의 환경을 개선하는 데 열정적인 새로운 회원을 찾고 있습니다. 2014 수능 변형

3 All travellers should ensure they have ______________ travel insurance before they depart.
모든 여행자들은 출발하기 전에 그들이 적절한 여행 보험에 들었는지 확실히 해야 한다. 2007 수능

4 In Picasso's panting *Guernica*, images of a cruel war ______________ the canvas.
Picasso의 그림 Guernica에는 잔인한 전쟁의 이미지들이 캔버스를 지배하고 있다. 16 고3 평가원 변형

5 Once the newspaper had a considerable ______________ but it is sharply declining these days.
그 신문은 한 때 상당한 판매부수를 가지고 있었지만 지금은 판매부수가 급격히 줄고 있다.

G 다음 〈보기〉 중 두 문장에 공통으로 사용할 수 있는 어휘를 고르시오.

1 ____________ with grief, he cried. 06 고3학평
The mother was totally ____________ with her son's rude manner.

① strained ② stunned ③ stacked ④ polished ⑤ assisted

2 Don't let poor communication damage the ____________ success of your ideas. 11 고2학평
The ____________ power is the power to get people to do as you wish. 11 고3평가원

① devastating ② cereal ③ climate ④ ultimate ⑤ abundant

3 The teachers' committee will ____________ each participant and decide on the winner. 08 고3평가원 변형
I don't ____________ people by their appearance or possessions. 04 고2평가원 변형

① induce ② dislike ③ substitute ④ diminish ⑤ evaluate

Study More

'in-' : [형용사, 부사, 명사에서] '부정,반대'의 뜻을 나타낸다.
[동사에서] '~의 상태가 되게 하다'의 뜻을 나타낸다.

- [incapacity] 명 무력, 무능
  Martin didn't recognize his **incapacity** for work. Martin은 그가 일할 능력이 없음을 깨닫지 못했다.
- [inflame] 동 격앙시키다, (상황을) 악화시키다
  Her attitude **inflamed** public anger. 그녀의 태도는 대중의 화를 악화시켰다.

Day 07

MP3

181 **friction** [fríkʃən]
명 마찰, 알력, 불화 유 conflict 투쟁, 전투, 분쟁
friction between two countries 두 국가 사이의 마찰

182 **indifferent** [indífərənt]
형 무관심한, 중요하지 않은, 관계없는
indifferent about social issues 사회 이슈에 무관심한

183 **allegory** [ǽləgɔ:ri]]
명 우화, 풍자 유 fable 우화
a political allegory 정치적 우화

184 **transport** [trǽnspɔ̀:rt]
명 수송, 이동 수단 동 수송하다, 이동시키다 유 transportation 수송, 운송
public transport 대중 교통

185 **identification** [aidèntəfəkéiʃən]
명 신원 확인, 신분증, 식별 유 recognition 알아봄, 인식
an identification number 신분증 번호

186 **federal** [fédərəl]
형 연방의, 연방 정부의
federal government 연방 정부

187 **wage** [weidʒ]
명 임금, 급료 동 (전쟁, 전투 등을) 벌이다, 계속하다
a minimum wage system 최저 임금제 a wage rise 임금 인상

188 **hardship** [há:rdʃip]
명 고난, 고충, 곤란
financial hardship 재정적 고난 undergo hardship 고난을 견디다

189 **guarantee** [gæ̀rəntí:]
동 보장하다, (품질을) 보증하다, 확신하다 명 약속, (품질) 보증서, 보장
guarantee the quality of a product 상품의 질을 보장하다

190 **intake** [íntèik]
명 섭취, 흡입, 채용, 수입
daily calorie intake 일일 칼로리 섭취 adequate intake 적절한 섭취

191 **modest** [mádist]
형 적절한, 겸손한
a modest and honest student 겸손하고 정직한 학생

192 **inexpensive** [ìnikspénsiv]
형 비싸지 않은, 값이 싼
a relatively inexpensive car 상대적으로 비싸지 않은 자동차

193 **intermediate** [ìntərmí:diit]
형 중간의
take an intermediate course 중간 과정을 등록하다

194 **neutral** [njú:trəl]
형 중립의, 중립국의, 중성의
neutral territory 중립 영토

195 **favorable** [féivərəbl]
형 유리한, 호의적인, 양호한
favorable position 유리한 위치

Daily Test

| 월 일 |

A 우리말에 맞게 빈 칸에 알맞은 단어를 쓰세요.

1 I think some politicians are ______________ to public opinion.
난 일부 정치인들이 대중의 의견에 무관심하다고 생각한다. 10 고3평가원 변형

2 It is important that workers be treated well and paid proper ______________.
노동자들이 대우를 잘 받고 적절한 임금을 받는 것은 중요하다.

3 Savings accounts are guaranteed by the ______________ government up to a certain dollar amount.
예금 계좌는 특정한 달러 액수까지 연방 정부에 의해 보장받는다. 15 고2학평 변형

4 The elephant and polar bear will be ______________ to a zoo next week.
그 코끼리와 북극곰은 다음 주에 동물원으로 옮겨질 것이다.

5 More and more elderly people find it difficult to lead a decent life due mainly to financial ______________.
점점 더 많은 노인들이 주로 재정적 고난으로 인해 제대로된 삶을 영위하기 어려워진다. 11 고3학평 변형

6 Moderate food ______________ is essential for the survival of every living organism.
적절한 음식 섭취는 모든 생물의 생존을 위해 필수적이다. 2016 수능 변형

7 You need 15 to 20 minutes of ______________ physical activity three times a week to stay in shape.
너에게는 몸매를 관리하기 위해서 일주일에 세 번, 15분에서 20분 정도의 적절한 신체적 운동이 필요하다. 11 고2학평 변형

8 We are looking for a slightly ______________ car.
우리는 다소 비싸지 않은 자동차를 찾고 있어요.

9 He plays badminton at an ______________ level.
그는 중급 수준으로 배드민턴을 친다.

10 Hundreds of celebrities fail to make a ______________ impression because they don't listen attentively to public opinion.
수많은 유명 인사들이 호의적인 인상을 주지 못하는 것은 대중의 의견을 귀 기울여 듣지 않지 때문이다. 05 고3학평 변형

Day 07

MP3

196 **urgent** [ə́:rdʒənt]
형 긴급한, 시급한
deliver an urgent message 긴급 메시지를 전달하다

197 **expansion** [ikspǽnʃən]
명 확대, 팽창
expansion and renovation 확장과 혁신

198 **grant** [grænt]
동 승인하다, 허락하다 명 보조금
grant permission to visit 방문 허가를 승인하다

199 **column** [kάləm]
명 기둥, 열, 세로줄, (신문, 잡지 등의) 기고란
the first column of the table 표의 첫 번째 열

200 **curriculum** [kəríkjələm]
명 교육과정, 이수과정
national curriculum 국가 교육과정 a basic curriculum 기본 교육과정

201 **input** [ínpùt]
명 투입, 입력, 조언 동 (정보 등을) 입력하다, (조언, 정보 등을) 제공하다
input of pollutants 오염물질의 투입 information input 정보 입력

202 **flesh** [fleʃ]
명 살, 고기
flesh and blood 살과 피 raw flesh 생고기

203 **exceed** [iksí:d]
동 넘다, 초과하다
exceed the weight limit 제한 중량을 초과하다

204 **usage** [jú:sidʒ]
명 사용(량), (단어의) 용법, 어법
annual water usage 연간 물 사용량

205 **wilderness** [wíldərnis]
명 황야, 황무지
a desolate wilderness 사람이 없는 황야

206 **breakthrough** [bréikθrù:]
명 돌파구, (난관의) 타개
make a breakthrough 돌파구를 찾다

207 **forage** [fɔ́(:)ridʒ]
동 먹이를 찾다 명 먹이, 사료
forage for food 음식을 찾다 forage crops 사료용 곡물

208 **substantial** [səbstǽnʃəl]
형 상당한, 실질적인, 본질적인 유 considerable 상당한, 적지않은
a substantial sum of money 상당한 양의 돈

209 **overnight** [óuvərnàit]
형 밤새도록, 밤 사이에
stay overnight 하룻밤을 묵다

210 **lifelong** [láiflɔ̀(:)ŋ]
형 평생의, 일생 동안의
his lifelong study 그의 일생 동안의 연구

Daily Test

| 월 일 |

A 우리말에 맞게 빈 칸에 알맞은 단어를 쓰세요.

1 Two million years ago, the ______________ of the human brain required energy rich food.
200만 년 전 인간의 뇌가 커지면서 에너지가 풍부한 음식물이 필요하게 되었다. 09 고2 평가원 변형

2 The backbone is sometimes called the spinal ______________.
등뼈는 때때로 척추의 기둥이라고 불린다.

3 Some experts think that parents should encourage children to get involved in the school ______________.
일부 전문가들은 부모들이 아이들을 학교 교육 과정에 보다 적극적으로 개입하도록 격려해야 한다고 생각한다. 08 고2 평가원 변형

4 A mummy is simply a corpse whose ______________ has been preserved by chemicals and low temperatures.
미라는 살이 화학 물질과 저온에 의해 보존된 단순한 시체이다.

5 The total time of this performance should not ______________ an hour.
전체 공연 시간이 한 시간을 넘어서는 안됩니다. 06 고3 평가원 변형

6 In most ______________, the majority of groups visiting the area are usually between four and eight people.
황무지 대부분에서, 그 지역을 방문하는 무리는 대부분 보통 네 명에서 여덟 명 사이다. 14 고3 학평 변형

7 The successful cloning of sheep was an enormous ______________ for science.
양 복제의 성공은 과학의 거대한 돌파구가 되었다.

8 In the past, people commonly ______________ for food in forests, riversides and caves.
과거에 사람들은 주로 숲, 강가, 그리고 동굴에서 음식을 찾아왔다. 11 고3 평가원 변형

9 The city's wealth originally came from the ______________ tolls it placed on passing merchants.
그 도시가 부유해진 것은 원래 지나가는 낙타 대상들에게 부과한 상당한 통행료에서 비롯되었다. 11 고3 평가원

10 The ______________ mail service and direct long distance telephone calls increased the speed of cross-national communication.
빠른 우편 서비스와 장거리 직통 전화는 국가 간 소통의 속도를 증가시켰다. 15 고1 학평 변형

Day 08

MP3

211 **rank** [ræŋk]
명 계층, 계급 동 (등급, 순위를) 매기다, 평가하다
be promoted to the rank of captain 대령으로 진급하다

212 **frost** [frɔ(:)st]
명 서리, 성에 동 성에로 뒤덮다, 성에가 끼다
severe frost 된서리 frost damage 서리 피해

213 **ridiculous** [ridíkjələs]
형 말도 안 되는, 웃기는 유 silly 어리석은, 지각없는
make a ridiculous mistake 말도 안 되는 실수를 하다

214 **dawn** [dɔ:n]
명 새벽, 시작
wake up before dawn 새벽이 오기 전에 깨다

215 **inappropriate** [ìnəpróupriət]
형 부적절한
inappropriate behavior 부적절한 행동

216 **accustomed** [əkʌ́stəmd]
형 익숙한, 평소의 유 familiar 잘 알려진, 익숙한
get accustomed to getting up early 일찍 일어나는데 익숙해지다

217 **domain** [douméin]
명 영역, 범위
protect their domain 그들의 영역을 보호하다

218 **update** [ʌ́pdèit]
동 업데이트하다, 가장 최근의 정보를 알려주다
update his software 그의 소프트웨어를 업데이트하다

219 **exclusive** [iksklú:siv]
형 독점적인, 배타적인 부 exclusively 배타적으로, 전적으로
exclusive rights 독점권 an exclusive contract 독점 계약

220 **sacrifice** [sǽkrəfàis]
동 희생하다 명 희생, 제물
sacrifice for his children 그의 아이들을 위해 희생하다

221 **contagious** [kəntéidʒəs]
형 전염되는, 옮기 쉬운
a contagious disease 전염병 highly contagious 전염이 잘 되는

222 **immense** [iméns]
형 굉장한, 막대한, 한없는 유 huge 거대한, 막대한
an immense crowd 굉장한 군중

223 **defensive** [difénsiv]
형 방어의, 방어적인, 수비적인
a defensive weapon 방어용 무기

224 **potter** [pátər]
명 도예가 명 pottery 도자기(그릇들), 도예, 도기 제조소
potter around the house 집에서 빈둥거리다

225 **shield** [ʃi:ld]
명 방패, 보호막, 보호장치 동 보호하다, 가리다
a shield-shaped bag 방패 모양의 가방 sword and shield 창과 방패

Daily Test

| 월 일 |

A 우리말에 맞게 빈 칸에 알맞은 단어를 쓰세요.

1 Although Mina's attitude was ______________ for the seminar, she couldn't realized that.
Mina의 태도가 그 세미나에 부적절했음에도 불구하고, 그녀는 이를 깨닫지 못했다.

2 Because I was not ______________ to earthquakes, I was so terrified.
나는 지진에 익숙하지 않았기 때문에, 매우 겁에 질려 있었다.

3 In many countries, soccer is a predominantly male ______________.
많은 나라에서, 축구는 대개 남자의 영역이다.

4 The flight to Dallas is delayed. We'll ____________ the flight information soon.
Dallas행 비행은 지연되었습니다. 우리는 곧 비행 정보를 업데이트 하겠습니다. 2016 수능 변형

5 Foot-and-Mouth Disease(FMD) is almost ______________ to cattle, sheep, swine, goats, and other cloven-hoofed animals.
구제역은 소, 양, 돼지, 염소와 다른 갈라진 발굽을 가진 동물들에게 전적으로 생긴다 15 고2 평가원 변형

6 Patriotism demands ______________ which some people think is disadvantageous.
애국심은 몇몇 사람들이 불리하다고 생각하는 희생을 요구한다. 12 고3 학평 변형

7 Some emotions such as sadness can quickly become ______________.
슬픔과 같은 몇몇 감정은 빠르게 전염될 수 있다. 16 고3 평가원 변형

8 There are ______________ pressures at work in the core, mantle and crust of the Earth.
지구의 중심핵, 맨틀, 그리고 지각 속 작용에는 엄청난 압력이 가해진다.

9 When a company comes out with a new product, its competitors typically go on the ______________, doing whatever they can.
한 회사가 신상품을 제안할 때, 그 회사의 경쟁자들은 전형적으로 그들이 할 수 있는 모든 것을 하면서 방어적 자세를 취한다.
14 고3 평가원 변형

10 ______________ are currently using approximately 600 trademarks that date to the Roman period.
도예가들은 현재 로마시대까지 거슬러 올라가는 600여개의 상표를 사용하는 중이다.

Day 08

MP3

226 **hesitation** [hèzitéiʃən]
명 주저, 망설임 　 동 hesitate 망설이다, 주저하다
show hesitation 주저하다

227 **retail** [ríːtèil]
명 소매
recommended retail price 권장 소매가

228 **latitude** [lǽtətjùːd]
명 위도 　 반 longitude 경도
calculate latitude 위도를 계산하다 　 latitude of Seoul 서울의 위도

229 **amateur** [ǽmətər]
명 비전문가 형 전문이 아닌, 아마추어인
team of amateur dancers 아마추어 댄스팀

230 **pest** [pest]
명 해충, 기생충
insect pest control 해충 방제 　 a garden pest 식물 기생충

231 **antibiotic** [æ̀ntaibaiátik]
명 항생제 형 항생의
take antibiotics 항생제를 복용하다 　 antibiotic resistance 항생 저항

232 **cottage** [kátidʒ]
명 오두막, 별장
stay in a cottage 오두막에 머무르다 　 a country cottage 시골 별장

233 **volcanic** [vɑlkǽnik]
형 화산의 　 명 volcano 화산
potential volcanic hazards 잠재적 화산 위험

234 **loan** [loun]
명 대출(금), 대여 동 (돈을)빌려주다, 대여하다
household mortgage loans 주택 담보 대출

235 **solely** [sóulli]
형 오로지, 단지
depend solely on her experience 오로지 그녀의 경험에 의존하다

236 **controversy** [kántrəvə̀ːrsi]
명 논란, 논쟁 　 형 controversial 논란이 많은
beyond controversy 논쟁의 여지없이

237 **assembly** [əsémbli]
명 의회, 조립 　 동 assemble 모으다, 집합시키다, 조립하다
state assembly 지방 의회 　 a simple assembly job 간단한 조립 작업

238 **fatal** [féitəl]
형 치명적인 　 유 disastrous 비참한, 피해가 막심한
a fatal injury 치명적 부상 　 carry a fatal disease 치명적 질병을 옮기다

239 **distress** [distrés]
명 고통, 고뇌 동 괴롭히다
psychological distress 정신적인 고통 　 deeply distressed 심히 괴로운

240 **precipitation** [prisìpitéiʃən]
명 강수(량)
accumulate the precipitation data 강수 데이터를 축적하다

Daily Test

| 월 일 |

A 우리말에 맞게 빈 칸에 알맞은 단어를 쓰세요.

1 We don't know why customers leave ______________ stores empty-handed.
우리는 왜 고객들이 빈 손으로 소매점을 떠나는지 알 수 없다. 11 고3학평 변형

2 When I was in high school, I was studying longitude and ______________ in geography class.
내가 고등학생 때, 나는 지리학 시간에 경도와 위도에 대해서 공부했었다. 16 고2학평 변형

3 The professor was impressed with the young ______________ powers of observation.
교수는 그 젊은 아마추어의 관찰력에 깊은 감명을 받았다. 13 고1학평 변형

4 The densely structured wood is resistant to invasion by insects and other potential ______________.
조밀하게 조직을 갖춘 나무는 곤충들이나 다른 잠재적인 해충들의 공격에 내성이 있다. 2011 수능 변형

5 ______________ are medicines that help make our bodies resistant to diseases.
항생제는 우리 몸이 질병에 저항할 수 있도록 돕는 약이다.

6 The teacher said that the island was formed as a result of a ______________ eruption.
선생님은 그 섬이 화산 폭발로 형성되었다고 말했다.

7 An estimated 73 million sharks are killed ______________ for their fins every year.
매년 7300만 마리의 상어가 단지 지느러미 때문에 죽음을 당한다. 11 고2학평 변형

8 There is an educational ______________ in science classrooms over how to teach the evolution of life on Earth.
과학시간에 지구 생명체의 진화를 어떻게 가르칠지에 대한 교육적 논쟁이 있다.

9 The McDonaldization of society does not refer just to the robot like ______________ of food.
사회의 맥도날드화는 기계적인 음식의 조합만을 의미하지는 않는다. 12 고3평가원

10 Empathetic ______________ occurs when people realize that their actions have caused pain to another person.
고통의 공감은 자신들의 행동이 다른 사람에게 고통을 일으켰음을 깨달을 때 생긴다. 2013 수능 변형

Review Test 04

A 우리말에 맞게 빈 칸에 알맞은 단어를 쓰시오.

1 ______________ about social issues 사회 이슈에 무관심한

2 undergo ______________ 고난을 견디다

3 information ______________ 정보 입력

4 annual water ______________ 연간 물 사용량

5 a ______________ sum of money 상당한 양의 돈

6 be promoted to the ______________ of captain 대령으로 진급하다

7 wake up before ______________ 새벽이 오기 전에 깨다

8 an ______________ contract 독점 계약

9 recommended ______________ price 권장 소매가

10 ______________ resistance 항생 저항

B 영어에 맞게 빈 칸에 알맞은 우리말을 쓰시오.

1 a wage rise ______________ 인상

2 adequate intake 적절한 ______________

3 neutral territory ______________ 영토

4 a basic curriculum 기본 ______________

5 forage for food 음식을 ______________

6 sacrifice for his children 그의 아이들을 위해 ______________

7 a defensive weapon ______________ 무기

8 a shield-shaped bag ______________ 모양의 가방

9 latitude of Seoul 서울의 ______________

10 stay in a cottage ______________에 머무르다

C 다음 영어 풀이에 알맞은 어휘를 〈보기〉에서 고르시오.

보기	hardship	controversy	ridiculous	update	forage

1 ______________ : to provide the most recent information or details

2 ______________ : a lot of arguments and disagreements about something

3 ______________ : a difficult or unpleasant situation

4 ______________ : to eat grass or search for food

5 ______________ : foolish and unreasonable

D 문맥에 맞게 다음 문장을 완성하시오.

1 The backbone is sometimes •

2 In many countries, soccer is •

3 There are immense pressures •

4 Potters are currently using •

5 An estimated 73 million sharks are •

• a called the spinal column.

• b at work in the core, mantle and crust of the Earth.

• c killed solely for their fins every year.

• d approximately 600 trademarks that date to the Roman period.

• e a predominantly male domain.

E 문장을 읽고 문맥에 적절한 단어를 고르시오.

1 Maintaining balanced nutritional (intake/overtake) is essential for your health.

2 We don't have much time. Let's do the most (modest/urgent) thing first.

3 I will (update/forage) my computer system to the newest version tonight.

4 Since this movie has a lot of violence, it is (exclusive/inappropriate) for children.

5 You will soon become (accustomed/neutral) to studying with new classmates.

F 문장의 빈칸에 알맞은 단어를 〈보기〉에서 찾아 쓰시오. (필요하면 형태를 고치시오.)

보기 breakthrough controversy contagious precipitation identification

1 Many ______________ diseases spread through carriers such as birds and mosquitoes.
많은 전염병이 새나 모기와 같은 매개체를 통해 확산된다. 10 고3학평

2 In Rome, the highest monthly ______________ occurs in October.
로마에서 강수량이 가장 많은 달은 10월이다. 06 고2학평 변형

3 Our understanding of context plays an important role for object ______________.
상황에 대한 이해는 개체 인식에 중대한 역할을 한다. 2008 수능 변형

4 The company made an important ______________ in robot technology.
그 회사는 로봇 기술에서 획기적인 돌파구를 마련했다.

5 There is now considerable ______________ over the notion of general intelligence.
이제는 일반 지능에 대한 상당한 논쟁이 있다. 15 고2학평

G 다음 〈보기〉 중 두 문장에 공통으로 사용할 수 있는 어휘를 고르시오.

1 An ____________ matter stopped Justin from attending the conference. 2012 수능 변형
I began to feel an ____________ need for a change to get closer to my goal. 15 고3평가원 변형

① macro ② flesh ③ urgent ④ indifferent ⑤ antibiotic

2 The size of your image file cannot ____________(e)d 100 megabytes. 12 고3평가원
To my surprise, the result ____________(e)d my expectations. 10 고3학평 변형

① transport ② exceed ③ grant ④ guarantee ⑤ substitute

3 When we are unable to set healthy limits, ____________ can enter our relationships. 2014 수능 변형
People in the village fell into ____________ due to the recent storm damage.

① distress ② wilderness ③ domain ④ latitude ⑤ curriculum

Study More

혼동하기 쉬운 단어 indifferent vs. different

- [indifferent] 형 무관심한
  Many students are **indifferent** to social problems. 많은 학생들은 사회 문제에 무관심하다.
- [different] 형 서로 다른
  The teacher said that James is **different** from other kids in his age group.
  선생님은 James가 또래 집단의 다른 아이들과는 다르다고 말했다.

Day 09

MP3

241 **facilitate** [fəsílitèit]
동 용이하게 하다, 촉진시키다
facilitate the intervention 개입을 촉진시키다

242 **ignorance** [ígnərəns]
명 무지, 무식
ignorance about the disease 그 병에 대한 무지

243 **sacred** [séikrid]
형 신성한, 성스러운
dress in sacred robes 신성한 예복을 입다

244 **trace** [treis]
동 쫓다 명 자취
trace pickpockets 소매치기를 쫓다 leave no trace 자취를 남기지 않다

245 **competent** [kámpitənt]
형 유능한, 능숙한, 만족할만한
recruit competent computer experts 능력 있는 컴퓨터 전문가를 모집하다

246 **equivalent** [ikwívələnt]
형 동등한, 맞먹는 명 (~에 상당하는) 대용물, 등가물
equivalent figure 동등한 수치

247 **hemisphere** [hémisfìər]
명 반구
the southern hemisphere 남반구

248 **impatient** [impéiʃənt]
형 참을성 없는, 조급한
impatient customers 참을성 없는 소비자들

249 **reception** [risépʃən]
명 수신, 환영 연회, 접수처, 평판
a wedding reception 결혼식 연회

250 **subsequent** [sʌ́bsəkwənt]
형 그 후의, 차후의 유 following 다음의, 다음에 계속되는
a subsequent discussion 그 후의 논의

251 **circumstance** [sə́ːrkəmstæ̀ns]
명 환경, 상황
the current circumstance 현재 상황

252 **symbolic** [simbálik]
형 상징적인
understand the symbolic meaning 상징적 의미를 이해하다

253 **vigorous** [vígərəs]
형 활발한, 격렬한 명 vigor 힘, 활력, 활기
a vigorous workout 격렬한 운동

254 **transmit** [trænsmít]
동 전달하다, 전송하다, 전염시키다 명 transmission 전파, 전염, 전달
transmit electricity 전기를 전달하다

255 **exceptional** [iksépʃənəl]
형 뛰어난, 아주 훌륭한
exceptional talent as a pianist 피아니스트로서 뛰어난 능력

Daily Test

| 월 일 |

A 우리말에 맞게 빈 칸에 알맞은 단어를 쓰세요.

1 The new terminal and airport will ______________ the development of tourism.
새 터미널과 공항이 관광 산업 발전을 촉진시킬 것이다.

2 Because of ______________ about the African continent, there were some enormous errors in mapmaking.
아프리카 대륙에 대한 무지 때문에, 지도 제작에서 일부 엄청난 오류가 있었다. 10 고2학평 변형

3 Scientists have ______________ the origins of shopping back to prehistoric times, when "shopping" was called "hunting."
과학자들은 "쇼핑"이 "사냥"으로 불렸던 선사시대로 거슬러 올라가 쇼핑의 기원을 추적해왔다. 08 고2평가원 변형

4 Jimmy got really ______________ because he wanted to master all the techniques as soon as possible.
Jimmy는 그가 가능한 빨리 모든 기술을 숙달하고 싶었기 때문에 매우 조급했다. 08 고1학평 변형

5 The device has a new antenna that helps with the ______________ of the signal.
그 장치는 신호의 수신을 돕는 새로운 안테나를 갖고 있다. 09 고3평가원 변형

6 ______________ event verified Sue's innocence.
그 후의 사건들이 Sue의 무죄를 입증하였다. 09 고2평가원 변형

7 Remember that refunds are not given under any ______________.
어떠한 상황에도 환불을 해 드리지 않음을 기억하세요.

8 Students who engage in ______________ activity outside of school have higher academic scores.
학교 밖에서 활발한 활동에 참여하는 학생들은 학업 점수가 더 높았다. 10 고3평가원 변형

9 Scientists do not know how mosquitoes ______________ the malaria virus.
과학자들은 어떻게 모기가 말라리아 바이러스를 옮기는지 알지 못한다.

10 Some people worshipped medical doctors as if they were ______________ beings possessing godlike qualities.
몇몇 사람들은 의사들이 마치 신과 같은 재능을 가진 뛰어난 존재인 것처럼 우러러보았다. 16 고2학평 변형

Day 09

MP3

256 **globalization** [gloʊbələzeiʃn]
명 세계화
era of globalization 세계화 시대

257 **voluntary** [vάləntèri]
형 자발적인
make a voluntary contribution 자발적인 기여를 하다

258 **gratitude** [grǽtitjùːd]
명 감사, 고마움
sincere gratitude 진지한 감사 love and gratitude 사랑과 감사

259 **autograph** [ɔ́ːtəgræ̀f]
명 사인 형 자필의
give an autograph 사인을 해주다

260 **dump** [dʌmp]
동 (쓰레기 등을) 버리다 명 쓰레기 더미
be dumped at the forest 숲에 쓰레기를 버리다

261 **reinforce** [rìːinfɔ́ːrs]
동 강화하다, 보강하다 유 strengthen 강하게하다, 튼튼하게 하다
reinforce a stereotype 고정관념을 강화하다

262 **humiliate** [hjuːmílièit]
동 창피를 주다, 모욕하다
humiliate him in front of his friends 친구들 앞에서 그를 모욕하다

263 **abuse** [əbjúːs]
명 남용 동 남용하다
drug abuse 약물 남용 abuse his rights 그의 권리를 남용하다

264 **farewell** [fὲərwél]
명 작별
give a farewell reception 송별회를 열다

265 **equator** [ikwéitər]
명 적도
above the equator 적도 위에 almost on the equator 거의 적도상에

266 **recite** [risait]
동 낭독하다, 열거하다
recite a poem 시를 낭독하다 recite a monologue 독백하다

267 **flock** [flαk]
명 떼, 무리 동 떼지어 가다
a flock of birds 한 떼의 새

268 **chaos** [kéiὰs]
명 혼란, 카오스 형 chootic 혼란한, 무질서한
order out of chaos 혼돈 속의 질서 economic chaos 경제 혼란

269 **vessel** [vésəl]
명 (대형) 선박, 혈관
the rapidly sinking vessel 빠르게 가라앉는 선박 blood vessel 혈관

270 **worthwhile** [wə̀ːrθhwáil]
형 가치 있는
worthwhile endeavor 가치 있는 노력

Daily Test

| 월 일 |

Ⓐ 우리말에 맞게 빈 칸에 알맞은 단어를 쓰세요.

1 ______________ gives us a chance to learn about other societies and cultures.
세계화는 우리에게 다른 사회와 문화에 대해서 배울 수 있는 기회를 준다. 15 고1 학평 변형

2 Helen sometimes does ______________ work at the local orphanage.
Helen은 지역 고아원에서 때때로 봉사활동을 한다.

3 Iron was used to ______________ a ship's internal frame.
철은 배의 내부 구조를 강화시키기 위해 사용된다.

4 I felt ______________ by the negative responses of the audience.
나는 관중들의 부정적인 반응에 모욕감을 느꼈다.

5 When I had to say ______________ to my friends, their eyes were full of tears.
내가 친구들에게 작별인사를 해야 했을 때, 그들의 눈은 눈물로 가득 찼다. 07 고2 학평 변형

6 This forest is a very warm and rainy area near the ______________.
이 숲은 적도 근처의 따뜻하고 비가 많이 내리는 지역이다.

7 I can ______________ the name of nearly every baseball player on the team.
나는 팀의 거의 모든 야구 선수들의 이름을 읊을 수 있다. 2005 수능 변형

8 A ______________ of birds would gather together in the tree, eating fruits and chattering.
새무리는 열매를 먹고 지저귀면서 나무 위에 모여들고는 했다. 08 고2 평가원 변형

9 Black Friday originated from describing the ______________ created by the massive traffic and the numerous people flocking to stores.
Black Friday는 가게로 모여드는 엄청난 교통량과 사람들로 인한 혼란을 묘사하는 데서 유래됐다. 11 고3 평가원 변형

10 Because the journey was truly ______________, I wasn't tired.
그 여행이 정말 가치 있었기 때문에, 나는 피곤하지 않았다. 10 고3 평가원 변형

Day 10

MP3

271 **deed** [di:d]
명 행위, 행동
her infamous deed 그녀의 악독한 행동

272 **negotiate** [nigóuʃièit]
동 협상하다
negotiate the date 날짜를 협상하다

273 **sensation** [senséiʃən]
명 감각, 느낌, 돌풍(선풍)을 불러 일으키는것
have a strange sensation 이상한 느낌을 갖다

274 **checkup** [tʃékʌ̀p]
명 점검, 건강검진, 시험
periodic checkup 주기적인 점검

275 **biography** [baiágrəfi]
명 전기, 자서전
biography of Kennedy 케네디 전기

276 **sting** [stiŋ]
동 쏘다, 찌르다, 따끔거리다 명 (곤충 등의) 침, 가시, 따가움
be stung by a bee 벌에 쏘이다 a bee sting 벌침

277 **sewage** [sjú:idʒ]
명 하수, 오물
sewage disposal 하수 처리

278 **spouse** [spaus]
명 배우자
my beloved spouse 내 사랑하는 배우자

279 **magnitude** [mǽgnətjù:d]
명 규모, 중요성
the magnitude of the earthquake 지진의 규모

280 **nursery** [nə́:rsəri]
명 탁아소, 아기 방
work at a nursery 탁아소에서 일하다

281 **terrain** [təréin]
명 지형, 지역
mountainous terrain 산악 지형 swampy terrain 습지대

282 **audition** [ɔ:diʃn]
명 (가수, 배우 등의) 오디션 동 오디션을 보다
audition for the role of Juliet 줄리엣 역에 대한 오디션을 보다

283 **brochure** [bróuʃuər]
명 (안내, 광고용) 책자
a brochure for tourists 관광객을 위한 안내책자

284 **ongoing** [ángòuiŋ]
형 계속 진행 중인
ongoing debate 계속 진행 중인 토론

285 **criminal** [krímənəl]
형 범죄의 명 범인
criminal investigation 범죄 수사 catch a criminal 범인을 잡다

Daily Test

| 월 일 |

A 우리말에 맞게 빈 칸에 알맞은 단어를 쓰세요.

1 Children must be taught to perform good ______________ for their own sake, not in order to receive a reward.
아이들은 보상을 받기 위해서가 아니라 그들 스스로를 위해서 좋은 일을 행해야 한다고 가르침을 받아야 한다. 2011 수능 변형

2 Paralysis means the loss of movement and ______________ of a particular part of the body.
마비는 움직임과 신체의 특정 부분의 감각 상실을 의미한다.

3 Father takes his car to the mechanic for regular ______________.
아버지는 정기 검진을 위해 그의 차를 기술자에게 맡겼다. 12 고1학평 변형

4 In 1989, a ______________ of Henson called "Dark Companion" was published.
1989년에 "어둠의 동반자"라 불리는 Henson의 자서전이 출간되었다. 12 고1학평 변형

5 I got ______________ by a bee when I was visiting my grandparents' farm.
난 할아버지 농장을 갔을 때 벌에 쏘였어. 14 고2학평 변형

6 Garbage landfills leak poison into the groundwater, and ______________ from homes pollutes local lakes and waterways.
쓰레기 매립지는 독을 지하수로 흘리고, 가정에서의 오물은 지역 호수와 수로를 오염시킨다.

7 Switching on the light in the ______________, Amy found her baby daughter giving out odd little cries.
아기 방에 불을 키면서 Amy는 그녀의 어린 딸이 이상한 작은 울음 소리를 내는 것을 알았다. 12 고3평가원 변형

8 We will be contacting clients soon to hear their decision regarding putting their remarks in the ______________.
우리는 홍보 책자에 고객의 소견을 싣는 것에 관한 그들의 결정을 듣기 위해 곧 연락할 것이다. 16 고3평가원 변형

9 We know that earning the trust of our clients is a permanent and ______________ endeavor.
우리는 고객들의 신뢰를 얻기 위해 지속적인 노력을 기울이고 있습니다. 11 고2학평 변형

10 Adults have a responsibility to protect children from ______________.
어른들은 아이들을 범죄로부터 보호해야 할 책임이 있다.

Day 10

MP3

286 **proceed** [prəsíːd]
동 진행하다, 나아가다, ~을 이어서 계속하다 유 contine 계속하다
proceed quickly 빠르게 진행하다

287 **coward** [káuərd]
명 겁쟁이, 비겁한 사람 형 겁이 많은, 소심한
a dirty coward 비겁한 겁쟁이 act like a coward 겁쟁이 같은 행동을 하다

288 **exploit** [éksplɔit]
동 (부당하게)이용하다, 착취하다
exploit workers 노동자를 착취하다

289 **desperation** [dèspəréiʃən]
명 자포자기, 필사적임 유 despair 절망, 자포자기
in desperation 자포자기하여 an act of desperation 자포자기한 행동

290 **cabin** [kæbin]
명 객실, 선실, 오두막집
cabin crew (비행기의) 객실 승무원

291 **comprehension** [kàmprihénʃən]
명 이해(력) 동 comprehend 이해하다, 파악하다
improve comprehension 이해력을 증진시키다

292 **intuitive** [intjúːitiv]
형 직관력 있는, 직감에 의한
intuitive faculty 직관력

293 **blade** [bleid]
명 (칼, 도구 등의) 날
a razor blade 면도날 a dull blade 무딘 날

294 **stiff** [stif]
형 뻣뻣한, 빽빽한, 경직된
the stiff competition 치열한 경쟁

295 **occupy** [ákjəpài]
동 차지하다, (토지, 건물 등을)사용하다, 점령하다 명 occupation 점령, 직업
occupy territory 영토를 차지하다

296 **transition** [trænzíʃən]
명 인수, 이동, 변천 형 transitional 변천하는, 과도기적인
a transition period 과도기 transition to the north 북쪽으로의 이동

297 **outbreak** [áutbrèik]
명 발생, 발발 동 break out 발생하다, 발발하다
an outbreak of food poisoning 식중독 발생

298 **barn** [baːrn]
명 곳간, 마구간
go into the barn 마구간에 들어가다

299 **notable** [nóutəbl]
형 주목할 만한, 눈에 띄는 유 remarkable 주목할만한, 두드러진
a notable artist 주목 할 만한 예술가

300 **disturbing** [distə́ːrbiŋ]
형 충격적인, 불안감을 주는
disturbing news 충격적인 소식

Daily Test

| 월 일 |

A 우리말에 맞게 빈 칸에 알맞은 단어를 쓰세요.

1 It is important to put the past behind and ______________ with life.
과거를 잊고 삶을 계속 이어가는 것은 중요하다.

2 It is evident that humans tend to ______________ natural resources to benefit themselves.
인간이 스스로의 이익을 위해 천연 자원을 이용하는 것은 자명한 일이다. 08 고3 평가원 변형

3 John has an ______________ sense of what consumers want.
John은 소비자가 원하는 것을 직감적으로 알고 있다.

4 You can harden a ______________ just by hammering it.
당신은 단지 칼날을 두드림으로써 그것을 단단하게 할 수 있다. 14 고2 학평 변형

5 Our primary sense is vision, ______________ up to one third of our brain.
우리의 주된 감각은 뇌의 3분의 1을 차지하고 있는 시각이다. 14 고2 학평 변형

6 According to the theory of demographic ______________, nations go through several developmental stages.
인구 이동 이론에 따르면, 국가는 몇 번의 개발 단계를 거친다. 08 고3 평가원 변형

7 An ______________ of cholera in 1830 killed nearly 13,000 people in Italy.
1830년의 콜레라 발병은 이탈리아 사람들을 거의 13000명 가량 죽였다. 09 고2 평가원 변형

8 Come and visit Fresh Farm, and enjoy our beautiful fields, ______________, fresh milk, and cheese shop.
Fresh 농장에 와서 우리의 아름다운 들판, 마구간, 신선한 우유와 치즈 가게를 즐겨보세요. 16 고3 평가원 변형

9 Richard Porson, one of Britain's most ______________ classical scholars, was born on Christmas in 1759.
영국의 가장 유명한 고전 학자 중 한 명인 Richard Porson은 1759년 크리스마스에 태어났다. 16 고3 평가원 변형

10 The theme of the movie was so ______________ to us.
그 영화의 소재는 우리에게 매우 충격적이었어요.

Review Test 05

A 우리말에 맞게 빈 칸에 알맞은 단어를 쓰시오.

1 ______________ about the disease 그 병에 대한 무지

2 the southern ______________ 남반구

3 understand the ______________ meaning 상징적 의미를 이해하다

4 make a ______________ contribution 자발적인 기여를 하다

5 ______________ him in front of his friends 친구들 앞에서 그를 모욕하다

6 ______________ the date 날짜를 협상하다

7 the ______________ of the earthquake 지진의 규모

8 ______________ workers 노동자를 착취하다

9 ______________ faculty 직관력

10 ______________ to the north 북쪽으로의 이동

B 영어에 맞게 빈 칸에 알맞은 우리말을 쓰시오.

1 facilitate the intervention 개입을 ______________

2 equivalent figure ______________ 수치

3 love and gratitude 사랑과 ______________

4 give a farewell reception ______________를 열다

5 economic chaos 경제 ______________

6 her infamous deed 그녀의 악독한 ______________

7 sewage disposal ______________ 처리

8 swampy terrain ______________

9 a dull blade 무딘 ______________

10 disturbing news ______________ 소식

C 다음 영어 풀이에 알맞은 어휘를 〈보기〉에서 고르시오.

보기	transmit	sting	occupy	deed	ongoing

1 ______________ : to continue to exist or happen

2 ______________ : to send something from one place to another

3 ______________ : to cause a pain with a sharp or pointed object

4 ______________ : to take or fill a space or use a certain amount of time

5 ______________ : something that is done or performed, e.g., an action

D 문맥에 맞게 다음 문장을 완성하시오.

1	Globalization gives us a chance	a	rainy area near the equator.
2	This forest is a very warm and	b	for regular checkups.
3	I can recite the name of	c	to learn about other societies and cultures.
4	Father takes his car to the mechanic	d	nearly every baseball player on the team.
5	In 1989, a biography of Henson	e	called "Dark Companion" was published.

E 문장을 읽고 문맥에 적절한 단어를 고르시오.

1 The investigation into the accident is still (symbolic/ongoing).

2 The wedding (reception/perception) will be held at Olympia Bar and Grill.

3 The remaining issues will be discussed in (frequent/subsequent) meetings.

4 A (flock/herd) of birds is flying over the mountains.

5 The guests left the house without leaving any (trace/equator).

F 문장의 빈칸에 알맞은 단어를 〈보기〉에서 찾아 쓰시오. (필요하면 형태를 고치시오.)

보기 sting reinforce abuse outbreak comprehension

1 What disturbs me is the idea that good behavior must be ______________ with incentives.
나를 불편하게 만드는 것은 선행이 보상으로 강화되어야 한다는 생각이다. 2011 수능

2 Some people ______________ public library Internet access, for example, to send spam emails.
어떤 사람들은 공공 도서관의 인터넷 접속을 스팸 메일 등을 보내기 위해 남용한다. 09 고3평가원 변형

3 Compared to his age, the boy's ______________ of economic issues is amazing.
나이에 비해 그 소년의 경제 문제에 관한 이해력은 놀랍다.

4 The greatest known ______________ of malaria happened in the 1920s in Russia.
가장 많이 알려져 있는 말라리아의 발병은 1920년 대 러시아에서 일어났다. 08 고2학평

5 Most bees ______________ when they feel threatened.
대부분의 벌은 위협을 느낄 때 침을 쏜다. 2016 수능

G 다음 <보기> 중 두 문장에 공통으로 사용할 수 있는 어휘를 고르시오.

1 Last class, we learned about insects that can ___________ certain diseases. 13 고2 평가원 변형
My daughter is wondering how power stations ___________ electricity to our home.

① dump ② transmit ③ trace ④ exploit ⑤ recite

2 About two billion tons of fruit and vegetables are ___________ around the world every year. 16 고3 학평
They recycle old shoes which have been ___________ in landfills. 11 고2 평가원 변형

① dumped ② humiliated ③ flocked ④ proceeded ⑤ occupied

3 Usually, ___________ achievement comes down to hard work. 13 고3 학평 변형
The pitcher was famous for his ___________ curveball. 12 고3 학평 변형

① vigorous ② impatient ③ exceptional ④ coward ⑤ stiff

Study More

tense의 다양한 의미

- [형용사] : '긴장한', '신경이 날카로운'
  If you are **tense**, take deep breaths. 만약 당신이 긴장했다면, 여러 번 심호흡을 해라.
- [명사] : 문장의 '시제'
  Today, we will learn the past tense and the present perfect **tense** in English.
  오늘, 우리는 영어의 과거 시제와 현재 완료 시제에 대해 배울 거에요.

Day 11

MP3

301 **impractical** [impræ̀ktəkəl]
형 터무니없는, 비현실적인
an impractical plan 터무니없는 계획

302 **outfit** [áutfit]
명 의상, 복장, 용품 유 costume 복장, 옷차림
a wedding outfit 결혼 예복 wear a new outfit 새로운 의상을 입다

303 **mentor** [mentɔ:(r)]
명 스승, 조언자
the important role of a mentor 조언자로서의 중요한 역할

304 **optimal** [áptəməl]
형 최적의, 최상의
optimal conditions 최적의 상태 an optimal temperature 최적 온도

305 **elastic** [ilǽstik]
형 탄력 있는, 신축적인 유 flexible 신축성(융통성) 있는, 유명한
elastic force 탄력 elastic fiber 탄력 섬유

306 **diameter** [daiǽmitər]
명 지름, 직경, 배율 명 radius 반지름
the diameter of a circle 원의 지름

307 **dignity** [dígnəti]
명 존엄, 위엄, 품위, 자존감
fundamental human dignity 근본적 인간 존엄성

308 **longevity** [lɑndʒévəti]
명 장수, 수명
contribute to his longevity 그의 장수에 기여하다

309 **illustrate** [íləstrèit]
동 설명하다, 삽화를 넣다 유 demonstrate 입증하다, (행동으로)보여주다
illustrate by example 예를 들어 설명하다

310 **minimal** [mínəməl]
형 최소의 반 maximal 최대한의
minimal participation 최소한의 참여 a minimal effect 최소한의 노력

311 **imperfect** [impə́:rfikt]
형 불완전한, 불충분한
imperfect knowledge 불충분한 지식

312 **exert** [igzə́:rt]
동 (권력, 영향력을) 행사하다, 가하다
exert a strong influence 강한 영향력을 행사하다

313 **editorial** [èditɔ́:riəl]
형 편집의, 편집과 관련된, 사설의 명 사설
the editorial staff 편집 부원

314 **imply** [implái]
동 암시하다, 함축하다 명 implication 함축, 암시, 영향
imply participation 참여를 암시하다

315 **irrigation** [ìrəgéiʃən]
명 관개, 물대기 동 irrigate 땅에 물을 대다
repair the irrigation canal 관개수로를 수리하다

Daily Test

| 월 일 |

A 우리말에 맞게 빈 칸에 알맞은 단어를 쓰세요.

1 I recently ordered an ______________ from your online store and I want to exchange it.
나는 최근에 당신의 온라인 가게에서 옷을 주문했고 저는 이것을 교환하고 싶습니다. 15 고3학평 변형

2 Meeting a good ______________ is a meaningful and precious experience.
훌륭한 스승을 만나는 것은 의미있고 귀중한 경험이다.

3 Olives and nuts are just some of the foods that provide the types of fats which we need in order to maintain ______________ health.
올리브와 견과류는 최적의 건강 상태를 유지시켜 주는데 필요한 지방 유형을 제공하는 몇몇 음식들이다. 08 고2학평 변형

4 Have you ever seen a tree trunk which is about one meter in ______________?
당신은 지름이 대략 1미터 정도 되는 나무 밑동을 본 적이 있나요? 07 고1학평 변형

5 Hurting a man's ______________ is a crime.
인간의 존엄성을 해치는 것은 범죄다. 06 고2평가원 변형

6 Exercise and a healthy diet are important, but they are not the only keys to ______________.
운동과 건강한 식사는 중요하지만, 이들이 장수의 유일한 요소는 아니다. 11 고1학평 변형

7 Sean was frustrated because he gained only ______________ recognition for his work.
Sean은 자기가 한 일에 대해 최소한의 인정 밖에 받지 못했기 때문에 좌절했다.

8 While experience is an essential means of improvement, it is nontheless an ______________ instrument.
경험은 향상하기 위한 학습의 필수적인 방법이지만 이는 그럼에도 불구하고 완벽하지 않은 도구다. 08 고3평가원 변형

9 The president ______________ all his authority when the council makes new policy.
대통령은 의회가 새 정책을 만들 때 그의 모든 영향력을 행사한다.

10 The craters of extinct volcanoes were used by farmers for their ______________ water.
그 사화산의 분화구는 농부들의 관개 용수를 위해 사용되었다. 10 고2학평 변형

Day 11

MP3

316 foster [fɔ́(ː)stər]
동 조성하다, 위탁 양육하다 형 친부모같이, 보살펴주는
foster innovations 혁신을 조성하다 foster children 양자를 양육하다

317 dietary [dáiətèri]
형 음식의, 식이요법의
dietary intake 음식 섭취량 a dietary supplement 식사 보충량

318 nasty [nǽsti]
형 더러운, 형편없는, (성격등이) 못된, 고약한 명 mean 비열한, 심술궂은
wear nasty socks 더러운 양말을 신다 taste nasty 형편없는 맛이 나다

319 equality [ikwάləti]
명 평등, 동등 반 inequality 불평등
the equality of all living things 모든 생명체의 동등함

320 disguise [disgáiz]
동 변장하다, 위장하다
disguised as a duck 오리로 변장한 a disguised attack 위장 공격

321 keen [kiːn]
형 간절히 하고 싶어하는, 예민한
keen to/on ~을 간절히 하기를 원하다 keen sense of smell 후각이 예민한

322 cube [kjuːb]
명 정육면체, (음식 재료 등) 정육면체 모양을 한 것
a cube-shaped box 정육면체 모양의 상자

323 hasty [héisti]
형 서두른, 성급한, 경솔한
a hasty meal 서두른 식사 make a hasty decision 성급한 결정을 내리다

324 hierarchical [hàiərάːrkikəl]
형 계급(계층)에 따른
hierarchical structure 계급 구조

325 donor [dóunər]
명 기부자, 기증자 반 recipient 수령자, 수령인
a blood donor 혈액 기증자

326 insufficient [ìnsəfíʃənt]
형 불충분한, 부족한 유 scant 거의없는, 부족한
insufficient supply of water 불충분한 물 공급

327 impulsive [impʌ́lsiv]
형 충동적인, 감정에 끌린 명 impulse (갑작스러운) 충동
an impulsive decision 충동적인 결정

328 endeavor [endévər]
명 노력, 시도 동 노력하다
an active endeavor 적극적인 노력

329 convert [kάnvəːrt]
동 전환하다, 바꾸다
convert steam into power 증기를 동력으로 전환하다

330 renowned [rináund]
형 유명한, 명성있는 유 famous 유명한, 이름난
a renowned photographer 유명한 사진가

Daily Test

| 월 일 |

A 우리말에 맞게 빈 칸에 알맞은 단어를 쓰세요.

1 Schools are in a unique position to promote healthy ______________ behaviors.
학교는 건강한 식습관 형성을 향상시킬 수 있는 유일한 공간이다. 15 고2학평 변형

2 Mom bought a chicken and she discovered after getting home that it was all dry and ______________.
엄마는 닭 한 마리를 사오셨고 집에 온 뒤에야 그것이 완전히 말라있고 맛이 형편없다는 것을 알았다. 14 고3학평 변형

3 Tax ______________ refers to the way taxes are distributed among people.
과세 평등은 세금이 사람들 사이에서 부과되는 방식을 일컫는 말이다. 10 고2학평 변형

4 To ______________ the damaged goods, retailers encouraged shoppers to have their purchases gift-wrapped.
손상된 상품을 위장하기 위해, 소매상들은 손님들에게 구입한 물건들을 포장하도록 권했다. 12 고3평가원 변형

5 I am always ______________ on taking photographs.
나는 항상 사진 찍기를 열심히 했다. 06 고2평가원

6 The more ______________ your culture or background, the greater the power gap is apt to be.
당신의 문화나 배경이 더 계층적일수록, 권력 차이가 더 큰 경향이 있다. 16 고3학평 변형

7 We issue membership cards to ______________ who can use them to borrow equipment free of charge.
우리는 기증자에게 무료로 용품을 빌려갈 수 있는 멤버십 카드를 발급합니다. 2016 수능 변형

8 I had an ______________ amount of chocolate to make chocolate cookies.
나는 초콜릿 쿠키를 만들 만큼 충분한 양의 초콜렛을 갖고 있지 않다.

9 Like water, waves can be ______________ to energy and electricity.
물과 같이, 파도는 에너지와 전기로 전환 될 수 있다.

10 Cathy is ______________ for her great writing skills.
Cathy는 훌륭한 글 솜씨로 유명하다.

Day 12

MP3

331 **pedestrian** [pədéstriən]
명 보행자 형 보행의
pedestrian only area 보행자 전용 구역

332 **reservoir** [rézərvwὰːr]
명 저수지, 저장소, 비축, 공급원
a reservoir of knowledge 지식의 축적

333 **trivial** [tríviəl]
형 사소한, 하찮은 유 unimportant 중요하지 않은, 사소한
trivial arguments 사소한 논쟁

334 **retain** [ritéin]
동 유지하다, 간직하다 유 maintain 유지하다, 지속하다
retain his wealth 그의 부를 유지하다

335 **absurd** [əbsə́ːrd]
형 터무니없는, 황당한
an absurd idea 터무니없는 생각 an absurd rumor 황당한 소문

336 **outrage** [áutreidʒ]
명 격분, 격노 동 (수동태로) 격분하게 만들다
express outrage 격분을 표하다

337 **sway** [swei]
동 흔들다, 흔들리다
sway his peers 그의 동료들을 흔들다 sway in the wind 바람에 흔들리다

338 **decisive** [disáisiv]
형 결정적인, 단호한
play a decisive role 결정적 역할을 하다

339 **aesthetic** [esθétik]
형 심미적, 미학의
aesthetic value 심미적 가치 aesthetic theory 미학적 이론

340 **stall** [stɔːl]
명 가판대 동 멈추게 하다
a newspaper stall 신문 가판대

341 **contradict** [kὰntrədíkt]
동 부정하다, 모순되다 명 contradiction 모순, 반박
contradict his opinion 그의 주장을 부정하다

342 **supervise** [sjúːpərvàiz]
동 감독하다, 지휘하다 명 supervision 감독, 지휘, 통제
supervise an election 선거를 감독하다

343 **loom** [luːm]
동 어렴풋이 나타나다, 곧 닥칠 듯 보이다 형 looming 어렴풋이 보이기 시작하는
loom on the horizon 수평선으로 흐릿하게 나타나다

344 **appreciation** [əprìːʃiéiʃən]
명 감상, 감사
great appreciation of the painting 그림에 대한 명확한 감상

345 **activate** [ǽktəvèit]
동 작동시키다, 활성화시키다
activate a machine 기계를 작동시키다

Daily Test

| 월 일 |

A 우리말에 맞게 빈 칸에 알맞은 단어를 쓰세요.

1 Red foxes have even been known to use a ______________ underpass rather than cross a highway.
붉은 여우는 고속도로를 무단횡단하기보다는 보행자용 지하도를 이용하는 것으로 알려져 있다. 08 고3 평가원 변형

2 The mayor said other canals needed to pump water from underground or faraway ______________.
그 시장은 다른 운하들이 지하 또는 멀리 떨어진 저수지에서 물을 끌어올 필요가 있다고 말했다.

3 I think the new traffic regulations are ______________.
난 새로운 교통 정책이 너무 터무니 없다고 생각한다.

4 The lawyer, assuming the accident to be an example of Latin American gender bias, was ______________.
그 사고가 라틴계 미국인의 성 편견의 예시라고 추측하는 그 변호사는 격분했다. 16 고3 학평 변형

5 If you don't know yourself, you could be ______________ by what others think you should think, and do.
만약 당신이 스스로를 모른다면, 당신은 다른 사람들이 바라는 대로 행동하고 생각하도록 흔들릴 것이다. 16 고3 평가원 변형

6 Some dark shapes ______________ up ahead of them.
그들 앞에 몇몇 검은 형체들이 나타났다. 13 고3 평가원 변형

7 Peter's actions ______________ his faith.
Peter의 행동은 그의 신앙과 모순되었다.

8 In ancient America, building a canoe was a specialized art ______________ by a high priest.
고대 미국에서, 카누를 만드는 것은 지위가 높은 주술사가 감독하는 전문화된 일이었다. 07 고2 학평 변형

9 People have different ______________ values.
사람들은 다른 미적 가치를 갖고 있다.

10 When we listen to words conveying negative thoughts, our brains immediately ______________ to feel that pain.
우리가 부정적인 생각을 전달하는 말을 들었을 때, 우리의 뇌는 즉시 그 고통을 느끼는 것을 활성화시킨다. 14 고1 학평 변형

Day 12

MP3

346 **advocate** [ǽdvəkit]
동 지지하다, 옹호하다 명 옹호자
advocate democracy 민주주의를 지지하다

347 **sustainable** [səsteinəbl]
형 (환경 등과 관련해서) 지속 가능한, 지속할 수 있는
initiate sustainable agriculture policies 지속 가능한 농업 정책을 개시하다

348 **cosmetic** [kazmétik]
명 (주로 복수형) 화장품 형 성형의, 겉치레에 불과한
the cosmetic industry 화장품 산업 cosmetic surgery 성형 수술

349 **reciprocal** [risíprəkəl]
형 상호간의 동 reciprocate (비슷한 방식으로) 화답하다
reciprocal assistance 상호 원조 a reciprocal treaty 상호간의 조약

350 **plentiful** [pléntifəl]
형 풍부한, 많은 유 abundant 풍부한, 풍족한
enjoy plentiful light 풍부한 일광을 즐기다 a plentiful harvest 풍작

351 **advent** [ǽdvent]
명 도래, 출현
the advent of death 죽음의 도래

352 **tense** [tens]
형 긴박한, 긴장한, 팽팽한 명 (동사의) 시제 명 tension 긴장(상태)
a tense atmosphere 긴장된 분위기

353 **regulation** [règjəléiʃən]
명 규정, 규제
set safety regulations 안전 규정을 정하다

354 **health care** [helθ kɛər]
명 의료 서비스
provide health care for the elderly 노인들에게 의료 서비스를 제공하다

355 **synthetic** [sinθétik]
형 인공의, 합성의
synthetic leather 인조가죽

356 **spiritual** [spíritʃuəl]
형 정신의
spiritual development 정신적 발달 spiritual heritage 정신적 유산

357 **perceptual** [pərséptʃuəl]
형 지각의,지각에 의한 *conceptual 형 개념의, 개념에 의한
perceptual cognitive mistakes 지각 인지의 오류

358 **honorable** [ɑ́nərəbl]
형 존경할 만한, 고결한
honorable conduct 고결한 행위

359 **legacy** [légəsi]
명 유산, 업적 유 inheritance 유산, 상속
inherit a legacy 유산을 상속하다 a lasting legacy 계속 내려오는 유산

360 **sorrow** [sɑ́rou]
명 슬픔, 비애 동 (대단히) 슬퍼하다
hide bitter sorrow 쓰라린 슬픔을 감추다

Daily Test

A 우리말에 맞게 빈 칸에 알맞은 단어를 쓰세요.

1 I think today's ______________ of free writing would probably agree with Poe's writing style.
난 오늘의 자유 글쓰기 옹호자들은 아마도 Poe의 글쓰는 방식에 동의할 거라고 생각한다. 2013 수능 변형

2 In the past, some people expected ______________ economic growth.
과거에, 몇몇 사람들은 지속 가능한 경제 성장을 기대했다.

3 The modern man's interest in grooming and ______________ products is not a new phenomenon.
현대 남성들의 몸단장과 화장품에 대한 흥미는 새로운 현상이 아니다. 12 고1학평 변형

4 Without ______________ sunlight, plants cannot survive in large numbers.
충분한 햇살이 없다면, 식물은 많은 개체로 살아 남지 못한다.

5 Eric's heart beat faster and his muscles grew ______________.
Eric의 심장은 더 빨리 뛰었고 그의 근육은 긴장했다. 09 고1학평 변형

6 Researchers claim that strict ______________ banning junk foods from schools are crucial.
연구원들은 교내에서 인스턴트 음식을 금지하는 엄격한 규제가 중요하다고 주장한다. 05 고3학평 변형

7 Plastics are ______________ materials, which means that they are made from chemicals in factories.
플라스틱은 인공 물질인데 이는 그들이 공장의 화학물질로부터 만들어졌음을 의미한다. 09 고1평가원 변형

8 Whenever you get the opportunity, read about the great figures in history, especially the ______________ ones.
당신이 기회를 얻을 때마다, 특히 정신적으로 위대했던 사람들과 같은 역사상 훌륭한 사람들에 대해서 읽어라. 04 고1평가원 변형

9 This old castle was a ______________ of my grandfather.
이 오래된 성은 내 할아버지의 유산이에요.

10 We are trained to control bad feelings such as ______________ in public.
우리는 대중 앞에서 슬픔과 같은 나쁜 감정을 통제하도록 훈련되었다. 04 고3평가원

Review Test 06

A 우리말에 맞게 빈 칸에 알맞은 단어를 쓰시오.

1 wear a new ________________ 새로운 의상을 입다

2 ________________ force 탄력

3 contribute to his ________________ 그의 장수에 기여하다

4 ________________ children 양자를 양육하다

5 a ________________-shaped box 정육면체 모양의 상자

6 ________________ only area 보행자 전용 구역

7 an ________________ rumor 황당한 소문

8 ________________ theory 미학적 이론

9 the ________________ industry 화장품 산업

10 ________________ leather 인조가죽

B 영어에 맞게 빈 칸에 알맞은 우리말을 쓰시오.

1 an optimal temperature ________________ 온도

2 imperfect knowledge ________________ 지식

3 imply participation 참여를 ________________

4 a dietary supplement ________________ 보충량

5 make a hasty decision ________________ 결정을 내리다

6 a reservoir of knowledge 지식의 ________________

7 express outrage ________________을 표하다

8 contradict his opinion 그의 주장을 ________________

9 spiritual heritage ________________ 유산

10 inherit a legacy ________________을 상속하다

C 다음 영어 풀이에 알맞은 어휘를 〈보기〉에서 고르시오.

보기 trivial mentor contradict disguise sustainable

1 ______________ : able to be used for long

2 ______________ : not important or valuable

3 ______________ : to change something to look like something else

4 ______________ : to speak the opposite of something

5 ______________ : someone who helps another person as a teacher or adviser

D 문맥에 맞게 다음 문장을 완성하시오.

1 Have you ever seen a tree trunk which •	• a is about one meter in diameter?
2 Hurting a man's dignity •	• b can use them to borrow equipment free of charge.
3 Tax equality refers to the way •	• c taxes are distributed among people.
4 We issue membership cards to donors who •	• d such as sorrow in public.
5 People are trained to control bad feelings •	• e is a crime.

E 문장을 읽고 문맥에 적절한 단어를 고르시오.

1 We need to take (decisive/elastic) measures to overcome the current difficulties.

2 Although this car looks nice, it will be (impulsive/impractical) in real life.

3 Since our budget is tight, we need to travel with (minimal/nasty) cost.

4 Gerald tried to ease the (tense/trivial) atmosphere of the meeting.

5 Most plants cannot live without (plentiful/grateful) sunlight.

F 문장의 빈칸에 알맞은 단어를 〈보기〉에서 찾아 쓰시오. (필요하면 형태를 고치시오.)

보기 irrigation regulation advent sustainable convert

1 Producing good quality wine depends on rain, and in some cases, ________________.
와인의 품질은 비와 경우에 따라서는 물대기에 달려있다. 2016 수능 변형

2 Our goal is to find ways to use natural resources at ________________ levels.
우리의 목표는 천연 자원을 지속 가능한 수준에서 이용하는 방법을 찾는 것입니다.

3 The government introduced a number of new ________________ on the use of plastic bags.
정부는 비닐 백 사용에 관한 새로운 규정을 도입했다. 06 고2학평 변형

4 Coconut oil can be used as a skin cream or ________________ into soap.
코코넛 오일은 피부에 바르는 크림으로 이용되거나 비누로 변환될 수 있다. 06 고2학평 변형

5 Professor Alfred will give a lecture on the ________________ of globalization.
Alfred 교수는 세계화의 도래에 대한 강연을 할 것이다.

G 다음 〈보기〉 중 두 문장에 공통으로 사용할 수 있는 어휘를 고르시오.

1 Adrian wasn't always __________ to take his dad's advice. 16 고3학평
Since his early childhood, Alvin was a __________ model-maker.

① difficult ② keen ③ certain ④ nasty ⑤ amazed

2 Brian is a __________ worker and has been doing his job very well. 16 고3평가원
After years of practice, he now feels __________ to speak in public.

① hierarchical ② renowned ③ sustainable ④ competent ⑤ dietary

3 For his new novel, the author wants to __________ how fragile trust can be.
Instead of imitating reality, some painters wanted to __________ social conditions within their art. 15 고3학평 변형

① contradict ② supervise ③ activate ④ illustrate ⑤ exert

Study More

minimal vs. **maximal**

- [minimal] 형 아주 적은, 최소의
  While the risks are **minimal**, the new solar panel is cost-effective.
  위험도는 최소한인 반면에, 새 태양열 판은 가격 효율이 높다.
- [maximal] 형 최대한의, 최고조의
  You should not exceed **maximal** loading of each piece of luggage.
  당신은 각 수화물의 최대 적재량을 초과하면 안 된다.

Day 13

MP3

361 ☐ **metropolitan** [mètrəpálitən]
형 대도시의, 수도권의
metropolitan areas 대도시 지역

362 ☐ **lottery** [látəri]
명 복권, 제비뽑기 유 draw 추첨, 제비뽑기
win a lottery 복권에 당첨되다 scratch a lottery ticket 복권을 긁다

363 ☐ **punch** [pʌntʃ]
동 주먹으로 치다, 때리다, 구멍을 뚫다 명 주먹으로 한대 침, 천공기
punch the wall 벽을 주먹으로 치다

364 ☐ **prolonged** [prəlɔ́:ŋd]
형 오래 계속되는, 장기적인 동 prolong 연장시키다, 연장하다
prolonged viewing of a computer 장기적으로 컴퓨터를 보는 것

365 ☐ **persuasion** [pərswéiʒən]
명 설득
have great powers of persuasion 강한 설득력을 갖다

366 ☐ **duration** [djuəréiʃən]
명 지속, 기간
long-duration missions 장기간 임무

367 ☐ **fertile** [fə́:rtəl]
형 (땅, 토양 등이) 비옥한, 기름진
settle on fertile land 비옥한 땅에 정착하다

368 ☐ **manipulate** [mənípjulèit]
동 조정하다, 조작하다
manipulate public opinion 여론을 조작하다

369 ☐ **layout** [léiàut]
명 배치, (출판물의) 지면 배정, 배열 유 arrangement 정리, 배열, 배치
magazine layout 잡지의 배치 (지면 배정)

370 ☐ **glimpse** [glimps]
동 언뜻 보다, 잠깐 보다 명 얼핏 봄, 희미한 빛
glimpse her son through the window 창문을 통해 그녀의 아들을 잠깐 보다

371 ☐ **intact** [intǽkt]
형 손상되지 않은, 온전한
keep their culture intact 자신들의 문화를 온전히 유지하다

372 ☐ **evergreen** [évərgrì:n]
명 상록수
an evergreen forest 상록수림

373 ☐ **incorporate** [inkɔ́:rpərit]
동 (일부로) 포함하다, 합병하다, 섞다 명 incorporation 법인, 결합, 합병
be incorporated in the plan 계획에 포함시키다

374 ☐ **inborn** [ínbɔ́:rn]
형 타고난, 선천적인
inborn talent for dancing 춤에 대한 타고난 재능

375 ☐ **revive** [riváiv]
동 되살아나다, 회복하다, 다시 제작하다 명 revival 회복, 재유행, 재공연
revive a musical 뮤지컬을 다시 제작하다

Daily Test

| 월 일 |

A 우리말에 맞게 빈 칸에 알맞은 단어를 쓰세요.

1 For individuals, getting a good job is like winning the ______________.
사람들에게 좋은 직업을 얻는 것은 복권에 당첨되는 것과도 같다. 09 고2 평가원 변형

2 The sharks had ______________ a huge hole in the boat's side, and water started to rush in.
상어들이 배 한 쪽에 큰 구멍을 뚫었고 물이 그 안으로 들어가기 시작했다. 06 고2 학평 변형

3 ______________ is the strategic use of language to move an audience.
설득은 관객들을 감동시키는 언어의 전략적인 사용이다. 13 고3 평가원 변형

4 France and Germany have the moderate climate and ______________ soil.
프랑스와 독일은 온화한 기후와 비옥한 토양을 가지고 있다.

5 Some companies use tricks to ______________ their consumer's minds.
일부 회사들은 그들의 소비자의 심리를 조작하기 위해 술수를 사용한다. 15 고2 학평 변형

6 Harry made model cars and model railroad ______________.
Harry는 모형 자동차, 모형 철도 배치를 만들었다. 11 고2 학평 변형

7 There is strong research evidence that children perform better in mathematics if music is ______________ in it.
음악이 수학에 통합되면 어린이들이 수학을 더 잘한다는 강력한 연구 증거가 있다. 16 고3 평가원 변형

8 Establishing protected areas with ______________ ecosystems is essential for species conservation.
온전한 생태계가 있는 보호 구역을 만드는 것은 종의 보존을 위해 필수적이다. 16 고3 학평 변형

9 I walked around the village and found the ______________ forest.
나는 마을 주변을 돌아다녔고, 상록수림을 발견했다.

10 Success will be gained only if the individual has great ______________ ability.
성공은 그 사람이 타고난 뛰어난 능력을 가질 때에만 얻을 수 있을 것이다. 13 고1 학평 변형

Day 13

MP3

376 **platform** [plǽtfɔːrm]
명 승강장, 플랫폼, 연단, 강단 유 podium 연단, 강단
stand on platform 3 3번 승강장에 서다

377 **manuscript** [mǽnjəskrìpt]
명 원고, 필사본, 사본
read a manuscript 원고를 읽다 edit a manuscript 원고를 편집하다

378 **discrimination** [diskrìmənéiʃən]
명 차별 동 discriminate 식별하다, 차별하다
racial discrimination 인종 차별

379 **microscope** [máikrəskòup]
명 현미경
an electronic microscope 전자 현미경

380 **radioactive** [rèidiouǽktiv]
형 방사능의
severe radioactive contamination 심각한 방사능 오염

381 **assure** [əʃúər]
동 장담하다, 보장하다, 확언하다 명 assurance 확언, 장담, (보장성) 보험
assure the safety of tourists 관광객들의 안전을 보장하다

382 **responsive** [rispánsiv]
형 즉각 반응하는, 민감한 유 sensitive 민감한, 민감하게 반응하는
responsive to a customer's needs 고객의 요구에 즉각 반응하다

383 **reject** [ridʒékt]
동 거부하다 명 rejection 거절, 배제
reject the proposal 그 제안을 거절하다 firmly reject 강하게 거부하다

384 **optimism** [áptəmìzəm]
명 낙관론, 낙관적 생각 반 pessimism 비관적 생각, 비관주의
optimism for the future 미래에 대한 낙관론

385 **sheer** [ʃiər]
형 순전히, 완전히
sheer coincidence 순전한 우연의 일치

386 **lessen** [lésən]
동 줄이다, 완화하다
lessen racial bias 인종적 편견을 줄이다

387 **rotation** [routéiʃən]
명 회전, 순환
make a rotation 회전하다 Earth's rotation 지구의 자전

388 **presumably** [prizjúːməbli]
부 아마(도)
Presumably, he is tired. 아마, 그는 피곤한 것 같다.

389 **unwilling** [ʌnwíliŋ]
형 꺼리는, 싫어하는, 본의 아닌 부 unwillingly 마지못해, 본의 아니게
unwilling to answer questions 질문에 답하기를 꺼리는

390 **spacious** [spéiʃəs]
형 넓은, 널찍한
need a more spacious bed room 더 넓은 침실이 필요하다

Daily Test

| 월 일 |

A 우리말에 맞게 빈 칸에 알맞은 단어를 쓰세요.

1 I submitted my ______________ and Mr. Park accepted it for publishing.
나는 내 원고를 제출했고 Mr. Park은 이를 출판하기 위해 수락했다.

2 Wage ______________ is one of the most serious problems in our society.
임금 차별은 우리 사회의 가장 심각한 문제 중 하나다.

3 Tiny nuclei particles were observed under the electronic ______________.
작은 원자핵 입자들은 전자 현미경을 통해 관찰되었다.

4 ______________ waste material can cause pollution.
방사능 폐기물은 오염을 유발 시킬 수 있다. 04 고2 평가원 변형

5 When Jane was born, all the neighbors ______________ her father that she was the most beautiful girl in Germany.
Jane이 태어났을 때, 모든 이웃들은 그녀의 아버지한테 그녀가 독일에서 가장 아름다운 소녀라고 장담했다. 12 고1 학평 변형

6 I know a lot of best-selling novels were ______________ many times before they were accepted and published.
나는 많은 베스트셀러 소설들이 채택되고 출판 되기 전에 수없이 거절당한 것을 알고 있다. 05 고3 평가원 변형

7 Young people are full of energy and ______________.
젊은 사람들은 활기와 낙관적 생각으로 가득하다.

8 Many people suffer from eating disorders and I think these are ______________ caused by mass media.
많은 사람들이 식이 장애를 겪고 있으며, 난 이 점에 있어 언론 매체가 원인이라고 생각한다. 06 고3 평가원 변형

9 I was ______________ to go to the party because I had a lot of work to do.
나는 할 일이 매우 많았기 때문에 파티에 가기를 꺼려했다. 09 고3 평가원 변형

10 The room was ______________ and there was a large window overlooking the garden.
그 방은 넓었고 정원을 내려다 볼 수 있는 큰 창문이 있었다. 15 고3 학평 변형

Day 14

MP3

391 **flap** [flæp]
동 펄럭이다, 퍼덕거리다 명 (봉투 등의) 덮개, 펄럭임, 펄럭이는 소리
flap in the breeze 바람에 펄럭이다

392 **dual** [djú(:)əl]
형 두 부분으로 된, 이중의
her dual role 그녀의 두 가지 역할 dual nationality 이중 국적

393 **cherish** [tʃériʃ]
동 소중히 여기다, 아끼다, (마음 속에) 간직하다
cherish his cat 그의 고양이를 소중히 여기다

394 **furious** [fjú(:)əriəs]
형 몹시 화가 난, 맹렬한, 격렬한
fast and furious 빠르고 맹렬한 furious sea 격렬한 바다

395 **mourn** [mɔːrn]
동 애도하다, 슬퍼하다
mourn Andy's death Andy의 죽음을 애도하다

396 **spontaneous** [spɑntéiniəs]
형 자발적인, 즉흥적인
spontaneous enthusiasm 자발적인 열정

397 **deceased** [disíːst]
형 사망한 명 고인
Sam's deceased grandmother Sam의 돌아가신 할머니

398 **boundary** [báundəri]
명 경계, 영역
boundary marker 경계 표지 national boundaries 국경

399 **withstand** [wiðstǽnd]
동 견디다, 이겨내다 유 bear 참다, 견디다
withstand hardship 어려움을 견디다

400 **abrupt** [əbrʌ́pt]
형 갑작스러운, 퉁명스러운 유 sudden 돌연한, 뜻밖의
an abrupt change 갑작스러운 변화

401 **timber** [tímbər]
명 목재, 수목, 산림(재) +log 명 통나무
harvest timber 목재를 수확하다 supply of timber 목재의 공급

402 **thrive** [θraiv]
동 번창하다, 잘 해내다
continue to thrive 계속해서 번창하다

403 **deliberate** [delíbərit]
형 고의의, 의도적인
make a deliberate mistake 고의로 실수를 하다

404 **weed** [wiːd]
명 잡초, 수초 동 잡초를 뽑다
pull up a weed by its roots 잡초를 뿌리째 뽑다

405 **undergo** [ʌ̀ndərgóu]
동 겪다, 받다, 경험하다, 견디다 유 go through ~을 겪다
undergo surgery 수술을 받다

Daily Test

| 월 일 |

A 우리말에 맞게 빈 칸에 알맞은 단어를 쓰세요.

1 He is a ______________ citizen of Germany and Sweden.
그는 독일과 스웨덴의 이중 시민이다.

2 The green dress evoked both ______________ and painful memories.
그 녹색 드레스는 소중하고 고통스러운 기억들 둘 다 떠오르게 했다. 2012 수능 변형

3 Sam glanced at his teacher who looked ______________ as she screamed at him.
Sam은 그를 향해 소리치면서 격분하고 있는 그의 선생님을 바라보았다. 08 고3평가원 변형

4 Lily's family ______________ the death of the dog.
Lily의 가족들은 강아지의 죽음에 슬퍼하였다. 07 고3학평 변형

5 In many situations, the ______________ between good behavior and bad behavior depends on the immediate circumstances.
많은 경우에서, 좋음과 나쁨의 경계는 시간이 지나면서 변하는 기준점이며 당면한 상황에 의해 결정된다. 2016 수능 변형

6 Mice can not only ______________ heat, they can also eat either your organic breakfast cereal or garden apples.
쥐는 열을 견딜 뿐만 아니라, 그들은 또한 당신의 아침 식사용 유기농 시리얼이나 정원의 사과를 먹을 수도 있다. 14 고3학평 변형

7 The supervisor made an ______________ decision to cancel the meeting.
관리자는 회의를 취소하라는 갑작스러운 결정을 내렸다.

8 A ______________ frame house is more vulnerable to fire than a cement one.
목재 구조의 집은 시멘트로 된 집보다 더 불에 타기가 쉽다.

9 Goats like eating ______________.
염소는 잡초를 잘 먹는다.

10 The theories of science are not fixed; rather, they ______________ change.
과학의 이론은 고정적이지 않고 오히려 그들은 변화를 겪는다. 12 고3학평

Day 14

MP3

406 **faraway** [fá:rəwèi]
형 먼, 멀리 떨어진
send people to a faraway region 사람들을 먼 지방으로 보내다

407 **competitor** [kəmpétitər]
명 경쟁자
defeat a competitor 경쟁자를 이기다

408 **ecology** [ikálədʒi]
명 생태(학)
study animal ecology 동물 생태를 연구하다

409 **withdraw** [wiðdrɔ́:]
동 철회하다, 철수하다, (계좌에서 돈을) 인출하다 명 withdrawal 철회, 철수, 인출
withdraw savings from his account 그의 계좌에서 돈을 인출하다

410 **decay** [dikéi]
명 부패, 부식, 쇠퇴 동 썩다, 부패하다, 쇠퇴하다
have tooth decay 충치가 생기다 decaying food 썩고 있는 음식

411 **stubborn** [stʌ́bərn]
형 완강한, 고질적인
stubborn resistance 완강한 저항 a stubborn cough 고질적인 기침

412 **starvation** [sta:rvéiʃən]
명 기아, 굶주림 동 starve 굶주리다, 굶어죽다
suffer from starvation 기아에 허덕이다

413 **willingness** [wíliŋnis]
명 의향, 기꺼이 하기
express willingness 의향을 표현하다

414 **extract** [ékstrækt]
동 추출하다, 발췌하다 명 추출물, 발췌
extract natural resources 천연 자원을 추출하다

415 **epidemic** [èpidémik]
명 유행병 *pandemic 명 전국적인(전세계적인) 유행병
a severe epidemic 심각한 유행병

416 **steer** [stiər]
동 조종하다, 돌리다, (어떤 방향으로) 나아가다
steer a ship 배를 조종하다 turn the steering wheel 운전대를 돌리다

417 **coordination** [kouɔ̀:rdənéiʃən]
명 조직, 합동
strengthen team work and coordination 팀워크와 합동을 강화하다

418 **amnesia** [æmní:ʒə]
명 기억상실(증)
suffer from amnesia 기억상실증으로 고통 받다

419 **suppress** [səprés]
동 억압하다, 진압하다, 억제하다 명 suppression 진압, 억제
suppress opposition 반대를 억압하다

420 **longitude** [lándʒətjù:d]
명 경도 반 latitude 위도
measure the longitude 경도를 측정하다

Daily Test

| 월 일 |

A 우리말에 맞게 빈 칸에 알맞은 단어를 쓰세요.

1 Millions of people require different lenses to see near and ______________ objects.
수백만 명의 사람이 가까운 물체와 멀리 떨어진 물체를 바라보기 위해 다양한 렌즈를 필요로 한다. 07 고3 평가원 변형

2 While Andy and Sarah are best friends, they are also each other's biggest ______________.
Andy와 Sarah는 친한 친구이지만, 그들은 서로에게 가장 큰 경쟁자이기도 하다. 14 고3 평가원 변형

3 Most living things ______________ and disappear after they die.
대부분의 생물들은 그들이 죽은 후에 썩고 사라진다.

4 Julia had always focused on the ______________ belief that writing a book was too big a project.
Julia는 항상 책을 쓴다는 것을 너무나도 큰 일이라는 완고한 믿음을 갖고 있었다. 06 고3 평가원 변형

5 Disease, enemies and ______________ were always menacing primitive man.
질병, 적, 그리고 빈곤은 항상 원시 인류에게 위협적이었다. 12 고3 평가원 변형

6 The DNA ______________ from the bits of whale skin gave us some important evidence about their natural characteristics.
고래 피부에서 소량 추출된 DNA는 우리에게 그들의 선천적 특성에 대한 중요한 증거들을 제공했다.

7 Normally, a large outbreak of a virus is called an ______________.
일반적으로, 바이러스의 광범위한 발생을 유행병이라 부른다.

8 When people trust each other more deeply, their ______________ becomes easier.
사람들이 서로에 대해 더 깊게 믿을 때, 협력도 더 쉬워진다. 14 고1 학평 변형

9 When people suffer from ______________, they may not even be able to recall their own name.
사람들이 기억상실증을 앓을 때, 그들은 심지어 그들의 이름을 기억해내지 못한다. 13 고3 평가원 변형

10 Every day for a week, Kate kept getting ______________ and latitude confused.
일주일 동안 매일 Kate는 계속 경도와 위도가 헷갈렸다. 16 고2 학평 변형

A 우리말에 맞게 빈 칸에 알맞은 단어를 쓰시오.

1 ________________ areas 대도시 지역

2 settle on ________________ land 비옥한 땅에 정착하다

3 edit a ________________ 원고를 편집하다

4 ________________ to a customer's needs 고객의 요구에 즉각 반응하다

5 Earth's ________________ 지구의 자전

6 fast and ________________ 빠르고 맹렬한

7 Sam's ________________ grandmother Sam의 돌아가신 할머니

8 supply of ________________ 목재의 공급

9 study animal ________________ 동물 생태를 연구하다

10 suffer from ________________ 기아에 허덕이다

B 영어에 맞게 빈 칸에 알맞은 우리말을 쓰시오.

1 scratch a lottery ticket ________________을 긁다

2 magazine layout 잡지의 ________________

3 keep their culture intact 자신들의 문화를 ________________ 유지하다

4 racial discrimination 인종 ________________

5 sheer coincidence ________________ 우연의 일치

6 dual nationality ________________ 국적

7 spontaneous enthusiasm ________________ 열정

8 pull up a weed by its roots ________________를 뿌리째 뽑다

9 decaying food ________________ 음식

10 steer a ship 배를 ________________

C 다음 영어 풀이에 알맞은 어휘를 〈보기〉에서 고르시오.

보기	abrupt	fertile	revive	withstand	epidemic

1 ________________ : good for growing something such as plants

2 ________________ : to make something live, usable, or active again

3 ________________ : an illness or disease that spreads quickly among people

4 ________________ : sudden and unexpected; happening without notice

5 ________________ : to resist or endure

D 문맥에 맞게 다음 문장을 완성하시오.

1 Persuasion is the strategic use •	• a found the evergreen forest.
2 I walked around the village and •	• b of language to move an audience.
3 Success will be gained only if •	• c the individual has great inborn ability.
4 Lily's family mourned •	• d their coordination becomes easier.
5 When people trust each other more deeply, •	• e the death of the dog.

E 문장을 읽고 문맥에 적절한 단어를 고르시오.

1 The famous song has been (revived/withdrawn) by later generations.

2 Since he is very (stubborn/intact) he will not be persuaded easily.

3 This machine helps to (withstand/extract) juice from oranges.

4 The (duration/layout) of the ceremony will be about 2 hours.

5 We are trying to (glimpse/lessen) the amount of paper waste.

F 문장의 빈칸에 알맞은 단어를 <보기>에서 찾아 쓰시오. (필요하면 형태를 고치시오.)

보기 cherish suppress manipulate reject epidemic

1 I was told by the insurance company that my claim was ______________.
나는 내 청구가 거절당했다고 보험회사에서 통보를 받았다. 06 고2학평 변형

2 With this new computer, I can record and ______________ all kinds of interesting sounds.
이 새로운 컴퓨터로 나는 모든 종류의 흥미로운 소리를 녹음하고 조작할 수 있다. 11 고2학평 변형

3 Vaccines control ______________ but have not eliminated them.
백신은 전염병들을 조절하지만 없애지는 못한다. 11 고3학평

4 If we ignore or ______________ health symptoms, they will become progressively louder and more extreme.
우리가 건강상의 증상을 무시하거나 억제한다면 그것들은 계속해서 더 시끄럽고 더 극단적이게 될 것이다. 15 고3학평

5 My theory is very simple: "______________ these moments now."
내 이론은 간단하다. "지금 현재를 소중히 여겨라." 05 고2평가원

G 다음 〈보기〉 중 두 문장에 공통으로 사용할 수 있는 어휘를 고르시오.

1 In the water of this pond, tiny organisms ___________. 05 고3학평
The birch is a tree that ___________(e)s in cold countries such as Sweden and Russia. 10 고2학평 변형

① thrive ② incorporate ③ punch ④ glimpse ⑤ steer

2 Nasrudin ___________(e)d him that he had not made a mistake at all. 10 고2학평
The committee ___________(e)d us of equal opportunities.

① withstand ② assure ③ convert ④ mourn ⑤ steer

3 The automobile industry is currently ___________ing great technological developments. 07 고2학평 변형
The doctor told my father he would have to ___________ knee surgery.

① sway ② decay ③ suppress ④ exert ⑤ undergo

Study More

'-logy' : [명사에서] '학문', '교리' 등의 뜻을 나타낸다.

- [psychology] 명 심리학
  Sarah is a generalist in the field of child psychology. Sarah는 아동 심리학 분야의 전문가이다.
- [zoology] 명 동물학
  If you want to find out more about zoology, visit our website www.AllaboutZoo.com
  만약 당신이 동물학에 대해 더 찾고 싶다면, 우리 웹사이트 www.AllaboutZoo.com에 방문하세요.

Day 15

MP3

421 **prompt** [prɑmpt]
형 신속한, 즉각적인 동 촉발하다
a prompt reply 즉답

422 **hostile** [hástəl]
형 적대적인, 불리한
a hostile attitude 적대적인 태도 hostile criticism 적대적 비평

423 **restless** [réstlis]
형 가만히 못 있는, 불안한
a restless student 가만히 못 있는 학생

424 **reckless** [réklis]
형 무모한, 부주의한
the outcome of reckless behavior 부주의한 행동의 결과

425 **morality** [mərǽləti]
명 도덕(성)
commercial morality 상도덕 an issue of morality 도덕성의 문제

426 **relevance** [réləvəns]
명 관련(성), 적절(성), 타당(성)
have relevance to ~와 관련이 있다

427 **regain** [rigéin]
동 되찾다, 회복하다 유 recover 되찾다, 도로 찾다
regain his prestige 그의 명성을 되찾다

428 **probe** [proub]
동 조사하다, 수사하다, 살피다 명 (철저한) 조사, 탐침
probe the sea floor 해저를 조사하다

429 **malnutrition** [mæ̀lnjuːtríʃən]
명 영양실조
extreme malnutrition 극단적 영양실조

430 **parasite** [pǽrəsàit]
명 기생충, 기생 동물 형 parasitic 기생충에 의한, 기생하는
eradicate parasites 기생충을 박멸하다

431 **geometric** [dʒìːəmétrik]
형 기하학의, 기하학적인
geometric style 기하학 양식

432 **retreat** [ritríːt]
동 물러서다 명 후퇴
retreat from his earlier position 그의 이전 입장에서 물러나다

433 **leopard** [lépərd]
명 표범
hunt a leopard 흑표범을 사냥하다

434 **inadequate** [inǽdəkwit]
형 부적절한, 불충분한
inadequate budget 불충분한 예산

435 **segment** [ségmənt]
명 부분, 분절, 조각 동 (여러부분으로) 나누다, 분할하다
divide the garden into segments 정원을 부분으로 나누다

Daily Test

A 우리말에 맞게 빈 칸에 알맞은 단어를 쓰세요.

1 Competition ______________ innovation and drives global markets.
경쟁은 혁신을 촉구하고 세계 시장을 이끈다. 15 고2학평 변형

2 The Himalayas are the highest mountains on earth and contain some of the most ______________ terrain.
히말라야 산맥은 지구에서 가장 높은 산이고 그들 중 일부는 매우 오르기 어려운 지형이다.

3 Roy seemed ______________ and afraid.
Roy는 불안하고 두려워보였다. 11 고1학평 변형

4 After you have completed the course, you must write a report explaining the content of the course and it's ______________ to your position.
교육 과정을 마친 다음에 당신은 교육 과정의 내용과 직무와의 관련성을 설명하는 보고서를 작성해야 합니다. 2010 수능 변형

5 For Andy, it was difficult to ______________ public trust and confidence.
Andy에게 있어서, 대중의 신뢰와 확신을 다시 얻는 것은 어려웠다.

6 African children were suffering from severe ______________.
아프리카 아이들은 심각한 영양실조로 고통 받고 있었다. 07 고2학평 변형

7 It is not mosquitoes that kill people but the ______________ they carry that causes malaria.
사람들을 죽인 건 모기가 아니라 모기들이 옮긴 말라리아를 유발하는 해충 때문이다. 08 고2학평 변형

8 The general was mortally wounded, so they decided to ______________.
그 장군이 치명적인 부상을 입었으므로, 그들은 후퇴하기로 결정했다.

9 Some researchers consider snow ______________ to be shy because they are rarely seen in the wild.
일부 연구원들은 눈 표범들이 야생에서 잘 발견되지 않기 때문에 조심성이 많은 것으로 여긴다. 10 고3학평 변형

10 Words such as fantastic and incredible are ______________ to describe the movie.
환상적과 대단하다는 것과 같은 말은 그 영화를 묘사하기에 불충분했다. 05 고3평가원 변형

Day 15

MP3

436 **intuition** [ìntjuːíʃən]
명 직관(력)
depend on intuition 직관에 의존하다

437 **gorgeous** [gɔ́ːrdʒəs]
형 아주 멋진, 화려한, 굉장한 유 magnificient 장엄한, 웅장한, 장대한
a gorgeous night view 멋진 야경

438 **assert** [əsə́ːrt]
동 주장하다, 단언하다
assert her innocence 그녀의 무죄를 주장하다

439 **outlook** [áutlùk]
명 관점, 전망, 견해
a positive outlook on life 인생에 대해 긍정적인 관점

440 **penetrate** [pénitrèit]
동 관통하다, 뚫고 들어가다
penetrate the window 창문을 관통하다

441 **immoral** [imɔ́(ː)rəl]
형 부도덕한, 비도덕적인
immoral conduct 부도덕한 행동

442 **leak** [liːk]
동 (액체, 기체가) 새다, (비밀등을) 누설하다, 유출하다 명 새는 곳
the blood leaks out 피가 새어 나오다

443 **infinite** [ínfənit]
형 무한한, 무한정의 명 infinity 무한성
infinite possibilities 무한한 가능성

444 **irrational** [iræ̀ʃənəl]
형 비이성적인
her irrational attitude 그녀의 비이성적인 태도

445 **mammal** [mǽməl]
명 포유동물
a higher mammal 고등 포유동물 a type of mammal 포유동물의 한 종류

446 **implement** [ímpləmənt]
동 실행하다, 실시하다 명 기구, 도구, 수단, 방법
implement a policy 정책을 실행하다 cutting implement 절단도구

447 **surgeon** [sə́ːrdʒən]
명 외과의사 형 surgical 외과(술)의, 외과적인, 외과의
a heart surgeon 심장 외과의사

448 **rust** [rʌst]
명 녹 동 녹슬다, 부식하다
a nail covered with rust 녹으로 뒤덮힌 못

449 **compromise** [kɑ́mprəmàiz]
동 타협하다, 손상하다 명 타협
compromise reasonably 합리적으로 타협하다

450 **suspend** [səspénd]
동 중지하다, 유예하다, 매달다 유 postpone 연기하다, 늦추다
suspend assistance 원조를 중단하다

Daily Test

| 월 일 |

A 우리말에 맞게 빈 칸에 알맞은 단어를 쓰세요.

1 If you give yourself freedom to follow your ______________, you will find your inner voice.
만약 당신이 스스로에게 직관을 따를 자유를 준다면, 당신은 내면의 목소리를 들을 수 있을 것이다. 16 고3 평가원 변형

2 Alice did not ask her friends if the hat made her look ______________.
Alice는 그녀의 친구들에게 그 모자가 그녀를 예쁘게 보이게 하는지 묻지 않았다. 08 고2 평가원 변형

3 Paul continued to ______________ that the rumor was true.
Paul은 그 소문이 사실이라고 계속해서 주장했다.

4 Jimmy wanted to develop a healthy, positive ______________ towards the future.
Jimmy는 미래에 대해 건강하고 긍정적인 견해를 키우길 원했다. 14 고3 평가원 변형

5 While the eye only sees what's on the surface, the ear tends to ______________ below it.
눈은 표면에서 보지만, 귀는 표면 아래로 침투하는 경향이 있다. 2015 수능 변형

6 Most psychologists think that young children are ______________ and impatient.
대부분의 심리학자들은 어린이들이 비이성적이고 조급하다고 생각한다. 10 고1 학평 변형

7 I didn't know bats are a type of ______________.
나는 박쥐가 포유류의 일종인 것을 알지 못했다.

8 Singapore has ______________ the strictest no-smoking laws on Earth.
싱가포르는 이 세상에서 가장 강력한 금연 법을 시행하고 있다. 07 고3 학평 변형

9 My uncle is Dr. Maxwell, a ______________ specializing in neurosurgery.
우리 삼촌은 신경외과 수술을 전문으로 하는 외과 의사인 Dr. Maxwell이다. 06 고2 평가원 변형

10 Although we hoped to reach a ______________, in the end we failed to do so.
우리는 타협점에 도달하기를 희망했음에도 불구하고, 결국에 우리는 그렇게 하는데 실패했다.

Day 16

MP3

451 **egocentric** [ì:gousέntrik]
형 자기 중심적인, 이기적인
an egocentric speech 자기중심적 발화

452 **patch** [pætʃ]
명 헝겊 조각 동 헝겊 조각을 대다
patch up a hole in the fence 울타리에 구멍을 메우다

453 **anticipate** [æntísəpèit]
동 예측하다, 기대하다 유 predict 예언하다, 예측하다
anticipate economic growth 경제 성장을 예측하다

454 **proclaim** [proukléim]
동 선포하다, 선언하다, 칭송하다 유 declare 선언하다, 공표하다
proclaim a state of emergency 비상사태를 선포하다

455 **swarm** [swɔːrm]
명 떼 동 떼를 지어 다니다
a swarm of flies 파리떼

456 **conflicting** [kənflíktiŋ]
형 상반되는, 모순되는
conflicting claims 상반되는 요구

457 **textile** [tékstil]
명 직물, 옷감
the textile industry 섬유 산업 export textiles 섬유를 수출하다

458 **agony** [ǽgəni]
명 (극도의) 고민, 고통, 격정
immense agony 심각한 고민

459 **warrior** [wɔ́(ː)riər]
명 용사, 전사
invincible warriors 천하무적의 용사들 the warrior class 무인 계급

460 **womb** [wuːm]
명 자궁
from the womb to the tomb 요람에서 무덤까지

461 **cuddle** [kʌ́dl]
동 껴안다 명 껴안기, 포옹 유 hug 꼭 껴안다
cuddle her daughter 그녀의 딸을 껴안다

462 **texture** [tékstʃər]
명 질감
the rough texture of the skirt 치마의 거친 질감

463 **choke** [tʃouk]
동 질식시키다, 막다, 숨이 막히다
almost choked to death 거의 죽을 정도로 질식시키다

464 **credible** [krédəbl]
형 믿을 수 있는 반 incredible 믿을 수 없는, 믿기 힘든
a credible source of information 믿을 수 있는 정보원

465 **tenant** [ténənt]
명 세입자, 임차인
a previous tenant 이전 세입자 a tenant farmer 소작농

Daily Test

| 월 일 |

A 우리말에 맞게 빈 칸에 알맞은 단어를 쓰세요.

1 Cindy was blamed for her ______________ behavior.
Cindy는 그녀의 자기 중심적인 행동 때문에 비난 받았다.

2 The woman began to cry in great ______________.
그 여자는 고통스럽게 울기 시작했다.

3 Have you ever seen hundreds of thousands of bees or millions of birds ______________ around?
당신은 수십, 수천만 마리의 벌이나 수백만 마리의 새가 떼지어 있는걸 본 적 있나요?

4 A tiny flap of tissue covers the windpipe when we swallow our food so that we don't ______________.
우리가 음식을 삼킬 때 질식하지 않기 위해서 조직의 작은 덮개들이 호흡기관을 덮는다.

5 ______________ and clothing have functions that go beyond just protecting the body.
직물과 의복은 단순히 몸을 보호하는 그 이상의 기능을 갖고 있다. 15 고3 평가원 변형

6 Horses were used to carry armored ______________ with shields and weapons in the Middle Ages.
중세 시대에, 말들은 방패와 무기로 무장한 전사들을 태우는 데 사용 되었다. 07 고3 학평 변형

7 Scientists said that babies in the ______________ taste, remember, and form preferences for what Mom has been eating.
과학자들은 자궁 속 아기들이 엄마가 먹는 것들에 대해 맛을 보고, 기억하고, 선호도를 형성한다고 말했다. 15 고1 학평 변형

8 In the orphanages in the early 1900s, visitors were not permitted to ______________ newborn babies.
1900년대 초반 고아원에서는 방문자들이 신생아들을 안는 것은 허락되지 않았다. 15 고1 학평 변형

9 Freezing helps to change tofu's ______________, making it chewier.
추운 날씨는 두부의 질감을 쫄깃쫄깃하게 변화 시키는 데 유용하다. 06 고3 학평 변형

10 As a ______________ of your apartment for seven years, I have paid the rent happily because it is in a terrific location.
7년 동안 당신 건물의 세입자로서, 나는 아주 좋은 위치 때문에 기쁘게 임대료를 지불했습니다. 06 고2 평가원 변형

Day 16

MP3

466 **ultraviolet** [ʌ̀ltrəváiəlit]
명 자외선
ultraviolet rays 자외선　　an ultraviolet lamp 자외선 램프

467 **ally** [ǽli]
명 동맹, 연합　동 편들다, 지지하다
a strong ally 강한 동맹　　ally against the enemy 적에 대항하여 연합하다

468 **burial** [bériəl]
명 매장, 장례식
burial ground 묘지　　a burial at sea 수장

469 **unrealistic** [ʌnri:əlistik]
형 비현실적인, 비사실적인
set an unrealistic goal 비현실적인 목표를 세우다

470 **abolish** [əbáliʃ]
동 (법률, 제도 등을) 폐지하다, 없애다
abolish slavery 노예제를 폐지하다

471 **adhere** [ædhíər]
동 들러붙다, 부착하다, 고수하다　명 adhesive 접착제
adhere to his principle 그의 원칙을 고수하다

472 **compulsive** [kəmpʌ́lsiv]
형 강박적인, 조절이 힘든, 상습적인　유 uncontrollable 제어할 수 없는
treat compulsive mental disorders 강박적 정신장애를 치료하다

473 **beforehand** [bifɔ́:rhæ̀nd]
부 미리, 사전에
two days beforehand 2일 전에 미리

474 **affirmative** [əfə́:rmətiv]
형 긍정의　명 긍정의 대답　유 positive 긍정적인, 낙관적인
answer in the affirmative 긍정적으로 답하다

475 **childish** [tʃáildiʃ]
형 유치한, 어린애같은
have a childish idea 유치한 생각을 갖다

476 **consent** [kənsént]
동 동의하다　명 동의
give consent to a proposal 그 제안에 동의하다

477 **collaborate** [kəlǽbərèit]
동 협력하다, 공동으로 작업하다　형 collaborative 공동의
collaborate on the art project 예술 프로젝트에서 협력하다

478 **absent-minded** [æbsənt-máindid]
형 멍한, 얼빠진　반 attentive 주의를 기울이는
look absent-minded 멍해 보이다

479 **intersection** [ìntərsékʃən]
명 교차로, 교차점
a dangerous intersection 위험한 교차로

480 **dim** [dim]
형 어두운　동 ~을 어둑하게 하다
walk along a dim street 어두운 거리를 걷다

Daily Test

A 우리말에 맞게 빈 칸에 알맞은 단어를 쓰세요.

1 Direct exposure to ______________ light can cause severe negative effects on the skin.
자외선의 직접적인 노출은 피부에 심각한 부정적 영향을 일으킬 수 있다. 15 고1학평 변형

2 Ants carry off dead members of their colony to ______________ grounds.
개미들은 그들 집단의 죽은 일원들을 그들의 매장지로 옮긴다. 16 고3평가원 변형

3 Some people did not want to ______________ capital punishment.
몇몇 사람들은 사형제도를 폐지하는 것을 원하지 않았다.

4 Some desingers tend to ______________ to the principles that produced success in the first place.
일부 디자이너들은 처음에 성공을 가져다준 원칙을 고수하는 경향이 있다. 12 고3평가원 변형

5 ______________ shopping is a serious disorder that can ruin lives.
충동 구매는 삶을 망칠 수 있는 심각한 장애 이다. 12 고1학평 변형

6 A movie or a novel is often robbed of much of its interest if you know the plot ______________.
영화나 소설은 줄거리를 미리 알게 되면 흥미가 대부분 없어진다. 14 고2학평 변형

7 Don't be so ______________! Stop behaving like a baby!
유치하게 굴지마! 어리광 부리는 것을 멈추렴!

8 Smart competitors ______________ whenever they can.
현명한 경쟁자는 가능하면 언제나 협력한다. 12 고1학평 변형

9 Children were waiting for the truck to leave the ______________.
어린이들이 그 트럭이 교차로에서 출발하기를 기다리고 있었다.

10 Reading in ______________ light doesn't affect the function of your eyes.
어두운 조명 속에서 글을 읽는 것은 당신의 눈 기능에 영향을 끼치지 않는다. 07 고2학평 변형

Review Test 08 Day 15 + Day 16 | 월 일 |

A 우리말에 맞게 빈 칸에 알맞은 단어를 쓰시오.

1 ________________ criticism 적대적 비평

2 extreme ________________ 극단적 영양실조

3 ________________ from his earlier position 그의 이전 입장에서 물러나다

4 depend on ________________ 직관에 의존하다

5 her ________________ attitude 그녀의 비이성적인 태도

6 an ________________ speech 자기중심적 발화

7 export ________________ 섬유를 수출하다

8 ________________ her daughter 그녀의 딸을 껴안다

9 ________________ ground 묘지

10 answer in the ________________ 긍정적으로 답하다

B 영어에 맞게 빈 칸에 알맞은 우리말을 쓰시오.

1 a restless student ________________ 학생

2 geometric style ________________ 양식

3 immoral conduct ________________ 행동

4 a type of mammal ________________의 한 종류

5 a nail covered with rust ________________으로 뒤덮힌 못

6 a swarm of flies 파리 ________________

7 the warrior class ________________ 계급

8 almost choke to death 거의 죽을 정도로 ________________

9 adhere to his principle 그의 원칙을 ________________

10 have a childish idea ________________ 생각을 갖다

C 다음 영어 풀이에 알맞은 어휘를 〈보기〉에서 고르시오.

보기	probe	prompt	consent	abolish	hostile

1 ______________ : to put an end to something such as a law, regulation, or custom

2 ______________ : to search or investigate carefully

3 ______________ : to agree to do something

4 ______________ : difficult to endure; showing unfriendly feelings

5 ______________ : done quickly; to cause to do something

D 문맥에 맞게 다음 문장을 완성하시오.

1 Competition prompts innovation and •	• a specializing in neurosurgery.
2 Roy seemed restless •	• b drives global markets.
3 My uncle was Dr. Maxwell, a surgeon, •	• c severe negative effects on the skin.
4 Freezing helps to change tofu's texture, •	• d and afraid.
5 Direct exposure to ultraviolet light can cause •	• e making it chewier.

E 문장을 읽고 문맥에 적절한 단어를 고르시오.

1 The bright sunlight (penetrated/implemented) the dark room.

2 Computer manufacturers have a positive (intuition/outlook) on next year.

3 The old and unfair restrictions have finally been (abolished/leaked).

4 Your essay has little (asset/relevance) to the subject of this class.

5 If you want to join the meeting, contact us (recklessly/beforehand).

F 문장의 빈칸에 알맞은 단어를 〈보기〉에서 찾아 쓰시오. (필요하면 형태를 고치시오.)

보기 parasite intersection compromise infinite probe

1 Do you remember when you were little and you imagined that adults had _______________ power?
여러분이 어렸을 때, 어른들은 무한한 힘을 가졌다고 상상하던 때를 기억하는가? 2008 수능

2 Contrary to what is known, only one sixth of mosquitoes transmit the malaria _______________.
알려져 있었던 것과 반대로 오직 모기들의 ⅙만이 말라리아 기생충을 옮긴다. 08 고2학평 변형

2 The research team designed a special robot to _______________ the sea floor.
그 연구팀은 해저를 조사하기 위해 특별한 로봇을 고안했다.

4 We've done everything we can to contain costs without _______________ quality.
우리는 질을 손상시키지 않으면서 비용을 억제하기 위해 우리가 할 수 있는 모든 일을 다했습니다. 13 고3평가원

5 At the _______________, turn left and go straight two blocks until you get to Earl Street.
교차로에서 왼쪽으로 돌아서 Earl Street에 도착할 때까지 두 블록을 계속 직진 하세요. 2014 수능

G **다음 〈보기〉 중 두 문장에 공통으로 사용할 수 있는 어휘를 고르시오.**

1 He faced a challenge that no one had ____________(e)d. 11 고2학평 변형
We did not ____________ such bad weather on our picnic day.

① retreat ② adhere ③ revive ④ lessen ⑤ anticipate

2 Customers are often easy to lose but hard to ____________. 14 고2학평
He ____________(e)d his confidence and made many new friends. 14 고3평가원 변형

① regain ② proclaim ③ leak ④ cherish ⑤ proceed

3 We have had to ____________ these classes during the winter. 10 고3학평
The two players were ____________(e)d from the team for violating team rules.

① activate ② suspend ③ endeavor ④ disguise ⑤ imply

Study More

childish vs. **childlike**

- [childish] 형 유치한
  Yesterday, your attitude was so **childish** and rude. 어제, 너의 태도는 너무 유치하고 무례했어.
- [childlike] 형 순수한, 아이 같은
  My brother has **childlike** curiosity. 내 남동생은 아이 같은 호기심을 갖고 있다.

Day 17

MP3

481 **diploma** [diplóumə]
명 졸업장, 학위
a college diploma 대학 졸업장

482 **prism** [prízəm]
명 프리즘, 분광기
an experiment involving a prism 프리즘을 이용한 실험

483 **prestigious** [prestídʒiəs]
형 명성 있는, 일류의
receive a prestigious award 명성 있는 상을 수상하다

484 **dilute** [dilúːt]
동 희석하다, 묽게하다 형 희석된, 묽은
dilute with water 물로 희석하다 diluted ink 희석된 잉크

485 **episode** [épisòud]
명 사건, 에피소드
a tragic episode 비극적 사건

486 **injure** [índʒər]
동 다치게 하다, 손상시키다 유 hurt 다치게하다, 아프게하다
injure passengers 승객들을 다치게 하다

487 **evoke** [ivóuk]
동 불러 일으키다, 환기시키다 유 arouse 자극하다, 환기하다
evoke sympathy 동정심을 불러 일으키다

488 **luxurious** [lʌgʒú(ː)riəs]
형 호화로운, 고급의
live in a luxurious house 호화로운 집에서 살다

489 **allocate** [ǽləkèit]
동 할당하다, 배치하다 유 assign 할당하다, 배당하다
allocate resources 자원을 할당하다

490 **diagnosis** [dàiəgnóusis]
명 진단 동 diagnose (질병, 문제의 원인을) 진단하다
make a wrong diagnosis 잘못 진단하다

491 **porch** [pɔːrtʃ]
명 현관
a car parked at a back porch 뒤 현관에 주차된 차

492 **dummy** [dʌ́mi]
명 인체 모형, 견본 형 모조의
a tailor's dummy 재단용 인체 모형 ride a dummy horse 목마를 타다

493 **nurture** [nə́ːrtʃər]
동 양육하다, 키우다 명 양육, 육성
nurture children 아이들을 양육하다 nurture creativity 창의력을 키우다

494 **dormitory** [dɔ́ːrmitɔ̀ːri]
명 기숙사
live in a dormitory 기숙사에서 살다

495 **implication** [ìmpləkéiʃən]
명 영향, 함축
an implication of the policy 그 정책의 영향

Daily Test

| 월 일 |

A 우리말에 맞게 빈 칸에 알맞은 단어를 쓰세요.

1 A ______________ is used to break visible light into its spectrum or range of colors.
프리즘은 가시광선을 그것의 빛의 띠 또는 일련의 색들로 분리하기 위해 사용된다.

2 If the Juice is too strong for you, you can ______________ it with water.
주스 맛이 너무 강하게 느껴지면 물을 섞어 묽게 하셔도 됩니다.

3 My coffee was too strong, so I ______________ it with more water.
내 커피가 너무 진해서, 나는 물을 더 탔다.

4 In the first test, the children watched an ______________ of a sitcom.
첫 번째 시험에서, 아이들은 시트콤의 한 에피소드를 보았다. 10 고2학평 변형

5 My brother was severely ______________ in the car accident.
오빠는 차 사고로 인해 큰 부상을 입었다.

6 Some music or movies can ______________ memories in particular age groups.
몇몇 음악 또는 영화들은 특정한 연령대 사람들에게 기억을 불러일으킬 수 있다. 16 고3학평 변형

7 After Smith's cancer ______________, he began visualizing the cancer cells being killed by soldiers.
Smith는 암 진단을 받은 후에 군인들에 의해 죽는 암세포의 모습을 머릿속에 그려보기 시작했다. 14 고3학평 변형

8 The ______________ job is to simulate a human being during a crash.
그 인체 모형의 할 일은 사고 동안 인간을 모의 실험을 하는 것이다. 10 고3학평 변형

9 You need to develop and ______________ your problem solving skills regularly just like your physical strength.
당신은 체력을 기르는 것과 같이 규칙적으로 문제 해결 능력을 개발하고 키울 필요가 있다. 09 고3평가원 변형

10 This poem represents the importance of true friendship by ______________.
이 시는 함축적으로 진실한 우정의 중요성을 나타낸다.

Day 17

MP3

496 **erode** [iróud]
동 침식 시키다, 약화 시키다 유 corrode 부식시키다, 침식하다
be eroded by the sea 바다에 의해 침식되다

497 **conservative** [kənsə́ːrvətiv]
형 보수적인, (실제 수나 양보다) 적게 잡은 명 보수당원
conservative view 보수적 관점 conservative policy 보수적 정책

498 **hinder** [háindər]
동 방해하다, 훼방하다 명 hindrance 방해(요인)
hinder their travel plans 그들의 여행 계획을 방해하다

499 **dread** [dred]
동 몹시 무서워하다, 두려워하다
dread riding a bike 자전거를 타는 것을 무서워하다

500 **enrich** [inrítʃ]
동 부유하게 하다, 풍성하게 하다
enrich the soil 토양을 비옥하게 하다

501 **intellect** [íntəlèkt]
명 지성, 지적 능력
a sharp intellect 날카로운 지성 train intellect 지적 능력을 연마하다

502 **ambition** [æmbíʃən]
명 야망, 포부
literary ambition 문학적 야망

503 **discern** [disə́ːrn]
동 식별하다, 분간하다 유 distinguish 구별하다, 식별하다
discern difference 차이를 식별하다

504 **marble** [máːrbl]
명 대리석, 구슬
a marble floor 대리석 바닥

505 **racism** [réisizəm]
명 인종 차별(주의)
a victim of racism 인종 차별의 희생자

506 **impose** [impóuz]
동 부과하다, 도입하다, 강요하다 반 lift (제재 등을) 해제하다
impose heavy taxes on alcohol 술에 과중한 세금을 부과하다

507 **gracious** [gréiʃəs]
형 품위 있는, 자애로운
his gracious attitude 그의 품위 있는 태도

508 **revenge** [rivéndʒ]
명 보복, 복수
Tim sought revenge. Tim은 복수를 꿈꾸었다.

509 **atomic** [ətámik]
형 원자의, 원자력의, 핵무기의
the atomic structure 원자 구조 an atomic explosion 원자 폭발

510 **plead** [pliːd]
동 애원하다, 호소하다 명 plea 애원, 간청
her pleading eyes 그녀의 애원하는 두 눈

Daily Test

| 월 일 |

A 우리말에 맞게 빈 칸에 알맞은 단어를 쓰세요.

1 Wind makes sand hills and wind-blown sand ______________ rocks.
바람은 모래 언덕을 만들고 바람에 불어온 모래는 바위를 침식시킨다.

2 The noise of the train passing by didn't ______________ our training.
지나가는 기차의 소음은 우리의 훈련을 방해하지 않았다.

3 When I was a small child, I ______________ Friday nights.
내가 조그만 아이였을 때, 난 금요일 밤을 무서워했다. 07 고2학평 변형

4 Wheat and maize are often ______________ with iron.
밀과 옥수수는 종종 철분이 강화된다. 10 고2학평

5 Anxiety often undermines the ______________.
긴장은 종종 지적 능력을 악화시킨다. 2013 수능 변형

6 The pattern of stripes on a zebra makes it hard for a cheetah to ______________ an individual zebra.
얼룩말의 줄무늬 패턴은 치타가 각각의 얼룩말을 분간하기 어렵게 만든다.

7 Because of the government's efforts, educational institutes are free from ______________.
정부의 노력 때문에, 교육 기관들은 인종차별로부터 자유롭다. 09 고3평가원 변형

8 Hundreds of years ago, the Duke of Tuscany ______________ a tax on salt.
수백 년 전에, 투스카니의 공작은 소금에 세금을 부과했다. 15 고2학평 변형

9 Although the Big Bang theory suggests an explosion as in an ______________ bomb, this is misleading.
빅뱅이론은 원자폭탄에서와 같은 폭발을 암시했지만 그것은 오해의 소지가 있다.

10 Amy denied the charge and kept ______________ innocent.
Amy는 경찰의 기소를 거부했고 계속해서 무죄를 호소했다. 12 고1학평 변형

Day 18

MP3

511 **hinge** [hinʤ]
명 경첩 동 ~여하에 달려있다
put a hinge on a door 문에 경첩을 달다

512 **shiver** [ʃívər]
동 (추위, 두려움, 흥분으로) 떨다 명 전율, 오한
shiver from the cold 추위에 떨다

513 **artifact** [ɑ́ːrtəfæ̀kt]
명 인공물, 인공 유물
ancient artifacts 고대 유물

514 **armor** [ɑ́ːrmər]
명 갑옷, 장갑, 방호구 동 갑옷을 입히다
a suit of armor 갑옷 한 벌 pierce body armor 갑옷을 뚫다

515 **simplify** [símpləfài]
동 간소화하다, 단순화하다
simplify enrollment procedures 등록절차를 간소화하다

516 **upcoming** [ʌ́pkʌ̀miŋ]
형 다가오는, 곧 있을 유 forthcoming 다가오는, 곧 있을
the upcoming election 다가오는 선거

517 **strand** [strænd]
명 가닥 동 오도가도 못하게 하다
a strand of red wool 빨간 털실 한 가닥

518 **sprout** [spraut]
명 싹 동 싹이 나기 시작하다
Potatoes sprout in the bag. 감자가 자루 안에서 싹을 틔우다.

519 **oblige** [əbláiʤ]
동 의무적으로 ~하게 하다, 강요하다 명 obligation (법적, 도덕적) 의무
be obliged to attend the meeting 회의에 의무적으로 참여 해야 한다

520 **soothe** [suːð]
동 진정시키다, 달래다, 누그러뜨리다
soothe symptoms 증상을 진정시키다

521 **dichotomy** [daikɑ́təmi]
명 양분, 이분법 형 dichotomous 양분된, 이분법의
an absolute dichotomy 완전한 양분 a false dichotomy 잘못된 이분법

522 **reassure** [rìːəʃúər]
동 안심시키다, 힘을 북돋우다 명 reassurance 안심시키기
try to reassure her daughter 그녀의 딸을 안심시키려 노력하다

523 **acupuncture** [ǽkjupʌ̀ŋktʃər]
명 침술
acupuncture treatment 침술 치료 do acupuncture 침술을 놓다

524 **tolerate** [tɑ́lərèit]
동 참다, 견디다, 용인하다
tolerate a sore throat 아픈 목을 참다 tolerate adversity 역경을 견디다

525 **bankrupt** [bǽŋkrʌpt]
형 파산한 명 bankruptcy 파산
go bankrupt 파산하다

Daily Test

| 월 일 |

A 우리말에 맞게 빈 칸에 알맞은 단어를 쓰세요.

1 A ______________ went through his body.
그의 온 몸에 전율이 흘렀다. 11 고2학평 변형

2 Researchers were surprised to find incredible amounts of ancient ______________ nearly 11 meters deep!
연구원들은 거의 11미터 깊이에서 엄청난 양의 고대 유물을 발견해서 깜짝 놀랐다.

3 Body ______________ is a protective bulletproof clothing worn underneath a soldier or police officer's uniform.
몸 갑옷은 군인이나 경찰의 유니폼 안에 입는 보호 방탄 의복이다.

4 ______________ the process of car manufacture was our main task.
자동차 제조 과정을 단순화 시키는 것이 우리의 주된 업무였다.

5 Hi, Denis. Do you plan to do anything special during the ______________ holiday?
Denis, 다가오는 휴가에 특별히 무엇이라도 할 계획이니?

6 She picked out some flowers, and ______________ of green ivy to make her wedding bouquet.
그녀는 자신의 결혼 부케를 만들기 위해 몇 송이의 꽃과 초록 담쟁이 줄기들을 꺾었다. 16 고3학평 변형

7 In May, clusters of red roses ______________ from the stem tips, attracting hummingbirds.
5월에, 붉은 장미 송이들이 가지 끝에서 벌새를 끌어들이면서 싹을 틔웠다. 14 고3학평 변형

8 The first Everesters were ______________ to trek 400 miles to reach the foot of the mountain.
최초의 에베레스트를 오른 사람은 산기슭까지 다다르기 위해 의무적으로 400마일을 걸어야만 했다. 2012 수능 변형

9 I had turned toward Nick in shock, but he did not cuddle or ______________ me.
나는 충격에 휩싸여 Nick을 향해 돌아 보았지만, 그는 나를 안아주거나 진정시켜주지 않았다. 11 고3평가원 변형

10 If self-esteem is taught improperly, you can raise a generation of kids who cannot ______________ frustration.
자존감 교육이 부적절하게 행해진다면, 당신은 좌절감을 견디지 못하는 세대의 아이들을 키우게 된다. 06 고2학평 변형

Day 18

MP3

526 **transplant** [trǽnsplæ̀nt]
동 이식하다 명 이식
need a heart transplant 심장이식이 필요하다

527 **particle** [pά:rtikl]
명 입자, 티끌, (문서 등의) 항목, 조항
tiny particles 아주 작은 입자 a dust particle 먼지 입자

528 **sympathetic** [sìmpəθétik]
형 동정적인, 동조하는, 호감이 가는
offer a sympathetic opinion 동정의 의견을 제시하다

529 **successive** [səksésiv]
형 연속적인, 연이은 유 consecutive 연속적인, 계속되는
our team's successive victories 우리 팀의 연승

530 **superb** [sju(:)pə́:rb]
형 최고의, 최상의
do a superb job 뛰어난 일을 해내다

531 **recession** [riséʃən]
명 불경기, 불황
the manufacturing recession 제조업 불경기

532 **soar** [sɔ:r]
동 (가치, 물가 등이) 치솟다, 날아오르다
soaring prices 치솟는 물가 soar into the sky 하늘로 날아오르다

533 **wreck** [rek]
명 난파선, (사고 등의) 잔해, 충돌 동 망가뜨리다, 난파시키다, 파괴하다
be trapped in the wreck 난파선에 갇히다

534 **shrine** [ʃrain]
명 성지, 사당
a historic shrine 역사적인 성지 pray at a shrine 사당에서 기도하다

535 **yeast** [ji:st]
명 효모균, 이스트
add yeast to dough 반죽에 이스트를 넣다

536 **vanish** [vǽniʃ]
동 사라지다, 없어지다 유 disappear 사라지다, 안보이게 되다
vanish without a trace 흔적도 없이 사라지다

537 **radical** [rǽdikəl]
형 급진적인 유 extreme 극도의, 극심한
the need for radical change 급진적 변화의 필요성

538 **refrain** [rifréin]
동 삼가다, 자제하다
refrain from traveling 여행을 자제하다

539 **humanitarian** [hju:mæ̀nitέ(:)əriən]
형 인도주의적인
provide humanitarian aid 인도주의적 원조를 제공하다

540 **distort** [distɔ́:rt]
동 (사실 등을) 왜곡하다, (형태, 모습 등을) 비틀다 명 distortion 일그러짐, 왜곡
distort the truth 진실을 왜곡하다

Daily Test

| 월 일 |

A 우리말에 맞게 빈 칸에 알맞은 단어를 쓰세요.

1 Her brother needed an organ ______________ to replace his failed kidney.
그녀의 오빠는 그의 기능이 정지된 신장을 교체 하기 위해 장기 이식이 필요했다.

2 Sweat is made mostly of water, but it also contains small ______________ of salt.
땀은 거의 물로 만들어지지만 또한 작은 소금 입자들을 포함하고 있다.

3 Jim failed his entrance exams to Philip dance school in two ______________ years.
Jim은 2년 연속 Philip 무용 학교의 입학 시험에 떨어졌다. 10 고3학평 변형

4 Thank you so much for your great service and ______________ delivery.
당신의 훌륭한 서비스와 최상의 배달에 매우 감사 드립니다. 09 고3학평 변형

5 ______________ eagles have the incredible ability to see a dog in the grass from a mile away.
날아오르는 독수리들은 1마일 떨어진 거리에서도 잔디밭에 있는 개를 볼 수 있는 믿기 힘든 능력을 지녔다. 08 고3평가원 변형

6 Many different religions have ______________.
많은 다양한 종교들이 사당을 가지고 있다.

7 ______________ cells growing on an orange skin obtain energy from nutrient molecules.
오렌지 껍질에서 자라는 효모 세포는 영양 분자로부터 에너지를 얻는다. 08 고3평가원 변형

8 The fairy saved me and ______________ quietly into the dark when doctors came to my side.
그 요정은 나를 구해주었고 의사가 내 쪽으로 왔을 때 어둠 속으로 조용히 사라졌다. 09 고2학평 변형

9 Some of the most recent government policies are much too ______________.
최근 정부 정책 중 일부는 너무 급진적이다. 11 고2학평 변형

10 In 2003, the organization was awarded the Nobel Peace Prize for their ______________ efforts.
2003년에 그 단체는 그들의 인도주의적 노력에 대해 노벨 평화상을 수상했다.

Review Test 09

A 우리말에 맞게 빈 칸에 알맞은 단어를 쓰시오.

1 receive a ______________ award 명성 있는 상을 수상하다

2 ______________ sympathy 동정심을 불러 일으키다

3 ______________ policy 보수적 정책

4 literary ______________ 문학적 야망

5 a victim of ______________ 인종 차별의 희생자

6 put a ______________ on a door 문에 경첩을 달다

7 Potatoes ______________ in the bag. 감자가 자루 안에서 싹을 틔우다.

8 do ______________ 침술을 놓다

9 a dust ______________ 먼지 입자

10 pray at a ______________ 사당에서 기도하다

B 영어에 맞게 빈 칸에 알맞은 우리말을 쓰시오.

1 diluted ink ______________ 잉크

2 allocate resources 자원을 ______________

3 nurture creativity 창의력을 ______________

4 train intellect ______________을 연마하다

5 his gracious attitude 그의 ______________ 태도

6 pierce body armor ______________을 뚫다

7 soothe symptoms 증상을 ______________

8 soar into the sky 하늘로 ______________

9 refrain from traveling 여행을 ______________

10 distort the truth 진실을 ______________

C 다음 영어 풀이에 알맞은 어휘를 〈보기〉에서 고르시오.

보기 dichotomy bankrupt luxurious prestigious discern

1 ______________ : highly influential and with good reputation

2 ______________ : very comfortable and expensive

3 ______________ : no longer able to pay debt or money owned

4 ______________ : the difference between two opposing things, parts, or qualities.

5 ______________ : to see or notice something; to distinguish

D 문맥에 맞게 다음 문장을 완성하시오.

1 A prism is used to break visible light •	• a watched an episode of a sitcom.
2 In the first test, the children •	• b to replace his failed kidney.
3 Wheat and maize are often •	• c into its spectrum or range of colors.
4 I had turned toward Nick in shock, •	• d but he did not cuddle or soothe me.
5 Her brother needed an organ transplant •	• e enriched with iron.

E 문장을 읽고 문맥에 적절한 단어를 고르시오.

1 Next year, Cindy will graduate from college and get her (diplomat/yeast).

2 My daughters (justify/dread) going to the dentist.

3 The boy (pleaded/coped) with his father to take him to the zoo.

4 What we need are gradual changes, not (radical/atomic) changes.

5 She was (soaring/shivering) because of the cold wind.

F 문장의 빈칸에 알맞은 단어를 〈보기〉에서 찾아 쓰시오. (필요하면 형태를 고치시오.)

보기 soothe superb tolerate upcoming impose

1 We have an important announcement regarding an _______________ special event.
다가오는 특별 행사에 대해 중대한 발표가 있습니다. 16 고3평가원

2 I taught Chloe to_______________ other cultures.
나는 Chole에게 다른 문화를 용인하도록 가르쳤다. 13 고3학평

3 My dad bought me a used piano. Surprisingly, it was in _______________ condition.
아버지는 내게 중고 피아노를 사주셨다. 놀랍게도 피아노는 최상의 상태였다.

4 The tourism department will _______________ a limit on the number of visitors to the park.
관광국은 그 공원의 방문객 수에 대한 제한을 도입할 것이다.

5 Not only did my explanation not _______________ her, it seemed to make things worse.
내 설명은 그녀를 진정시키지 못했을 뿐만 아니라 상황을 오히려 악화시켰다. 14 고2학평

G 다음 〈보기〉 중 두 문장에 공통으로 사용할 수 있는 어휘를 고르시오.

1 I got so badly ____________(e)d that I couldn't swim or come up for air. 13 고3평가원
In some cases, pets have been ____________(e)d or killed by wild animals. 14 고3평가원

① dilute ② injure ③ discern ④ vanish ⑤ hinge

2 I had started doing this just to ____________ the task of managing people. 15 고2학평
Research shows that we need to ____________ reality in a way that best serves our purposes. 07 고2학평

① enrich ② revenge ③ evoke ④ simplify ⑤ erode

3 When we have an experience on ____________ occasions, we quickly begin to adapt to it. 11 고2학평
His hard work made him achieve three ____________ world chess championships.

① prestigious ② luxurious ③ marble ④ successive ⑤ humanitarian

Study More

'succeed'의 다양한 뜻

- [succeed] 동 성공하다
  Mina **succeeded** in passing the graduation exam. 미나는 졸업 시험에 합격하는 데 성공했다.
- [succeed] 동 잇다, 상속하다
  William will **succeed** to the throne next year. William은 내년에 왕위를 계승 할 것이다.

Day 19

MP3

541 **flame** [fleim]
명 불꽃, 화염
spout out flames 불꽃을 내뿜다　the Olympic flame 올림픽 성화

542 **bureaucracy** [bjuərákrəsi]
명 관료(제)
the power of state bureaucracy 국가 관료의 권력

543 **doom** [du:m]
명 죽음, 파멸　동 ~을 운명짓다, (수동으로) ~할 운명이다
go to one's doom 죽다　impending doom 임박한 파멸

544 **glacier** [gléiʃər]
명 빙하
glacier in Alaska 알라스카의 빙하　the top of a glacier 빙하의 끝

545 **epic** [épik]
명 서사시, 장편 서사 영화　형 서사시의, 장대한
a folk epic 민족 서사시

546 **commentary** [káməntèri]
명 해설, 논평, 주석
give a commentary 해설을 하다　a political commentary 정치 논평

547 **clarify** [klǽrəfài]
동 명백히 하다, 분명히 하다　명 clarification 맑게 함, 설명, 해명
clarify the cause 원인을 명백히 하다

548 **diaper** [dáiəpər]
명 기저귀
change his daughter's diaper 그의 딸의 기저귀를 갈다

549 **complementary** [kàmpləméntəri]
형 상호 보완적인　명 서로 보완하는 것
enhance the complementary relationships 상호보완적 관계를 강화하다

550 **graze** [greiz]
동 풀을 뜯다, 방목하다
graze by the river 강 근처에서 풀을 뜯다

551 **indigenous** [indídʒənəs]
형 고유의, 토착의
indigenous human trait 인간 고유의 특성

552 **chronic** [kránik]
형 (병, 질환 등이) 만성의, 만성적인
suffer from chronic asthma 만성 천식에 시달리다

553 **eternal** [i(:)tə́:rnəl]
형 영원한, 끊임없는　유 everlasting 영원히 계속되는, 불후의
our eternal love 우리의 영원한 사랑

554 **coarse** [kɔ:rs]
형 (피부, 천 등이) 거친, (알갱이 등이) 굵은
her coarse hand 그녀의 거친 손　coarse salt 굵은 소금

555 **dose** [dous]
명 (약의) 복용량 (투여량)　동 투약시키다, 복용시키다
a dose of medicine 약의 1회 복용량　a fatal dose 치사량

Daily Test

| 월 일 |

A 우리말에 맞게 빈 칸에 알맞은 단어를 쓰세요.

1 I saw my son's black motorcycle exploding with ______________.
나는 내 아들의 오토바이가 불꽃에 휩싸여 폭발하는 것을 보았다. 07 고1학평 변형

2 Greenhouse gases lead to melting ______________ and cause the ocean water to warm up.
온실 가스는 빙하를 녹이고 바닷물을 따뜻하게 만든다.

3 Student frequently ______________ and interpret their teacher's instructions concerning what they should be doing.
학생들은 흔히 그들이 무엇을 하고 있어야 하는지에 관한 교사의 지시를 분명히 하고 해석한다.

4 Students frequently ______________ and interpret their teacher's instructions.
학생들은 자주 그들 선생님의 지시를 분명히 하고 해석한다. 15 고3학평 변형

5 We noticed Youngjin talking on the phone while simultaneously changing his baby's ______________.
우리는 영진이 그의 아기의 기저귀를 갈면서 동시에 전화를 받고 있음을 알아차렸다. 2004 수능 변형

6 The land that was previously used by animals to ______________ became useless.
이전에 동물들을 방목하기 위해 사용되었던 그 땅은 쓸모 없어졌다.

7 We discussed the main environmental issues: Extinction, Biodiversity and ______________ Healing.
우리는 멸종, 생물학적 다양성, 토착 치료법과 같은 주된 환경 문제에 대해 토론했다. 06 고3학평 변형

8 Early philosophers considered the world stable, ______________, and unshakable.
초기 철학자들은 세계는 안정적이고 영원하며 흔들리지 않는다고 여겼다. 10 고3평가원 변형

9 The ______________ white sand stuck to the back of my legs and thighs but provided a cool feeling.
거친 흰 모래가 내 다리 뒤와 허벅지에 묻었지만 시원한 느낌을 주었다. 14 고3학평 변형

10 Small ______________ of pesticides on crops can adversely affect people.
곡식에 있는 소량의 해충제의 복용도 사람들에게 심각하게 영향을 미칠 수 있다.

Day 19

MP3

556 cling [kliŋ]
동 꼭 붙잡다, 매달리다, 애착을 갖다
cling together 밀착하다 cling to the ceiling 천장에 매달리다

557 copyright [kápiràit]
명 저작권, 판권 동 저작권을 얻다
copyright on this movie 이 영화의 저작권

558 cuisine [kwizíːn]
명 요리, 요리법
royal court cuisine 궁중요리

559 curb [kəːrb]
동 억제하다, 제한하다 명 구속, 속박, 억제
curb global warming 지구 온난화를 억제하다

560 discard [diskáːrd]
동 버리다, 폐기하다 유 abandon 버리고 떠나다, 포기하다, 버리다
discard her old shoes 그녀의 오래된 신발을 버리다

561 evaporate [ivǽpərèit]
동 증발하다, 증발시키다
evaporate in the air 공기 중에서 증발하다

562 inhabit [inhǽbit]
동 거주하다, 서식하다
inhabit a remote island 외딴 섬에 거주하다

563 congestion [kəndʒéstʃən]
명 (교통 등의) 혼잡, 밀집, 정체
cause serious traffic congestion 심각한 교통 혼잡을 야기하다

564 handshake [hǽndʃèik]
명 악수 동 악수하다
a warm handshake 따뜻한 악수

565 connectivity [kànektívəti]
명 연결(성), 연결상태
resolve server connectivity problems 서버 연결 문제를 해결하다

566 flee [fliː]
동 도망치다, 달아나다
flee from enemies 적을 피해 도망치다 flee to Korea 한국으로 도망치다

567 decent [díːsənt]
형 제대로 된, 품위 있는, 예의 바른
provide decent education 제대로 된 교육을 제공하다

568 corpse [kɔːrps]
명 시체, 송장
bury a corpse 시체를 매장하다

569 lump [lʌmp]
명 덩어리, 혹 동 한 덩어리로 만들다
a lump of cheese 치즈 덩어리

570 overhear [òuvərhíər]
동 우연히 듣다, 엿듣다
overhear their conversation 그들의 대화를 엿듣다

Daily Test

| 월 일 |

A 우리말에 맞게 빈 칸에 알맞은 단어를 쓰세요.

1 Most music companies ______________ their songs.
대부분의 음악 회사는 그들의 음악에 대한 저작권을 가지고 있다.

2 Wine is an important part of the French ______________.
와인은 프랑스 요리의 중요한 부분이다. 10 고2학평 변형

3 After it rains, it's fun to watch the puddles ______________ in the hot sun.
비가 온 뒤에, 뜨거운 태양에 물 웅덩이가 증발되는 것을 보는 것은 재밌다.

4 Seal fish are known ______________ very deep water, off the edge of the continental shelf.
물개 어류는 대륙붕 가장자리에서 떨어진 아주 깊은 물에서 서식하는 것으로 알려져있다. 14 고3평가원 변형

5 Building multi-billion dollar skyscrapers can cause traffic ______________.
수십억 달러의 고층 건물들을 짓는 것은 교통 혼잡을 유발할 수 있다.

6 "It's time to celebrate!" Eric lined up for hugs and ______________ alongside the winner.
"축하할 시간이야!" Eric은 우승자 옆에서 포옹과 악수를 위해 줄을 섰다. 14 고2학평 변형

7 The group of deer ______________ from the tiger created confusion.
호랑이를 피해 도망치는 한 무리의 사슴들이 혼란을 빚었다. 14 고3평가원 변형

8 If your computer breaks down, check its ______________.
만약 당신의 컴퓨터가 고장이 나면 연결 상태를 확인해 보십시오.

9 Lastly, he would say, "Behold!" and a ______________ of precious gold would be found in the bottom of his pot.
마지막으로, 그가 말하길, " 보아라!" 그러자 그의 항아리 바닥에서 귀한 금 한 덩어리가 발견되곤 했다. 07 고3평가원 변형

10 The strong point of the marketing strategy is that you don't know that the conversation you ______________ is just a performance.
그 마케팅 전략의 가장 큰 강점은 당신이 엿들은 대화가 단순한 퍼포먼스라는 걸 모른다는 것이다. 07 고2학평 변형

Day 20

MP3

571 **pavement** [péivmənt]
명 인도, 보도, 포장도로 동 pave (길을) 포장하다
improve the pavement 포장도로를 개선하다

572 **multitask** [ˈmʌltitæsk]
동 다중 작업 처리를 하다
multitask effectively 효과적으로 여러 가지 일을 처리하다

573 **precede** [prisíːd]
동 앞서다, 선행하다, 먼저 일어나다
precede all matters 모든 문제를 앞서다

574 **renew** [rinjúː]
동 재개하다, 갱신하다
renew the discussion 토론을 재개하다

575 **morale** [mərǽl]
명 사기, 의욕
boost morale 사기를 북돋우다

576 **pessimistic** [pèsəmístik]
형 비관적인 반 optimistic 낙관적인, 낙관하는
pessimistic about the accident 그 사고에 대해 비관적이다

577 **provision** [prəvíʒən]
명 (법률 등의) 조항, 규정, 단서, 공급, 제공
the lack of housing provision 주택 공급의 부족

578 **prescribe** [priskráib]
동 처방을 내리다, 처방전을 쓰다 명 prescription 처방전
prescribe the medication 약을 처방하다

579 **livelihood** [láivlihùd]
명 생계, 생계수단
write for his livelihood 그의 생계를 위해 글을 쓰다

580 **mortgage** [mɔ́ːrgidʒ]
명 저당, 담보대출
get a second mortgage 재융자를 받다 mortgage rate 담보율

581 **primate** [práimèit]
명 영장류
important research on primates 영장류에 대한 중요한 연구

582 **oval** [óuvəl]
형 계란형의, 타원형의
her oval face 그녀의 계란형 얼굴 an oval frame 타원형 액자

583 **remedy** [rémidi]
명 치료(약), 해결책 동 바로잡다, 개선하다
a new flu remedy 새로운 감기 치료약

584 **precaution** [prikɔ́ːʃən]
명 예방(책), 조심, 경계
take precautions against fire 화재에 대해 경계를 하다

585 **ornament** [ɔ́ːrnəmənt]
명 장식(품)
a garish ornament 화려한 장식

Daily Test

| 월 일 |

A 우리말에 맞게 빈 칸에 알맞은 단어를 쓰세요.

1 Scientists say that it is hard for street trees to survive with only foot-square holes in the ______________.
과학자들은 포장도로 위 겨우 발이 들어갈만한 정사각형 구멍에서 가로수들이 살아남는 것은 힘들다고 말한다. 10 고3 평가원 변형

2 Lina focused on a single task instead of trying to ______________.
Lina는 여러가지 일을 처리하는 대신 한 가지 일에 집중했다. 16 고3 평가원 변형

3 Jessie has to ______________ her driver's license.
Jessie는 그녀의 운전 면허증을 갱신해야 한다. 2014 수능 변형

4 For example, voluntary labor, such as helping mom clean the house constitutes an unpaid service ______________.
예를 들어, 집 청소를 하는 엄마를 돕는 것과 같은 자발적 노동은 돈을 받지 않는 서비스에 해당된다. 15 고1 학평 변형

5 It is important to ______________ equal doses of medication across the course of the day.
하루에 같은 양의 약을 처방하는 것은 중요하다. 12 고3 학평 변형

6 The Industrial Revolution brought commerce as an alternative means of ______________.
산업혁명은 무역을 하나의 대안적인 생계수단으로 가져왔다.

7 The bank can sell your property if you fail to keep up your ______________ payments.
만약 당신이 담보대출을 계속해서 지불하지 못한다면, 은행은 당신의 자산을 팔 수 있다. 07 고2 학평 변형

8 Anthropologists observed a correlation between the sizes of ______________ brains and frequency of social contacts.
인류학자들은 영장류의 뇌 크기와 사회적 접촉의 빈도 간의 연관성을 관찰했다. 11 고3 학평 변형

9 The causes of anorexia are often quite simple and easy to ______________.
거식증의 원인은 종종 꽤 단순하고 치료하기 쉽다.

10 You should take every necessary ______________ before embarking on a major mountain climbing trip.
당신은 중대한 산악 여행을 시작하기 전에 모든 필수적인 예방 조치를 취해야 한다.

Day 20

MP3

586 □ **inquiry** [inkwáiəri]
명 조사, 수사, 연구, 탐구
scientific inquiry 과학적 조사

587 □ **radiate** [réidiət]
동 내뿜다, (사방으로) 퍼지다　유 emit 방사하다, 내뿜다
radiate heat 열을 방사하다

588 □ **irresponsible** [ìrispánsəbl]
형 무책임한, 책임감이 없는
promote irresponsible spending 무책임한 소비를 조장하다

589 □ **overload** [óuvərlòud]
동 과적하다　명 과부하
drive the overloaded truck 과적된 트럭을 몰다

590 □ **naive** [nɑːíːv]
형 순진한, 고지식한, 속기 쉬운　유 innocent 순진한, 천진난만한
a naive answer 순진한 대답

591 □ **meteorite** [míːtiəràit]
명 운석, 유성체
fragments of meteorite 운석의 파편들

592 □ **mutation** [mju(ː)téiʃən]
명 돌연변이, (형태·구조상의) 변화　동 mutate 돌연변이를 만들다
a genetic mutation 유전자 돌연변이

593 □ **irritate** [íritèit]
동 거슬리게 하다, 몹시 짜증내다　형 irritating 흥분시키는, 아리게하는
irritate his nerves 그의 신경을 거슬리게 하다

594 □ **pledge** [pledʒ]
명 약속, 맹세　동 약속하다
pledge to support his plan 그의 계획을 지지하기로 약속하다

595 □ **quote** [kwout]
동 인용하다, 예를 들다, 견적을 내다　명 인용(문), 견적액
quote the sentence 그 문장을 인용하다

596 □ **linguistic** [liŋgwístik]
형 언어의, 언어적인
linguistic diversity 언어적 다양성

597 □ **murmur** [mə́ːrmər]
동 중얼거리다, 속삭이다　명 속삭임, 소곤거림
start to murmur 중얼거리기 시작하다

598 □ **qualified** [kwáləfàid]
형 자격이 있는　동 qualify 자격을 갖추다
fully qualified for the job 그 직업에 전적으로 자격을 갖춘

599 □ **cluster** [klʌ́stər]
동 떼를 지어 모이다　명 무리, 떼
cluster around the center 중심으로 떼를 지어 모이다

600 □ **omission** [oumíʃən]
명 생략, 누락　동 omit 빠뜨리다, 누락하다, 생략하다
without omission 생략 없이　a serious omission 심각한 누락

Daily Test

| 월 일 |

A 우리말에 맞게 빈 칸에 알맞은 단어를 쓰세요.

1 In much of scientific ______________, there are no right or wrong answers.
많은 과학 연구에서, 맞거나 틀린 답은 없다. 14 고2학평 변형

2 The oven ______________ heat which could be felt throughout the kitchen.
오븐은 부엌 전체에서 느낄 수 있을 만큼의 열을 방출했다.

3 Because Andy was ______________ behind the wheel, he caused the accident.
Andy의 무책임한 운전이 사고를 일으켰다.

4 Environmental factors can cause genetic ______________ .
환경적 요소가 유전적 돌연변이를 초래할 수도 있다. 15 고3학평 변형

5 Bronchitis is a virus that ______________ the inside of the nose.
기관지염은 코 속을 자극하게 하는 바이러스이다.

6 Helen simply said that she ______________ to support the village's recycling program.
Helen은 그녀가 마을의 재활용 프로그램을 지지할 것을 약속했다고 말했다. 14 고1학평 변형

7 It is sometimes incorrectly ______________ that mosquitoes kill more people than any other animal.
모기가 다른 어떤 동물들보다 사람을 많이 죽인다는 것으로 부정확하게 인용되는 경우가 간혹 있다. 08 고2학평 변형

8 Traditional second language learning has focused its attention on ______________ knowledge.
전통적인 제2언어 학습은 언어 지식에 초점을 두어 왔다. 10 고1학평 변형

9 Our well-______________ and well-paid teachers will be able to teach more effectively.
우리의 자격을 잘 갖추고 좋은 급여를 받는 선생님들은 더 효율적으로 가르칠 수 있을 거에요. 06 고3평가원 변형

10 In June, ______________ of red flowers sprout from the stem tips, attracting humming birds.
6월에, 줄기 끝에서 빨간 꽃이 무리를 지어 피면서 벌새를 불러들인다. 09 고3학평 변형

A 우리말에 맞게 빈 칸에 알맞은 단어를 쓰시오.

1 the power of state ______________ 국가 관료의 권력

2 change his daughter's ______________ 그의 딸의 기저귀를 갈다

3 suffer from ______________ asthma 만성 천식에 시달리다

4 ______________ her old shoes 그녀의 오래된 신발을 버리다

5 ______________ to Korea 한국으로 도망치다

6 improve the ______________ 포장도로를 개선하다

7 ______________ about the accident 그 사고에 대해 비관적이다

8 ______________ the medication 약을 처방하다

9 drive the ______________ truck 과적된 트럭을 몰다

10 a serious ______________ 심각한 누락

B 영어에 맞게 빈 칸에 알맞은 우리말을 쓰시오.

1 a folk epic 민족 ______________

2 our eternal love 우리의 ______________ 사랑

3 cling together ______________

4 inhabit a remote island 외딴 섬에 ______________

5 bury a corpse ______________를 매장하다

6 precede all matters 모든 문제를 ______________

7 mortgage rate ______________율

8 take precautions against fire 화재에 대해 ______________를 하다

9 a naive answer ______________ 대답

10 pledge to support his plan 그의 계획을 지지하기로 ______________

C 다음 영어 풀이에 알맞은 어휘를 〈보기〉에서 고르시오.

보기 flee lump clarify evaporate decent

1 _______________ : to change from liquid, e.g., water, to gas

2 _______________ : to make more understandable ; make clear

3 _______________ : a small piece or pile of something with no fixed shape

4 _______________ : good enough or suitable for something

5 _______________ : to run away from a place or escape

D 문맥에 맞게 다음 문장을 완성하시오.

1	I saw my son's black motorcycle •	• a	irritates the inside of the nose.
2	Students frequently clarify and interpret •	• b	their teacher's instructions concerning what they should be doing.
3	Wine is an important part •	• c	her driver's license.
4	Jessie has to renew •	• d	of the French cuisine.
5	Bronchitis is a virus that •	• e	exploding with flames.

E 문장을 읽고 문맥에 적절한 단어를 고르시오.

1 The boy (overheard/curbed) his parents talking about his study.

2 Craig was (discarded/irritated) by his little brother asking him endless questions.

3 The researchers explore (indigenous/decent) cultures in the Amazon Rainforest.

4 We are late because we got caught in serious traffic (mortgage/congestion).

5 The man (murmured/preceded) something, but we could not understand it.

F 문장의 빈칸에 알맞은 단어를 〈보기〉에서 찾아 쓰시오. (필요하면 형태를 고치시오.)

보기 radiate livelihood primate linguistic quote

1 The land needs people to heal it, and the people need the land to sustain their ______________.
땅은 치유를 위해 인간이 필요하고 인간은 생계를 유지하기 위해 땅이 필요하다. 10 고3학평

2 Some nonhuman ______________ use sign language to communicate.
인간을 제외한 몇몇 영장류는 소통하기 위해 손짓 언어를 배웠다. 14 고2학평 변형

3 People often ______________ the saying "Good fences make good neighbors."
사람들은 종종 "좋은 울타리는 좋은 이웃을 만든다."라는 말을 인용한다. 08 고2학평

4 These paved surfaces and structures heat up and ______________ energy into the atmosphere.
이 포장된 표면과 구조물들은 뜨거워져 에너지를 대기로 방출한다. 06 고2평가원

5 India is a prime example of ______________ diversity; more than 122 major languages are spoken in the country.
인도는 언어적 다양성의 아주 좋은 예이다; 122개 이상의 주요 언어가 이 나라에서 사용된다.

G 다음 〈보기〉 중 두 문장에 공통으로 사용할 수 있는 어휘를 고르시오.

1 The Journal 'Times' is looking for a ____________ student reporter. 11 고2학평 변형
The hardest part was getting a ____________ instructor. Did you find someone? 15 고3평가원

① chronic ② primate ③ irresponsible ④ naïve ⑤ qualified

2 Nevertheless, scientific ____________ seldom involves a series of logical steps. 08 고2학평
Researchers conducted an ____________ into the causes of the new infectious disease.

① cluster ② inquiry ③ omission ④ flame ⑤ pavement

3 Using ice for your back pain is only a temporary ____________. You had better go see a doctor. 2011 수능 변형
Regular and mild exercise will be the best natural ____________ for your sleep problem.

① cuisine ② commentary ③ bureaucracy ④ remedy ⑤ ornament

Study More

혼동하기 쉬운 단어 complementary vs. complimentary

- [complementary] 형 상호 보완적인
  Your proposal and Yuna's proposal are **complementary.** 당신과 유나의 제안은 서로 상호 보완적이군요.
- [complimentary] 형 무료의
  A **complimentary** breakfast is served every morning. 매일 아침 무료 조식이 제공됩니다.

Day 21

MP3

601 **panel** [pǽnəl]
명 (사각형) 판, 조각, 토론단, 위원단
operate solar panels 태양 판을 가동하다

602 **subordinate** [səbɔ́ːrdənit]
형 종속된, 부차적인 명 종속자, 하급자
her direct subordinates 그녀의 직속 부하들

603 **envision** [invíʒən]
동 마음속에 그리다, 상상하다
envision the future of our school 우리 학교의 미래를 상상하다

604 **dine** [dain]
동 식사를 하다, 만찬을 들다
dine at a traditional Korean restaurant 한국 전통 식당에서 식사를 하다

605 **deception** [disépʃən]
명 속임, 사기 유 deceit 사기, 기만
practice deception 속임수를 쓰다

606 **accommodation** [əkɑ̀mədéiʃən]
명 숙소, 거처, 수용, 화해, 조정
many types of accommodation 다양한 유형의 숙소

607 **tame** [teim]
동 길들이다 형 길들여진 유 domesticated 길들여진
tame wild animals 야생동물을 길들이다 a tame dog 길들여진 강아지

608 **swamp** [swɑmp]
명 늪 동 늪에 빠지다
tropical swamps 열대 늪지대 swamped with emails 이메일이 쇄도하는

609 **viewpoint** [vjúːpɔ̀int]
명 관점, 견해, 시각
global viewpoint 세계적인 관점

610 **stabilize** [stéibəlàiz]
동 안정시키다, 안정되다
stabilize the oil price 유가를 안정시키다

611 **await** [əwéit]
동 ~을 기다리다
await the winter vacation 겨울 방학을 기다리다

612 **astonish** [əstɑ́niʃ]
동 깜짝 놀라게 하다 유 amaze (대단히) 놀라게 하다
astonish her family 그녀의 가족들을 놀라게 하다

613 **simultaneously** [sàiməltéiniəsli]
부 동시에
happen simultaneously 동시에 일어나다

614 **interchange** [ìntərtʃéindʒ]
명 (생각·정보 등의) 교환, 교차로 동 (생각·정보 등을) 교환하다
important information interchange 중요한 정보의 교환

615 **amend** [əménd]
동 개정하다, 수정하다
amend the Constitution 헌법을 개정하다

Daily Test

| 월 일 |

A 우리말에 맞게 빈 칸에 알맞은 단어를 쓰세요.

1 Solar ______________ on our roof can rotate independently of the building to follow the sun.
우리 지붕의 태양열 판은 태양을 따라가기 위해서 건물과 관계 없이 회전할 수 있다. 11 고3학평 변형

2 We ______________ a society with equal opportunities.
우리는 기회가 균등한 사회를 마음속에 그린다.

3 Women who ______________ with two or three friends eat an average of 500 calories, or double that of solo diners.
두세 명의 친구들과 함께 식사를 하는 여성들이 평균적으로 500칼로리 혹은 혼자 식사하는 사람의 두 배의 양을 먹는다. 08 고3평가원 변형

4 Law enforcement invented a new tool for detecting ______________.
법의 집행은 속임수를 간파하는 새로운 도구를 발명했다. 15 고3학평 변형

5 The word "diamond" comes from the ancient Greek word, which means "impossible to ______________."
그 단어는 "길들여 질 수 없는" 의 뜻을 가진 고대 그리스어에서 왔다. 05 고1평가원 변형

6 One day, Yoda told his colleague to lift his sunken ship out from the ______________.
어느 날, Yoda는 동료에게 늪에서 그의 침몰한 배를 들어올려달라고 말했다. 05 고1평가원 변형

7 People tend to pay attention to information that supports their ______________.
사람들은 그들의 관점을 지지해주는 정보에 관심을 기울이는 경향이 있다. 16 고3학평 변형

8 Interest rates and exchange rates now ______________ more rapidly than ever before.
현재 이자율과 환율은 그 어느 때보다 더 빠르게 안정화 되었다. 12 고3학평 변형

9 Sarah stood in the doorway ______________ her father.
Sarah는 그녀의 아빠를 기다리며 문간에 서있었다.

10 We had sighted each other ______________.
우리는 동시에 서로를 쳐다보았다. 12 고3학평 변형

Day 21

MP3

616 **archery** [ɑ́ːrtʃəri]
명 활쏘기, 궁술
practice archery 활쏘기를 연습하다

617 **enchant** [intʃǽnt]
동 황홀하게 만들다
designed to enchant people 사람들을 황홀하게 만들기 위해 제작되다

618 **uncover** [ʌnkʌ́vər]
동 밝히다, 발견하다
uncover a hidden motivation 숨겨진 동기를 밝히다

619 **vapor** [véipər]
명 증기, 증발 기체 동 증발하다
emit a vapor 증기를 내뿜다 water vapor in the air 공기 속 수증기

620 **footprint** [fútprìnt]
명 발자국, (무엇이) 차지하는 공간
leave a footprint in the snow 눈 위에 발자국을 남기다

621 **surpass** [sərpǽs]
동 능가하다, 뛰어넘다 유 exceed 넘다, 상회하다
surpass expectations 기대를 능가하다

622 **repetitive** [ripétitiv]
형 반복적인, 반복되는
repetitive movements 반복적인 움직임

623 **vacant** [véikənt]
형 (객실, 방 등이) 비어 있는, 공석인 유 empty 빈, 인적이 없는
find a vacant seat 빈 좌석을 찾다

624 **craving** [kreiviŋ]
명 갈망, 열망 동 crave 갈망하다, 열망하다
a craving for winning 승리에 대한 열망

625 **superficial** [sjùːpərfíʃəl]
형 피상적인, 얄팍한, 깊이 없는 유 shallow 얄팍한, 피상적인
a superficial analogy 피상적인 유추

626 **dimension** [diménʃən]
명 치수, 차원
measure the dimensions of the table 탁자의 치수를 재다

627 **weave** [wiːv]
동 짜다, 엮다 유 knit 뜨다, 짜다
weave a net 그물을 짜다 weave threads together 실을 함께 엮다

628 **supplement** [sʌ́pləmənt]
명 보충(추가)물, 추가 요금 동 보충하다, 추가하다
a Vitamin A supplement 비타민 A 보충제

629 **ventilate** [véntəlèit]
동 환기하다, 통풍시키다 명 ventilation 통풍, 환기, 환기 장치
ventilate a room with a fan 환풍기로 방을 환기하다

630 **clutch** [klʌtʃ]
동 움켜잡다 명 움켜 쥠, (자동차의) 클러치, 무리, 집단
clutch power 권력을 쥐다 clutch a chair 의자를 움켜쥐다

Daily Test

| 월 일 |

A 우리말에 맞게 빈 칸에 알맞은 단어를 쓰세요.

1 Scientists are working hard to ______________ the secrets of our world.
과학자들은 우리 세계의 비밀을 밝혀내기 위해 열심히 일하고 있다.

2 When the air cools, ______________ particles join up as water droplets that form clouds.
공기가 냉각되면, 수증기 입자는 구름을 형성하는 작은 물방울로 결합된다. 06 고2학평 변형

3 Certain imprints, like ______________, can give scientists hints of an animal's behavior.
발자국 같은 확실한 자국은 과학자에게 동물의 행동에 대한 힌트를 줄 수 있다.

4 Last year, hybrid cars suddenly increased in popularity in Asia, ______________ the U.S.A. in sales for the first time.
작년에 하이브리드 자동차는 아시아에서 갑작스럽게 인기가 상승했으며 처음으로 판매량에서 미국을 능가했다. 12 고1학평 변형

5 It is unusual for a book of thirty or more pages to be full of ______________ phrases.
한 책이 30 페이지 이상 반복되는 구절로 가득 찬 것은 드문 일이다. 10 고3학평 변형

6 Go to any ______________ chair and sit and look around.
빈 의자에 어디든 가서 앉고 주변을 둘러보아라. 05 고3학평 변형

7 Image formation is the first step towards seeing ______________ analogies between the eye and a camera.
이미지 형성은 눈과 카메라 사이에 피상적 유추를 보는 첫번째 단계이다. 2013 수능 변형

8 Mom sat at the loom and started to ______________.
엄마는 베틀에 앉아 천을 짜기 시작했다.

9 When molecules are extracted from fruits and made into ______________, the form of the molecules changed.
분자가 과일에서 추출되어 보충제로 만들어질 때, 분자의 형태는 변한다. 14 고3평가원 변형

10 ______________ her precious vase tightly, Yuna made her way six blocks to the local flower shop.
그녀의 귀중한 꽃병을 꽉 쥐면서, Yuna는 동네 꽃집으로 여섯 블럭을 걸어갔다. 06 고2평가원 변형

Day 22

MP3

631 **adorable** [ədɔ́:rəbl]
형 사랑스러운, 귀여운
an adorable baby 사랑스러운 아기

632 **blister** [blístər]
명 물집 동 물집이 생기게 하다
get blisters on the right hand 오른 손 위에 물집이 생기다

633 **counterpart** [káuntərpɑ̀:rt]
명 상대, 상대역, 등가물, 복사본
a formidable counterpart 버거운 상대

634 **contend** [kənténd]
동 싸우다, 주장하다, 논쟁하다 유 argue 논하다, 논쟁하다
contend with misfortune 불운에 맞서 싸우다

635 **adverse** [ædvə́:rs]
형 부정적인, 불리한 부 adversely 불리하게, 반대로
adverse effect 부정적인 영향

636 **appliance** [əpláiəns]
명 (가정용) 기기, 적용, 응용
kitchen appliance 가정용 기기

637 **auction** [ɔ́:kʃən]
명 경매 동 경매로 팔다
participate in the auction 경매에 참여하다

638 **bless** [bles]
동 축복하다, 은혜를 베풀다
God bless you! 당신께 신의 축복이 있기를!

639 **apologetic** [əpɑ̀lədʒétik]
형 사과하는, 미안해하는, 변명의
write an apologetic letter 사과의 편지를 쓰다

640 **conceal** [kənsí:l]
동 숨기다, 감추다
conceal her purpose 그녀의 목적을 숨기다

641 **baggage** [bǽgidʒ]
명 짐, 수화물 유 (미국식) luggage (여행용) 짐, 수화물
a baggage handler 수화물 담당자

642 **continual** [kəntínjuəl]
형 끊임없는, 거듭되는, 빈번한 유 repeated 되풀이된, 거듭된
continual complaints 끊임없는 불평

643 **ample** [ǽmpl]
형 풍부한, 넓은, 충분한
ample opportunity 충분한 기회 an ample terrace 넓은 테라스

644 **attic** [ǽtik]
명 다락방
clean the attic 다락방을 치우다 a dusty attic 먼지 쌓인 다락방

645 **compel** [kəmpél]
동 강요하다, 강제하다 유 force 억지로 ~하게 하다, 강요하다
compel students to study English 학생들에게 영어 공부를 강요하다

Daily Test

| 월 일 |

A 우리말에 맞게 빈 칸에 알맞은 단어를 쓰세요.

1 Wearing high heels can cause ______________ that can be painful and ugly.
하이힐을 신는 것은 고통스럽고 흉한 물집을 유발할 수 있다. 07 고1학평 변형

2 Red silk ties are much cheaper and simpler than their woven ______________.
붉은 실크 타이는 실로 짜여진 타이보다 훨씬 싸고 더 단순하다. 08 고3평가원 변형

3 Critics ______________ that hybrid cars might only be popular if they are small cars.
비평가들은 하이브리드 자동차가 소형차일 경우에만 인기가 있을거라고 주장한다.

4 Let's meet in front of the Home ______________ department.
가전 매장 앞에서 만나요.

5 A young boy named Tom went to the park for the ______________ of bicycles.
Tom이라는 어린 소년은 자전거 경매를 위해 공원으로 갔다. 08 고3학평 변형

6 Minji said, "God ______________ you! You can do it!"
민지가 말했다, "당신께 신의 축복이 가득하길! 당신은 할 수 있어요!". 07 고3평가원 변형

7 Polar bears evolved white fur because it better ______________ them in the Arctic.
북극곰은 북극에서 자신을 더 잘 숨길 수 있기 때문에 털이 하얀 색깔로 진화했다. 09 고2평가원 변형

8 Passengers won't be allowed to access their carry on ______________ or have any items in their laps.
승객들은 기내에 가지고 간 가방에 접근하거나 무릎 위에 어떤 물건을 두는 것도 허락되지 않는다. 10 고1학평 변형

9 The baseball team in our school has a ______________ problem with behavior.
우리 학교 야구팀은 행동에 있어 거듭되는 문제가 있다. 07 고1학평 변형

10 If you have to stay in your house, do not go into the ______________ or basement.
만약 당신이 집에 머물러야 한다면, 다락방이나 지하실은 가지 마세요.

Day 22

MP3

646 **blueprint**
[blú:prìnt]
명 청사진, 계획
draw a blueprint 청사진을 그리다

647 **aristocracy**
[æ̀ristάkrəsi]
명 귀족(제)
명 aristocrat 귀족
belong to the aristocracy 귀족에 속하다

648 **carbohydrate**
[kὰ:rbouhάidreit]
명 탄수화물
a low-carbohydrate diet 저탄수화물 식품

649 **beware**
[biwέər]
동 조심하다, 경계하다
유 mind 주의하다, 조심하다
beware of avalanche 눈사태를 조심하다

650 **bruise**
[bru:z]
동 타박상을 입히다 명 멍, 상처
a bruised arm 타박상을 입은 팔

651 **contemplate**
[kάntəmplèit]
동 고려하다, 심사 숙고하다, 응시하다 유 ponder 숙고하다
contemplate the meaning of life 삶의 의미에 대해 심사 숙고하다

652 **blur**
[blə:r]
동 흐리게 하다, 흐릿해지다 명 흐릿함, 침침함, 흐려보이는 것
blurred vision 흐릿한 시야(시력 저하)

653 **corruption**
[kərʌ́pʃən]
명 부패, 타락
political corruption 정치적 부패

654 **categorize**
[kǽtəgəràiz]
동 분류하다, ~의 범주에 넣다
categorize people according to age 사람을 나이에 따라 분류하다

655 **confront**
[kənfrʌ́nt]
동 직면하다, 맞서다
유 face 정면으로 대하다, 맞서다
confront a serious problem 심각한 문제에 직면하다

656 **comprise**
[kəmpráiz]
동 포함하다, ~을 구성하다, 차지하다
comprise a significant component 중요한 요소를 포함하다

657 **broaden**
[brɔ́:dən]
동 넓히다, 확장하다
broaden her view 그녀의 시야를 넓히다

658 **bribe**
[braib]
명 뇌물 동 뇌물을 주다
turn down a bribe 뇌물을 거절하다

659 **condense**
[kəndéns]
동 농축하다, 응축하다, 응축되다
명 condensation 응결, 응축, (책 등의) 압축 요약
condense milk 우유를 응축하다

660 **creep**
[kri:p]
동 기다, 살금살금 움직이다
creep up the wall 벽을 기어 올라가다

Daily Test

| 월 일 |

A 우리말에 맞게 빈 칸에 알맞은 단어를 쓰세요.

1 In a country without a landed ______________, judges formed a privileged but public-spirited class.
지주 귀족이 없는 나라에서, 법조인들은 특권층이지만 공공심을 가진 계층을 형성했다. 09 고3평가원 변형

2 Glucose is a simple form of sugar and comes from the ______________ a person eats.
Glucose는 단순한 당의 형태이고 사람이 먹는 탄수화물에서 온다.

3 The most important factor causing poverty in Latin America is governmental ______________.
라틴 아메리카의 빈곤을 유발하는 가장 중요한 요인은 정부의 부패이다. 05 고3학평 변형

4 When you go swimming, be careful not to ______________ yourself against the rocks.
수영하러 갈 때, 바위에 부딪혀 상처 입지 않도록 조심해야 한다. 09 고2평가원 변형

5 We have to slow down a bit and take the time to ______________ and relax.
우리는 조금 느긋해져야 하고 심사숙고하고 휴식을 취할 시간을 가져야 한다. 13 고3평가원 변형

6 Mike's vision was ______________ by the tears in his eyes.
눈에 눈물이 가득 고여 Mike의 시야가 흐려졌다. 08 고2평가원 변형

7 When ______________ with a threat, the brain would send the signal, "danger!"
위협과 마주할 때, 뇌는 "위험!"이라는 신호를 보낸다. 15 고1학평 변형

8 Nowadays, women ______________ the majority of small business owners.
요즘, 여성들이 중소 기업 소유주들의 대다수를 차지하고 있다.

9 Traveling to many other countries can be helpful to ______________ your view.
많은 나라를 여행하는 것은 당신의 시야를 넓히는데 도움이 될 수도 있다. 06 고3평가원 변형

10 For rain to occur, water has to ______________.
비가 오기 위해서, 물이 응축되어야 한다.

A 우리말에 맞게 빈 칸에 알맞은 단어를 쓰시오.

1 operate solar ______________ 태양 판을 가동하다

2 many types of ______________ 다양한 유형의 숙소

3 ______________ the winter vacation 겨울 방학을 기다리다

4 water ______________ in the air 공기 속 수증기

5 find a ______________ seat 빈 좌석을 찾다

6 get ______________ on the right hand 오른 손 위에 물집이 생기다

7 kitchen ______________ 가정용 기기

8 a ______________ handler 수화물 담당자

9 ______________ people according to age 사람을 나이에 따라 분류되다

10 turn down a ______________ 뇌물을 거절하다

B 영어에 맞게 빈 칸에 알맞은 우리말을 쓰시오.

1 practice deception ______________를 쓰다

2 stabilize the oil price 유가를 ______________

3 leave a footprint in the snow 눈 위에 ______________을 남기다

4 a craving for winning 승리에 대한 ______________

5 weave threads together 실을 함께 ______________

6 adverse effect ______________ 영향

7 write an apologetic letter ______________ 편지를 쓰다

8 draw a blueprint ______________을 그리다

9 a bruised arm ______________ 팔

10 broaden her view 그녀의 시야를 ______________

C 다음 영어 풀이에 알맞은 어휘를 〈보기〉에서 고르시오.

보기	envision	vacant	conceal	swamp	simultaneously

1 ______________ : to have an image of something in mind

2 ______________ : happening at the same time

3 ______________ : to hide something carefully or to keep something from being seen

4 ______________ : a large piece of wet land, often filled with water

5 ______________ : empty; not used or lived in; available

D 문맥에 맞게 다음 문장을 완성하시오.

1 Law enforcement invented a new tool •

2 People tend to pay attention to •

3 It is unusual for a book of thirty or •

4 The baseball team in our school •

5 Mike's vision was blurred •

• a has a continual problem with behavior.

• b information that supports their viewpoints.

• c by the tears in his eyes.

• d for detecting deception.

• e more pages to be full of repetitive phrases.

E 문장을 읽고 문맥에 적절한 단어를 고르시오.

1 The government is trying to (stabilize/clutch) the currency.

2 Personal privacy laws have been (amended/tamed) several times.

3 Against my will, I was (compelled/enchanted) to go through the whole process again.

4 Sue rolled down the windows to (radiate/ventilate) her car.

5 No need to hurry. We have (ample/multiple) time to prepare for the meeting.

F 문장의 빈칸에 알맞은 단어를 〈보기〉에서 찾아 쓰시오. (필요하면 형태를 고치시오.)

보기 simultaneously contemplate dimension comprise conceal

1 The advantages of reading can be discussed in personal and in social ________________.
독서의 이점은 개인적인 차원과 사회적인 차원에서 논의될 수 있다. 15 고3학평 변형

2 The museum's student council is ________________ of 12 students who love the arts.
박물관의 학생 협의회는 예술을 사랑하는 12명의 학생으로 구성되어 있다. 15 고3학평 변형

3 He ________________ his fear of roller coasters by talking about other things.
그는 롤러코스터에 대한 두려움을 다른 것들에 대해 이야기하는 것으로 감추었다.

4 Lisa is ________________ whether to continue her studies in nursing.
Lisa는 간호학 공부를 계속 할 것인가를 숙고하고 있다.

5 The City of Arcata saved millions of dollars and improved its environment ________________.
Arcata 시는 수백만 달러를 아꼈고 동시에 환경도 개선했다. 14 고2학평 변형

G 다음 〈보기〉 중 두 문장에 공통으로 사용할 수 있는 어휘를 고르시오.

1 It was a stunning record that was not ___________(e)d for 28 years. 2012 수능 변형
The hotel's excellent facilities and atmosphere ___________(e)d our expectations.

① surpass ② dine ③ broaden ④ categorize ⑤ irritate

2 The ___________(e)d executive just stood there, stunned. 10 고3학평
We were all ___________(e)d to see the boy's terrific memorizing skills.

① supplement ② astonish ③ contend ④ confront ⑤ await

3 Stone tools, animal bones, arrowheads and other artifacts were ___________(e)d in the village. 07 고3학평
The essence of science is to ___________ patterns and regularities in nature based on accurate data analysis. 12 고3평가원 변형

① overload ② discard ③ precede ④ vanish ⑤ uncover

Study More

'inter-' : [동사, 명사, 형용사, 부사에서] '~사이의', '상호간의' 라는 뜻을 나타낸다.

- [international] 형 국제적인
  The Olympics is one of most famous **international** events in the world.
  올림픽은 세계에서 유명한 국제 행사들 중 하나이다.

- [interact] 동 소통하다, 교류하다
  It is important to **interact** with people of different culture and age.
  다른 문화와 연령대의 사람들과 교류하는 것은 중요하다.

Day 23

MP3

661 **idiom** [ídiəm]
명 관용구, 숙어, (특정 지역, 시기의) 어법 형 idiomatic 관용적인
study English idioms 영어 숙어를 공부하다

662 **improper** [imprɑ́pər]
형 부적절한, 잘못된 유 inappropriate 부적당한, 타당하지 않은
an improper conclusion 부적절한 결론

663 **eradicate** [irǽdəkèit]
동 근절(퇴치)하다, 뿌리뽑다, 박멸하다
eradicate the bacteria 박테리아를 퇴치하다

664 **frail** [freil]
형 허약한, 노쇠한
a frail child 허약한 아이

665 **furnish** [fə́:rniʃ]
동 (가구를) 비치하다, 제공하다, 공급하다 유 furnished (집, 방 등이) 가구가 구비된
need to furnish the room 방에 가구를 비치할 필요가 있다

666 **immature** [imətjúər]
형 미숙한, 미완성의
mentally immature 정신적으로 미성숙한

667 **fortress** [fɔ́:rtris]
명 요새 유 fort 보루, 요새, 진지
build a fortress 요새를 짓다 an ancient fortress 고대 요새

668 **hospitality** [hàspitǽləti]
명 환대, 후대
warm hospitality 따뜻한 환대 impressive hospitality 인상 깊은 후대

669 **dispense** [dispéns]
동 나누어주다, 베풀다, 없애다
dispense medical supplies 의약품을 나누어주다

670 **drastic** [drǽstik]
형 과감한, 극단적인
make a drastic decision 과감한 결정을 하다

671 **escort** [éskɔ:rt]
명 호위대(원) 동 호위하다 유 accompany 동반하다, 수행하다
an armed escort 무장한 호위대

672 **geometry** [dʒiɑ́mitri]
명 기하학, 기하학적 구조
help Steve with his geometry homework Steve의 기하학 숙제를 돕다

673 **inflate** [infléit]
동 부풀리다, 부풀다, 가격이 오르다 명 inflation 인플레이션, 통화 팽창
inflate students' grade 학생들의 성적을 부풀리다

674 **crave** [kreiv]
동 갈망하다, 열망하다
crave spicy food 매운 음식을 갈망하다

675 **empower** [impáuər]
동 권한(권리)을 주다 유 authorize 권위를 부여하다, 위임하다
be empowered to change the schedule 일정을 변경할 권한을 갖다

Daily Test

| 월 일 |

A 우리말에 맞게 빈 칸에 알맞은 단어를 쓰세요.

1 The 'elephant in the room' is an English ______________ for an obvious truth that is being ignored.
'방 안의 코끼리'는 무시되거나 언급되지 않는 명백한 진실을 가리키는 영어 표현이다. 11 고2학평 변형

2 The goal of natural control is not to ______________ pests and diseases.
자연 통제의 목적은 해충과 질병을 뿌리뽑는 것이 아니다. 14 고1학평 변형

3 When Smith returned to the house, he was shocked to see his brother so thin and ______________.
Smith가 집에 돌아왔을 때, 그는 남동생이 마르고 허약해 진 것을 보고 충격 받았다. 16 고3학평 변형

4 At home, children may have a room ______________ with a personal computer and television.
가정에서, 아이들은 개인용 컴퓨터와 텔레비전이 갖춰진 방을 가지고 있을 것이다. 06 고3학평 변형

5 Outraged French citizens attacked Bastille, a ______________-prison in Paris, in the hope of capturing weapons.
성난 프랑스 시민들은 무기를 차지하겠다는 희망 하에 파리의 요새 감옥 바스티유를 공격했다.

6 I hang the picture in my bed room as a pleasant reminder of Jane's ______________.
나는 Jane의 환대를 즐겁게 상기시켜주는 것으로써 그 그림을 내 침실에 걸어두었다. 14 고3평가원 변형

7 Every day, I was going through ______________ changes.
매일, 나는 엄청난 변화를 경험하는 중이었다.

8 The bird ______________ its stomach with air and floated across the water.
그 새는 공기로 그의 배를 부풀렸고 물 위를 떠서 건너갔다. 09 고3학평 변형

9 Consumers ______________ more information, especially for the potentially harmful ingredients included in the product.
고객들은 특히 그 상품이 포함하고 있는 잠재적으로 유해한 요소에 대해 더 많은 정보를 갈망한다. 14 고1학평 변형

10 The king ______________ the prince to do everything.
그 왕은 왕자에게 모든 것을 할 수 있는 권한을 부여하였다.

Day 23

MP3

676 **exhale** [ekshéil]
동 (숨 등을) 내쉬다, 내뿜다
exhale deeply 깊게 숨을 내쉬다 exhale smoke 연기를 내뿜다

677 **deplete** [diplíːt]
동 고갈시키다, 격감시키다 유 use up 다 써버리다
deplete natural resources 천연 자원을 고갈시키다

678 **fermentation** [fəːrmentéiʃən]
명 발효 동 ferment 발효되다, 발효시키다
a secret fermentation process 비밀 발효 과정

679 **glare** [glɛər]
동 노려보다, 쏘아보다, 번쩍번쩍 빛나다 명 노려봄, 섬광, 눈부심
glare at her silently 조용히 그녀를 노려보다

680 **embassy** [émbəsi]
명 대사관
send a letter to the Korean embassy 한국 대사관에 편지를 보내다

681 **dictate** [díkteit]
동 받아쓰게 하다, 좌우하다, ~에 영향을 주다
dictate a letter to a secretary 비서에게 편지를 받아쓰게 하다

682 **exterior** [ikstí(ː)əriər]
형 외부의, 옥외의 명 (건물의) 외부, (사람의) 겉모습
exterior of the building 건물의 외부 an exterior view 외관

683 **divine** [diváin]
형 신성한
a divine song 신성한 노래 her divine efforts 그녀의 신성한 노력

684 **enclose** [inklóuz]
동 동봉하다, 둘러싸다
the enclosed documents 동봉된 자료

685 **futile** [fjúːtəl]
형 헛된, 소용없는 유 vain 헛된, 무익한
a futile gesture 헛된 손짓 make a futile attempt 소용없는 시도를 하다

686 **counterproductive** [kàuntərprədʌ́ktiv]
형 역효과를 낳는, 비생산적인
useless and counterproductive 쓸모 없고 역효과를 낳는

687 **dip** [dip]
동 살짝 담그다, 적시다 명 살짝 담금, 움푹한 곳
dip his hands in water 그의 손을 물에 (살짝) 담그다

688 **harness** [háːrnis]
동 이용하다, 마구를 채우다 명 마구
harness horses to a carriage 말들에 마구를 채워 마차에 연결하다

689 **cozy** [kóuzi]
형 아늑한, 안락한
a cozy little kitchen 아늑하고 작은 부엌

690 **locomotive** [lòukəmóutiv]
명 기관차, 견인차 형 기관차의, 이동하는
an electric locomotive 전기 기관차

Daily Test

| 월 일 |

A 우리말에 맞게 빈 칸에 알맞은 단어를 쓰세요.

1 Biomass is plant-derived material usable as a renewable energy source which does not ______________ existing supplies.
생물 자원은 현존하는 자원들을 고갈시키지 않는 재생에너지원으로 사용할 수 있는 식물에서 얻을 수 있는 자원이다. 08 고3 학평

2 Through ______________, bacteria along with yeast consume most of the lactose or milk sugar.
발효를 통해서, 박테리아는 이스트와 함께 젖당 또는 유당의 대부분을 소비한다. 11 고3 학평 변형

3 Don't forget that your attitude ______________ whether you are living life or life is living you.
당신의 태도가 당신이 삶을 살고 있는지 삶이 당신을 살고 있는지 좌우 한다는 것을 잊지 마세요. 05 고3 평가원 변형

4 Denny and his father are ______________ a garden with a fence.
Denny와 그의 아버지는 정원을 울타리로 둘러싸는 중이다.

5 My ______________ attempts to open the door only increased my panic.
문을 열려는 나의 헛된 시도는 그저 내 공포감을 크게 할 뿐이었다. 11 고3 평가원 변형

6 Forcing your children to eat, especially if they don't like what is on the plate, is absolutely ______________.
당신의 아이들에게 특히 그들이 접시 위에 음식을 싫어하는데도 강제로 먹이는 것은 전적으로 역효과를 낳는다. 16 고3 평가원 변형

7 The hawk started to ______________ its wing into the lake.
매는 그의 날개를 호수에 살짝 담그기 시작했다. 04 고1 평가원 변형

8 Wind power ______________ the force of the wind to turn large fans that create electricity.
풍력은 전기를 만드는 큰 팬을 돌리기 위해 바람의 힘을 이용한다.

9 The fisherman gave the student a ______________ room in which to sleep and a big breakfast the next morning.
그 어부는 학생에게 잘 수 있는 아늑한 방을 주었고 다음날 아침 근사한 아침을 차려주었다. 04 고3 평가원 변형

10 Most of the people didn't know he invented the electric ______________.
대부분의 사람들은 그가 전기 기관차를 발명한 것을 몰랐다.

Day 24

MP3

691 eligible [élidʒəbl]
형 자격이 있는, 권한이 있는
eligible to vote 투표할 자격이 있는

692 reform [rifɔ́ːrm]
동 개혁하다, 개선하다 명 개혁, 개정, 개선
reform the social system 사회 시스템을 개혁하다

693 indulge [indʌ́ldʒ]
동 빠지다, 탐닉하다, ~을 마음껏 하다 명 indulgence 하고 싶은 대로 함, 관대
indulge in sports 운동에 빠지다

694 itch [itʃ]
동 가렵다, (~을 하고 싶어) 근질거리다 명 가려움, 욕망
a persistent itch 지속적인 가려움 scratch an itch 가려운 곳을 긁다

695 provoke [prəvóuk]
동 자극하다, 유발하다, 화나게 하다 유 irritate 짜증나게 하다, 화나게 하다
provoke an allergic reaction 알레르기 반응을 유발하다

696 meditate [méditèit]
동 명상하다, 묵상하다, 숙고하다 명 meditation 명상, 묵상
meditate all day 하루 종일 명상하다

697 sin [sin]
명 죄, 죄악 동 (종교, 도덕 상의) 죄를 짓다
commit a sin 죄를 범하다 forgive his sin 그의 죄를 용서하다

698 prose [prouz]
명 산문(체)
poetry and prose 시와 산문

699 minority [minɔ́(ː)rəti]
명 소수
ethnic minorities 민족적 소수자 a minority opinion 소수 의견

700 refugee [rèfjudʒíː]
명 난민, 망명자
a refugee camp 난민 수용소 an economic refugee 경제 난민

701 patriotism [péitriətìzəm]
명 애국심 형 patriotic 애국적인
emphasize patriotism 애국심을 강조하다

702 omit [oumít]
동 빠뜨리다, 제외하다 명 omission 생략, 빠짐, 누락
omit an important question 중요한 질문을 빠뜨리다

703 patron [péitrən]
명 후원자, 보호자, 단골손님
a patron of the arts 그 예술의 후원자

704 refinement [rifáinmənt]
명 정제, 제련, 개선 동 refine 정제하다, 개선하다
the refinement of gold 금 정제 aesthetic refinement 미적 개선

705 protest [próutèst]
동 항의하다 명 시위, 항의
protest against the decision 결정에 대해 항의하다

Daily Test

| 월 일 |

A 우리말에 맞게 빈 칸에 알맞은 단어를 쓰세요.

1 Artists during the Renaissance ______________ painting and sculpture.
르네상스 시기의 예술가들은 그림과 조각을 개혁했다. 2005 수능 변형

2 Some students may ______________ in fantasies of violence by watching the movie.
몇몇 학생들은 그 영화를 봄으로써 폭력에 대한 환상에 빠질지도 모른다. 2015 수능 변형

3 If the ______________ do not disappear, you should stop scratching and take the medicine.
가려움이 사라지지 않는다면, 당신은 긁는 것을 멈추고 약을 먹어야 한다. 2010 수능 변형

4 Jessica's theory has ______________ a lot of debates on what art actually is.
Jessica의 이론은 예술이 실제로 무엇인가에 대해 많은 토론을 유발했다. 05 고3학평 변형

5 The people and governments of Korea, China, and Taiwan regularly hold large ______________ against Yasukuni Jinja.
한국, 중국, 그리고 대만의 국민과 정부는 정기적으로 야스쿠니 신사에 대항하는 큰 시위를 열었다.

6 The king declared that the price of this ______________ is death.
왕은 이 죄의 대가는 죽음이라고 소리쳤다.

7 The reporter said that ______________ from burning cities were desperate to find safe refuge.
기자는 불타는 도시들을 떠나는 피난민들은 안전한 피난처를 찾기 위해 필사적이었다고 말했다. 15 고1학평 변형

8 When you edit the manuscript, be careful not to ______________ the important sentences.
당신이 원고를 편집할 때, 중요한 문장을 빠트리지 않도록 조심해라.

9 Anderson was the ______________ of many artists.
Anderson은 많은 예술가들의 후원자였다.

10 The ______________ of theories is a strength of science, not a weakness.
이론의 개선은 과학의 약점이 아니라 강점이다. 12 고3학평 변형

Day 24

MP3

706 erect [irékt]
형 똑바로 선 동 똑바로 세우다
with ears erect 귀를 쫑긋 세우고 erect a fence 울타리를 세우다

707 persevere [pə̀:rsəvíər]
동 인내하며 계속하다 명 perseverance 인내심
persevere with her tasks 그녀의 일을 쉬지 않고 계속하다

708 seize [si:z]
동 붙잡다, 움켜잡다, 체포하다
seize on the last chance 마지막 기회를 붙잡다

709 proficient [prəfíʃənt]
형 능숙한, 숙달한 명 proficiency 숙달, 능숙
proficient in running 달리기에 능숙한

710 originate [ərídʒənèit]
동 비롯하다, 유래하다
originate from mutual distrust 상호간 불신에서 비롯하다

711 integrate [íntəgrit]
동 통합하다, 합병하다 형 통합된, 완전한
integrate materials 재료를 통합하다

712 shave [ʃeiv]
동 면도하다 명 면도
cut himself shaving 면도를 하다가 베다 have a shave 면도를 하다

713 lodge [lɑdʒ]
명 오두막
stay inside a lodge 오두막 안에 머무르다

714 ponder [pándər]
동 심사 숙고하다 유 contemplate 심사숙고하다, 묵상하다
ponder the question 그 질문에 대해 심사 숙고하다

715 prophecy [práfisi]
명 예언 유 prediction 예언, 예보
rosy prophecy 낙관적인 예언

716 mock [mɑk]
형 가짜의, 모의의 동 놀리다, 무시하다
hold a mock trial 모의 재판을 개최하다

717 dispute [dispjú:t]
동 분쟁하다, 반박하다 명 분쟁
dispute a decision 결정에 반박하다 labor dispute 노동 분쟁

718 inject [indʒékt]
동 주사하다, 주입하다 명 injection 주사, 투입, 주입
inject a drug 약물을 주사하다

719 prosperous [práspərəs]
형 번영하는, 번창하는
the most prosperous business in Korea 한국에서 가장 번창하는 사업

720 supreme [sjuprí:m]
형 최고의, 최대의 유 paramount 최고의, 탁월한
make the supreme vehicle 최고의 자동차를 만들다

Daily Test

| 월 일 |

A 우리말에 맞게 빈 칸에 알맞은 단어를 쓰세요.

1 The phrase 'jack-of-all-trades' refers to those who claim to be ______________ at countless tasks, but cannot perform a single one of them well.
'jack-of-all-trades'라는 구절은 많은 일들에 능숙하지만 그들 중 한가지도 제대로 하지 못하는 사람을 일컫는다. 11 고3 평가원 변형

2 Despite the accident, Alfred ______________ and discovered how to make the new substance safer to handle.
그 사고에도 불구하고, Alfred는 인내심을 갖고 계속해서 다루기 더 안전한 새로운 물질을 만드는 법을 발견했다.

3 According to legend, the tangram puzzle ______________ in China.
전설에 따르면, 탱그램 퍼즐은 중국에서 유래되었다. 06 고3 학평 변형

4 Traditional television is ______________ as it contains images, sound and text.
전통적인 텔레비전은 이미지와 소리, 글자를 포함함으로써 통합되었다. 2015 수능 변형

5 Max lathered his face and started to ______________.
Max는 그의 얼굴에 비누거품을 칠하고 면도를 하기 시작했다.

6 People are sometimes ______________ Tim's silly behavior.
사람들은 때때로 Tim의 어리석은 행동을 놀린다. 12 고3 학평 변형

7 Mike ______________ for a long time but confessed that he didn't know the answer.
Mike는 오랜 시간 심사숙고했지만 답을 몰랐다고 고백했다. 04 고3 평가원 변형

8 Dr. Lee will deliver a lecture about the necessity of intervening in ______________ between siblings.
Dr. Lee는 형제간의 다툼에 개입하는 것의 필요성에 관한 강의를 할 것이다. 2015 수능 변형

9 Spiders are able to control how much venom they ______________ into their prey.
거미들은 그들의 먹이에 얼마나 많은 독을 주입할지 조절할 수 있다.

10 During the Renaissance, many people in Europe were becoming ______________.
르네상스 시기에, 유럽의 많은 사람들이 번영했다. 11 고3 학평 변형

A 우리말에 맞게 빈 칸에 알맞은 단어를 쓰시오.

1 study English ________________ 영어 숙어를 공부하다

2 an ancient ________________ 고대 요새

3 a secret ________________ process 비밀 발효 과정

4 her ________________ efforts 그녀의 신성한 노력

5 a ________________ little kitchen 아늑하고 작은 부엌

6 ________________ the social system 사회 시스템을 개혁하다

7 ________________ an allergic reaction 알레르기 반응을 유발하다

8 an economic ________________ 경제 난민

9 cut himself ________________ 면도를 하다가 베다

10 hold a ________________ trial 모의 재판을 개최하다

B 영어에 맞게 빈 칸에 알맞은 우리말을 쓰시오.

1 eradicate the bacteria 박테리아를 ________________

2 mentally immature 정신적으로 ________________

3 crave spicy food 매운 음식을 ________________

4 exhale deeply 깊게 숨을 ________________

5 dictate a letter to a secretary 비서에게 편지를 ________________

6 scratch an itch ________________ 곳을 긁다

7 poetry and prose 시와 ________________

8 a minority opinion ________________ 의견

9 ponder the question 그 질문에 대해 ________________

10 inject a drug 약물을 ________________

C 다음 영어 풀이에 알맞은 어휘를 〈보기〉에서 고르시오.

보기	eradicate	reform	exhale	protest	seize

1 ______________ : to show that you disagree with or stand up against something

2 ______________ : to erase or to remove something completely

3 ______________ : to breathe out or to force out air from the lungs

4 ______________ : to get hold of something forcefully or to capture something

5 ______________ : to improve or enhance through moderate change

D 문맥에 맞게 다음 문장을 완성하시오.

1	The goal of natural control is not •	• a	with air and floated across the water.
2	The bird inflated its stomach •	• b	to eradicate pests and diseases.
3	Anderson was the patron •	• c	of violence by watching the movie.
4	The hawk started to dip •	• d	of many artists.
5	Some students may indulge in fantasies •	• e	its wing into the lake.

E 문장을 읽고 문맥에 적절한 단어를 고르시오.

1 The most serious problem of the report is the (supreme/improper) use of statistical data.

2 We think that Randy is (eligible/visible) to become student president.

3 The house was (exhaled/furnished) with antique sofas and tables.

4 Local governments are taking (drastic/cozy) measures to cut down on unnecessary spending.

5 Applicants to this school should be (proficient/efficient) in more than three languages.

F 문장의 빈칸에 알맞은 단어를 <보기>에서 찾아 쓰시오. (필요하면 형태를 고치시오.)

보기 originate harness futile dispense integrate

1 The artist likes to ______________ environmental issues into his artwork.
그 예술가는 환경 문제를 자신의 예술 작품에 통합하기를 좋아한다.

2 Many of the different kinds of coffee drinks we enjoy today ______________ in Italy.
오늘 날 우리가 즐기는 다른 많은 종류의 커피는 이탈리아에서 비롯되었다. 10 고2학평 변형

3 So they decided to ______________ with the old man's services.
그래서 그들은 그 노인의 업무를 없애기로 결정했다. 05 고3평가원

4 The two kingdoms finally agreed to end the ______________ war that lasted for a decade.
두 왕국은 마침내 10년 동안 지속된 헛된 전쟁을 끝내기로 동의했다.

5 In prehistoric times, any attempt to ______________ nature meant forcing nature against her will.
선사 시대에는 자연을 이용하려는 어떤 시도도 자연이 자신의 의지를 거스르도록 강요하는 것을 의미했다. 12 고2학평

G 다음 〈보기〉 중 두 문장에 공통으로 사용할 수 있는 어휘를 고르시오.

1 When I was young, the only love I experienced was the ___________, selfish love. 11 고3 평가원 변형
I strongly urge the stricter laws to limit opportunities for ___________ judgment that have harmful consequences. 05 고3 평가원 변형

① seize ② immature ③ mock ④ erect ⑤ dispute

2 Scientific theories evolve as they go through stages of redefinition and ___________. 12 고3 학평
Oil in its original form should go through several steps of ___________ before being used for cars and machines.

① prose ② geometry ③ fermentation ④ refinement ⑤ hospitality

3 I don't mean that we shouldn't ___________ against what's wrong. 06 고2 학평 변형
Many people have ___________(e)d against the additional tax on cars.

① escort ② dictate ③ protest ④ inflate ⑤ indulge

Study More

'counter-' : [명사, 동사, 형용사, 부사에서] '반대', '~에 대응하는'의 뜻을 나타낸다.

- [counterattack] 명 역습, 반격
  Our team is looking for a chance to **counterattack.** 우리 팀은 반격의 기회를 엿보는 중이다.
- [counterpart] 명 상대
  a formidable **counterpart** 버거운 상대

Day 25

MP3

721 **thrust** [θrʌst]
동 찔러 넣다, 밀다 명 (주장, 정책 등의) 요지, 찌르기, 추진력
thrust his hands into his pockets 주머니에 그의 손을 찔러 넣다

722 **statesman** [stéitsmən]
명 정치인
ambition to be a famous statesman 유명한 정치인이 되겠다는 야망

723 **stance** [stæns]
명 입장, 자세 유 attitude 태도, 마음가짐
a neutral stance 중립적 입장 take a stance 자세를 취하다

724 **tribute** [tríbjuːt]
명 감사의 표시, 경의, 헌사, 공물 유 compliment 찬사, 칭찬의 말
a tribute to her visit 그녀의 방문에 대한 감사의 표시

725 **surgical** [sə́ːrdʒikəl]
형 외과의, 수술의
surgical instruments 외과용 기구

726 **beam** [biːm]
명 광선, 빛, 기둥 동 활짝 웃다, 비추다
the beam of a flashlight 손전등 불빛 a beam of hope 희망의 빛

727 **tempt** [tempt]
동 유혹하다, 꾀다, 자극하다 명 temptation 유혹, 유혹하는 것
tempt him with chocolate 그를 초콜릿으로 꾀다

728 **afflict** [əflíkt]
동 괴롭히다, 가하다
be afflicted with poverty 가난에 시달리다

729 **wipe** [waip]
동 닦다, 없애다, 지우다
wipe the salad bowl 샐러드 그릇을 닦다

730 **terminate** [tə́ːrmənèit]
동 끝내다, 끝나다, (버스, 기차 등이) 종점에 닿다 명 termination 종료
terminate the contract 계약을 끝내다

731 **ego** [íːgou]
명 자아, 자존심
boost his ego 그의 자존심을 높이 올리다

732 **wicked** [wíkid]
형 못된, 사악한, 장난기 있는 부 wickedly 나쁘게, 심술궂게
her wicked habits 그녀의 못된 습관 a wicked murderer 사악한 살인마

733 **submerge** [səbmə́ːrdʒ]
동 잠수하다
a village submerged by the flood 홍수로 물에 잠긴 마을

734 **skull** [skʌl]
명 두개골
the skull of a wild wolf 야생 늑대의 두개골

735 **landslide** [lǽndslàid]
명 산사태, 압도적인 승리
prevent a landslide 산사태를 예방하다

Daily Test

| 월 일 |

A 우리말에 맞게 빈 칸에 알맞은 단어를 쓰세요.

1 The pilum was a heavy spear, used for ______________ by Roman soldiers.
투창은 로마 병사들이 찔러 넣는데 사용한 무거운 창이었다. 11 고3학평 변형

2 In addition to being a great ______________ and writer, Jefferson was also a scientist.
위대한 정치인과 작가일 뿐 아니라, Jefferson은 또한 과학자였다.

3 In hospitals, the X-ray energy ______________ can see through skin tissue to detect broken bones, tumors or other injuries.
병원에서, x-ray 에너지 빛은 부러진 뼈, 종양, 또는 다른 부상들을 감지하기 위해 피부 조직을 관통해서 볼 수 있다.

4 Researchers didn't know what ______________ elephants to wander out of their protected habitat.
연구원들은 코끼리들이 그들의 보호구역 밖을 방황하도록 유혹하는 것이 무엇인지 몰랐다. 06 고3학평 변형

5 Students ______________ an expression from their faces and appear to be interested in something else.
학생들은 아무 표정도 짓지 않고 다른 것에 관심 있는 것처럼 보인다. 06 고3학평 변형

6 His ______________ on the issue differs from mine.
그 문제에 대한 그의 입장은 저와는 다릅니다.

7 The officer was shocked because the cities he'd visited were full of ______________ liars and barbarians.
사무관은 그가 방문했던 도시가 사악한 거짓말쟁이와 야만인으로 가득 찼기 때문에 충격을 받았다. 06 고3학평 변형

8 Submarines ______________ beneath the surface of the ocean and snuck up on the enemies.
잠수함은 해양의 표면 아래로 잠수했고 적에게 슬금슬금 다가갔다.

9 The anthropologists started to study the ______________ of prehistoric man.
인류학자들은 선사시대 인간의 두개골을 연구하기 시작했다.

10 The hazards include ______________, constant fog, and tropical downpours.
위험 요인에는 산사태와 굴러 떨어지는 바위들, 지속적인 안개, 열대성 폭우가 포함된다. 16 고3학평 변형

Day 25

MP3

736 **abnormal** [æbnɔ́:rməl]
형 비정상적인 유 unusual 보통이 아닌, 비범한
abnormal behavior 비정상적인 행동

737 **elude** [ilú:d]
동 (교묘히) 피하다, 빠져나가다, 이해하기가 쉽지 않다
elude the police 경찰을 교묘히 피하다

738 **utmost** [ʌ́tmòust]
형 최고의, 극도의
do his utmost 그의 전력을 다하다 at the utmost 기껏해야

739 **broker** [bróukər]
명 중개인 동 (협상 등을) 중개하다
a real estate broker 부동산 중개인

740 **surrender** [səréndər]
동 항복하다, 넘겨주다 명 항복, 굴복
surrender to the enemy 적에게 항복하다

741 **adolescent** [æ̀dəlésənt]
명 청소년 형 사춘기의, 청춘의
adolescent problems 청소년 문제들

742 **subscribe** [səbskráib]
동 구독하다, 가입하다, (의견 등에) 동의하다
subscribe to a daily newspaper 일간 신문을 구독하다

743 **brand-new** [brænd nju:]
형 신품의, 아주 새로운
buy a brand-new computer 신형 컴퓨터를 구입하다

744 **exclaim** [ikskléim]
동 소리치다, 외치다 명 exclamation 외침, 절규, 감탄사
She exclaimed, "I won!" 그녀는 "내가 이겼다!" 라고 소리쳤다.

745 **garment** [gá:rmənt]
명 의복, 옷
a sports garment 운동복 sew a garment 옷을 재봉질하다

746 **workaholic** [wə̀:rkəhɔ́:lik]
명 일 중독자 형 일에 중독된
be described as a workaholic 일 중독자로서 묘사되다

747 **weep** [wi:p]
동 울다, 눈물을 흘리다
weep all night 울며 밤을 새다

748 **accuse** [əkjú:z]
동 고발하다, 혐의를 제기하다, 비난하다 명 accusation 혐의 제기, 비난
accuse him of stealing a car 그를 차 절도로 고발하다

749 **veteran** [vétərən]
명 전문가, 참전용사
veteran martial artists 무술 전문가

750 **devastate** [dévəstèit]
동 완전히 파괴하다, 엄청난 충격을 주다
devastate much of the forest 숲의 대부분을 완전히 파괴하다

Daily Test

| 월 일 |

A 우리말에 맞게 빈 칸에 알맞은 단어를 쓰세요.

1 The tomb of King Tutankhamen ______________ even the cleverest of tomb robbers.
투탕카멘 왕의 무덤은 가장 똑똑한 무덤 도굴꾼도 교묘히 피했다.

2 I expected to have the ______________ cooperation.
나는 최대한의 협조를 기대했다. 12 고3학평 변형

3 The thief finally put up his hands in ______________ and waited for the police to arrive.
도둑은 마침내 항복의 의미로 손을 들었고 경찰이 도착하기를 기다렸다. 12 고3학평 변형

4 Sometimes, ______________ have a dislike of adult advice.
때때로, 청소년들은 어른들의 충고에 반감을 가진다.

5 I have ______________ to your newspaper for about 15 years.
나는 15년간 당신의 신문을 구독해왔습니다. 14 고1학평 변형

6 A few years ago we purchased a ______________ digital camera.
몇 년 전에 우리는 신형 디지털 카메라를 구입했다. 12 고3평가원 변형

7 Suddenly I heard a woman ______________ while I was making some cookies.
쿠키를 만드는 동안에 난 갑자기 어떤 여자가 울고 있는 것을 들었다. 05 고3평가원 변형

8 Often, DNA evidence can be used to find a person ______________ of a crime innocent.
종종, DNA 증거는 피소당한 사람이 무죄라는 것을 밝히는데 사용될 수 있다. 06 고3학평 변형

9 Andrew was a ______________ airplane mechanic.
Andrew는 항공수리 전문가였다.

10 The doctor attending Glenn recommended amputating his legs, and his parents were ______________.
Glenn의 주치의는 그의 다리를 절단할 것을 추천했고 그의 부모는 엄청난 충격에 휩싸였다. 15 고3학평 변형

Day 26

MP3

751 **commemorate** [kəméməréit]
동 기념하다, 축하하다 유 celebrate 축하하다, 경축하다
commemorate the victory 승리를 기념하다

752 **delegate** [déləgèit]
명 대표(자) 동 위임하다, (대리자로) 파견하다 유 representative 대표자, 대리인
delegates from 60 countries 60개국의 대표

753 **depiction** [dipíkʃən]
명 묘사, 서술
an accurate depiction of the hero 그 영웅에 대한 정확한 묘사

754 **cognition** [kɑgníʃən]
명 인식, 인지
mental cognition 정신적 인식 impair cognition 인지를 손상시키다

755 **confess** [kənfés]
동 자백하다, 고백하다 명 confession 고백, 자백
confess his crime 그의 죄를 자백하다

756 **arouse** [əráuz]
동 불러일으키다, 깨우다, 각성시키다 명 arousal 각성, 환기, 자극
arouse passion 열정을 불러일으키다

757 **cathedral** [kəθí:drəl]
명 대성당
live in a cathedral 대성당에 살다

758 **archeology** [ɑ̀:rkiɑ́lədʒi]
명 고고학
major in archeology 고고학을 전공하다

759 **chunk** [tʃʌŋk]
명 큰 덩어리, 상당히 많은 양
a chunk of cheese 치즈 한 덩어리

760 **dart** [dɑ:rt]
명 가늘고 짧은 화살 동 돌진하다
throw a poisoned dart 독화살을 던지다

761 **alleviate** [əlí:vièit]
동 완화하다, 경감하다 반 aggravate 악화시키다
alleviate pain 고통을 완화하다 alleviate heat 열을 내리다

762 **blush** [blʌʃ]
동 얼굴이 붉어지다 명 얼굴이 붉어짐
blush with embarrassment 당황함에 얼굴이 붉어지다

763 **confidential** [kɑ̀nfidénʃəl]
형 기밀의, 비밀의
a confidential report 기밀 문서

764 **betray** [bitréi]
동 배신하다, 저버리다, 누설하다 명 betrayal 배신, 배반
betray his colleague 그의 동료를 배신하다

765 **comply** [kəmplái]
동 따르다, 준수하다
comply with the safety rules 안전 규칙을 따르다

Daily Test

| 월 일 |

A 우리말에 맞게 빈 칸에 알맞은 단어를 쓰세요.

1 The paintings can be used to ______________ events or individuals.
그 그림은 행사나 개인을 기념할 때 사용될 수 있다. 09 고3학평 변형

2 Historically, daylight saving time was first suggested by Benjamin Franklin as an American ______________ in France.
역사적으로, 일광 절약 시간제 미국 대표였던 벤자민 프렝클린에 의해 프랑스에서 처음 제안되었다. 11 고3학평 변형

3 I ______________ to having been a bit homesick during my first fall away from home.
나는 처음 집에서 나왔던 가을 동안 약간의 향수병을 앓았던 것을 고백했다. 10 고1학평 변형

4 Amy was appointed Honorary Professor in Mexican ______________ at the Peabody Museum of Harvard University.
Amy는 하버드 대학 Peabody 박물관의 멕시코 인류학 명예 교수로 임명되었다. 14 고3평가원 변형

5 Playing ______________ is the most popular activity among adolescents.
다트 던지기는 청소년들 사이에서 가장 인기있는 활동이다.

6 Trauma can result in decline in memory, in ______________, and in agility.
트라우마는 기억, 인지, 그리고 명민함에 대한 감소를 일으킬 수 있다.

7 When the teacher praised Lina, a ______________ came over her face.
선생님이 Lina를 칭찬했을 때, 그녀의 얼굴이 온통 빨개졌다.

8 Helen's father became her ______________ friend, and he also became her literary adviser.
Helen의 아버지는 그녀의 비밀 친구가 되었고, 그는 또한 그녀의 문학적 조언자가 되었다. 08 고3평가원 변형

9 We have to trust that the search engine will not spill our secrets, but it's a trust that has repeatedly been ______________.
우리는 검색 엔진이 우리의 비밀을 누설하지 않을 것이라고 믿어야 하지만, 그것은 이미 여러 차례 배반당한 믿음에 불과하다. 11 고2학평 변형

10 ______________ with the safety rules before you dive into the pool.
풀장으로 뛰어들기 전에 안전 규칙을 따르세요. 12 고3평가원 변형

Day 26

MP3

766 **barometer** [bərámitər]
명 기압계, (여론, 상황 등의) 지표
mercury barometer 수은 기압계

767 **blunder** [blʌ́ndər]
명 (어리석은) 실수 동 (어리석은) 실수를 하다
make a terrible blunder 큰 실수를 하다 a fatal blunder 치명적인 실수

768 **assassin** [əsǽsin]
명 암살자 동 assassinate 암살하다
a trained assassin 훈련 받은 암살자 arrest an assassin 암살자를 체포하다

769 **chatter** [tʃǽtər]
동 수다를 떨다, (요란하게) 지저귀다 명 수다, (동물 등의) 재잘거림
chatter about the weather 날씨에 대해 수다를 떨다

770 **consecutive** [kənsékjətiv]
형 연속되는, 연속적인
for six consecutive days 6일 연속으로

771 **constitution** [kɑ̀nstitjúːʃən]
명 헌법, 구조, 조직, 관행
a written constitution 성문 헌법 Constitution Day 제헌절

772 **anonymous** [ənánəməs]
형 익명인, 작자 미상의
an anonymous call 익명의 전화

773 **cripple** [krípl]
동 불구로 만들다, 무력하게 만들다
be crippled by war 전쟁으로 인해 불구가 되다

774 **cemetery** [sémitèri]
명 묘지 유 graveyard 묘지, 묘소
a national cemetery 국립 묘지

775 **deepen** [díːpən]
동 ~을 깊게하다, 악화되다, 악화시키다
deepen a river 강을 깊게 하다

776 **brisk** [brisk]
형 빠른, 활발한, 상쾌한
a brisk walk 빠른 걸음 expect brisk exports 활발한 수출을 기대하다

777 **creek** [kriːk]
명 작은 만, 개울, 시내
cross a creek 개울을 건너다

778 **conclusive** [kənklúːsiv]
형 결정적인, 명확한 부 conclusively 결정적으로
find conclusive evidence 결정적 증거를 찾다

779 **constraint** [kənstréint]
명 제약, 제한, 통제 유 restriction 제한, 한정
financial constraints 경제적 제약 without constraint 강제성 없이

780 **enlighten** [inláitən]
동 계몽하다, 깨우침을 주다
enlighten the general readers 일반 독자들을 계몽하다

Daily Test

| 월 일 |

A 우리말에 맞게 빈 칸에 알맞은 단어를 쓰세요.

1 The scientist knew that studying people's eyes is a surer ______________ of pain and pleasure than any spoken word.
그 과학자는 사람들의 눈을 주의 깊게 살펴보는 것이 그 어떤 말보다 더 확실한 고통과 즐거움의 척도라는 것을 알았다.
11 고3학평 변형

2 Our goal is to win two ______________ World Baseball Classics.
우리의 목표는 2년 연속 세계 야구 선수권 대회에서 우승하는 것이다.

3 Squirrels were ______________ and birds were singing.
다람쥐는 떠들고 있었고 새들은 노래를 부르고 있었다. 05 고3학평 변형

4 The article will not be published until it has undergone the examination of the journal's editor and two or three ______________ volunteer referees.
그 기사는 신문의 편집자와 두 세명의 익명 추천인들의 검토가 있기 전까지는 게재되지 않을 것이다.

5 If God allowed us to go through our lives without any obstacles, it would ______________ us.
신이 우리에게 어떤 장애물도 없는 삶을 겪게 허락한다면, 그것은 우리를 무력하게 만들 것이다. 10 고3학평 변형

6 Durrington Walls was a place for the living and Stonehenge was a ______________ and memorial.
Durrington 벽은 생활을 위한 장소였고 Stonehenge는 묘지이자 기념비였다. 07 고3학평 변형

7 Researchers were convinced that the recession would ______________ further.
연구원들은 경기침체가 더 악화 될 것이라 확신했다.

8 A ______________ walk near your house, two times a week, satisfies your daily exercise requirement.
일주일에 두 번 힘차게 동네 주변을 걷는 것은 당신의 일일 운동 요구량을 충족 시킨다. 11 고1학평 변형

9 The ______________ was located deep in the woods.
그 계곡은 깊은 숲 속에 위치해있다.

10 Society, through ethical and economic ______________, exerts a powerful influence on what science accomplishes.
윤리적이고 경제적인 제약을 통해서 사회는 과학이 성취한 것에 강한 영향력을 행사한다. 16 고3평가원 변형

Ⓐ 우리말에 맞게 빈 칸에 알맞은 단어를 쓰시오.

1 ________________ instruments 외과용 기구

2 ________________ the salad bowl 샐러드 그릇을 닦다

3 a real estate ________________ 부동산 중개인

4 She ________________, "I won!" 그녀는 "내가 이겼다!"고 소리쳤다.

5 ________________ all night 울며 밤을 새다

6 impair ________________ 인지를 손상시키다

7 major in ________________ 고고학을 전공하다

8 ________________ with embarrassment 당황함에 얼굴이 붉어지다

9 an ________________ call 익명의 전화

10 expect ________________ exports 활발한 수출을 기대하다

Ⓑ 영어에 맞게 빈 칸에 알맞은 우리말을 쓰시오.

1 boost his ego 그의 ________________ 을 높이 올리다

2 the skull of a wild wolf 야생 늑대의 ________________

3 surrender to the enemy 적에게 ________________

4 sew a garment ________________ 을 재봉질하다

5 be described as a workaholic ________________ 로서 묘사되다

6 arouse passion 열정을 ________________

7 throw a poisoned dart 독 ________________ 을 던지다

8 chatter about the weather 날씨에 대해 ________________ 를 떨다

9 deepen a river 강을 ________________

10 find conclusive evidence ________________ 증거를 찾다

C 다음 영어 풀이에 알맞은 어휘를 〈보기〉에서 고르시오.

보기	anonymous	brisk	subscribe	surrender	submerge

1 ______________ : moving quickly or actively

2 ______________ : to give up or stop fighting and accept defeat

3 ______________ : with names unknown or kept secret

4 ______________ : to pay money to get magazines or certain services regularly

5 ______________ : to go underwater; to make something go or sink underwater

D 문맥에 맞게 다음 문장을 완성하시오.

1 In addition to being a great statesman and writer, •	• a deep in the woods.
2 The tomb of King Tutankhamen eluded •	• b commemorate events or individuals.
3 I expected to have •	• c Jefferson was also a scientist.
4 The paintings can be used to •	• d the utmost coordination.
5 The creek was located •	• e even the cleverest of tomb robbers.

E 문장을 읽고 문맥에 적절한 단어를 고르시오.

1 The baseball team finally (terminated/blushed) the contract of the player.

2 He is (subscribing/surrendering) to a number of sports magazines.

3 This information is extremely important. So it should be kept (anonymous/confidential).

4 Many children in this school are (afflicted/provided) with an infectious disease.

5 His dog began to show (abnormal/healthy) behavior.

F 문장의 빈칸에 알맞은 단어를 〈보기〉에서 찾아 쓰시오. (필요하면 형태를 고치시오.)

보기 constraint alleviate tribute devastate enlighten

1 Many citizens gathered to pay ______________ to the life of the great musician.
많은 시민들이 그 위대한 음악가의 삶에 경의를 표하려고 모였다.

2 There are only a few ______________ people left in this world.
한 세기에 명확한 생각과 고상한 취향을 지닌 개화된 사람은 아주 적다. 2006 수능

3 High dependence on oil imposed a major ______________ on the economy of the country.
석유에 대한 높은 의존도가 그 국가 경제에 중대한 제약을 가했다.

4 The chemist discovered a chemical that can ______________ pain and make people sleepy.
그 화학자는 고통을 완화하고 사람들을 졸리게 만드는 화학물질을 발견했다.

5 The whole city was ______________ by the severe flood and typhoon.
온 도시가 심한 홍수와 태풍으로 완전히 파괴되었다.

G 다음 〈보기〉 중 두 문장에 공통으로 사용할 수 있는 어휘를 고르시오.

1 The man was ___________(e)d of stealing money from shoppers.
The jury decides whether an ___________(e)d person is guilty or not. 10 고3학평 변형

① accuse ② weep ③ wipe ④ commemorate ⑤ betray

2 The boys ___________(e)d that they broke the classroom windows.
He ___________(e)d his wrongdoings to his parents and made an apology.

① comply ② inject ③ confess ④ deepen ⑤ amend

3 We are often ___________ed to interrupt our listening by thinking about other things. 05 고2평가원 변형
Jamie's friends ___________ed him to skip his violin lesson and went to the movies instead.

① pinpoint ② uncover ③ confront ④ overload ⑤ tempt

Study More

혼동하기 쉬운 단어 arise vs. arouse

- [arise] 동 생기다, 발생하다
  People worry as the economic crisis **arises.** 경제 위기가 발생하자 사람들이 걱정하고 있다.
- [arouse] 동 (느낌, 태도를) 불러 일으키다
  The movie succeeded in **arousing** global interest. 그 영화는 세계인의 관심을 불러 일으키는데 성공했다.

Day 27

MP3

781 flaw [flɔ:]
명 (사물의) 결함, 결점
the fundamental flaw 근본적인 결함

782 intrude [intrú:d]
동 침해하다, 방해하다 형 intrusive 침입의, 거슬리는, 참견하는
intrude on her privacy 그녀의 사생활을 침해하다

783 drip [drip]
동 (방울 등이) 뚝뚝 떨어지다 명 (작은 액체) 방울, 물방울 소리
drip down the wall 벽을 타고 뚝뚝 떨어지다

784 hectic [héktik]
형 정신 없이 바쁜, 빡빡한
a hectic schedule 정신 없이 바쁜 일정

785 insane [inséin]
형 미친, 정신 이상의, 제정신이 아닌 반 sane 제정신인, 분별있는
go completely insane 완전히 미치다 an insane act 정신 이상적 행동

786 elevate [éləvèit]
동 들어올리다, 승격시키다, (기분을) 좋게 하다
elevate a weight 무거운 것을 들어올리다

787 fruitless [frú:tlis]
형 성과 없는, 보람없는
fruitless labor 헛수고 a fruitless attempt 소득 없는 시도

788 lure [ljuər]
동 유혹하다, 꾀다 명 유혹, 매력
lure a deer into a trap 사슴을 덫으로 유인하다

789 insulation [ìnsjəléiʃən]
명 절연체, 절연처리, 격리, 고립 동 insulate 절연(단열, 방음) 처리를 하다
inadequate insulation 부적절한 절연체

790 capitalize [kæpitəlaiz]
동 대문자로 쓰다, 자본화하다
capitalize a word 단어를 대문자로 시작하다

791 inherit [inhérit]
동 상속하다, 물려받다
inherited real estate 상속된 부동산

792 doze [douz]
동 깜빡 잠이 들다, 졸다
doze in an armchair 안락의자에서 졸다 doze off 꾸벅꾸벅 졸다

793 intelligible [intélidʒəbl]
형 (쉽게) 이해할 수 있는
an intelligible explanation 이해하기 쉬운 설명

794 linger [líŋgər]
동 오래 머물다, 오래 끌다 형 lingering 오래가는, 오래 끄는
linger over a cup of coffee 커피 마시며 오래 머물다

795 fragrance [fréigrəns]
명 향기, 향, 향수
subtle fragrance 은은한 향기 the fragrances of flowers 꽃 향기

Daily Test

| 월 일 |

Ⓐ 우리말에 맞게 빈 칸에 알맞은 단어를 쓰세요.

1 We all have a tendency to look at our own ______________ with a magnifying glass.
우리는 모두 자신의 결점을 확대경으로 바라보는 경향이 있다. 15 고3학평 변형

2 Andrew felt something begin to ______________ from his eyes.
Andrew는 그의 눈에서 무언가 뚝뚝 떨어지기 시작하는 것을 느꼈다. 07 고2학평 변형

3 On Christmas Eve in 2002, the Z-Mart in Seoul was jammed and ______________.
2002년 크리스마스 이브에, 서울의 Z마트는 혼잡스럽고 정신없이 바빴다. 15 고2학평 변형

4 Some large parrots are likely to seem to go ______________ if subjected to long periods of isolation.
몇몇 큰 앵무새들이 만약 오랜 기간 고립되어 있다면 미쳐가는 것처럼 보일 가능성이 있다. 14 고3학평 변형

5 Doctors warn that serious stress can ______________ your blood pressure.
의사들은 심한 스트레스가 혈압을 상승시킬 수 있다고 경고한다.

6 Nylon is used in everything from parachutes and ropes to ______________.
나일론은 낙하산과 밧줄에서부터 절연체까지 모든 것에 사용되었다. 07 고3학평 변형

7 People wondered who will ______________ the castle when the king dies.
사람들은 왕이 죽을 때 누가 그 성을 물려받을지에 대해 궁금해했다.

8 While I watched the movie, I ______________ off.
그 영화를 보는 동안, 난 내내 졸았어요. 09 고3학평 변형

9 Britney's performance will ______________ long in people's memory.
Britney의 공연은 오래도록 사람들의 기억 속에 남을 것이다.

10 Some ______________ might make you feel gloomy, while others might make your senses active.
몇몇 향기는 당신을 더 우울하게 만드는 반면에 다른 향기는 당신의 감각을 활발하게 만든다. 06 고3학평 변형

Day 27

MP3

796 **inconsistent** [ìnkənsístənt]
형 일치하지 않는, 일관성 없는
an inconsistent statement 일치하지 않는 진술

797 **glitter** [glítər]
동 반짝반짝 빛나다, 번들거리다 명 반짝거림, 빛남, 광채
glitter in the sunlight 햇빛 속에서 빛나다

798 **inhale** [inhéil]
동 들이마시다 반 exhale 내쉬다
inhale the fresh air 신선한 공기를 들이마시다

799 **intervene** [ìntərví:n]
동 개입하다, 끼어들다 명 intervention 개입, 중재, 간섭
intervene personally in the situation 상황에 개인적으로 개입하다

800 **frontier** [frʌntíər]
명 국경, 변경, 한계
frontier dispute 국경 분쟁 cross a frontier 국경을 넘다

801 **hygiene** [háidʒi(:)n]
명 위생, 위생학 형 hygienic 위생적인
personal hygiene 개인 위생 major in hygiene 위생학을 전공하다

802 **diagnose** [dáiəgnòus]
동 진단하다, 밝혀내다
diagnose cancer 암을 진단하다

803 **fling** [fliŋ]
동 (거칠게) 내던지다, (어떤 상태에) 빠뜨리다 명 내던지기, 약진, 돌진
fling his book on the desk 책상 위로 그의 책을 내던지다

804 **flourish** [flə́:riʃ]
동 번성하다, 번창하다, 잘 자라다
flourish for a while 한때 번창하다

805 **flush** [flʌʃ]
동 붉어지다 명 홍조
flush with anger 화가 나서 얼굴이 빨개지다

806 **homesick** [hóumsìk]
형 향수에 잠긴, 향수병의
homesick for his country 그의 고향에 대한 향수

807 **diplomatic** [dìpləmǽtik]
형 외교의 명 diplomacy 외교(술), 사교 능력
diplomatic relations 외교 관계 a diplomatic crisis 외교적 위기

808 **foremost** [fɔ́:rmòust]
형 가장 중요한, 선두의 유 leading 이끄는, 선도하는
her foremost duty 그녀의 가장 중요한 의무

809 **spectator** [spékteitər]
명 관중, 구경꾼, 목격자
attract spectators 관중을 모으다

810 **cannon** [kǽnən]
명 대포, 기관포 동 대포를 쏘다
fire a cannon 대포를 발사하다 the boom of a cannon 대포의 굉음

Daily Test

| 월 일 |

A 우리말에 맞게 빈 칸에 알맞은 단어를 쓰세요.

1 We were disturbed by Jack's _______________ behaviors.
우리는 Jack의 일관성 없는 행동으로 인해 방해 받았어요. 16 고3평가원 변형

2 _______________ gems called diamonds are among the most precious of Nina's possessions.
다이아몬드라 불리는 반짝반짝 빛나는 보석은 Nina의 소지품 중에 가장 귀중한 것이다. 04 고3평가원 변형

3 Even plants have respiratory systems, but they exhale oxygen and _______________ carbon dioxide.
심지어 식물들도 호흡 기관이 있지만, 그들은 산소를 배출하고 이산화탄소를 흡입한다.

4 Augustus made sure the empire had natural _______________ and placed soldiers there.
Augustus는 제국을 자연적으로 생긴 국경선을 둘러싸이게 하고 군인들을 거기에 배치했다. 08 고1학평 변형

5 Thomas was _______________ with a terminal illness and given six months to live.
Thomas는 불치병 말기로 6개월 밖에 살 수 없다는 진단을 받았다. 10 고3평가원 변형

6 All the villagers at the banquet began to _______________ tomatoes into the pot.
연회에 온 모든 마을 사람들은 그 항아리로 토마토를 던지기 시작했다. 11 고3평가원 변형

7 Some plants _______________ in a dry climate.
일부 식물들은 건조한 기후에서 잘 자란다.

8 Although the freezing wind pounds upon me, Allen felt _______________ with warmth of the fire.
찬 바람이 날 스침에도 불구하고, Allen은 화롯불의 온기에 볼이 붉어졌다. 10 고3평가원 변형

9 After separating from my parents, I have been a little _______________.
부모님으로부터 독립한 후에, 나는 약간의 향수병이 있었다.

10 All the _______________ congratulated the winner on his victory.
모든 관중들이 우승자에게 승리를 축하했다. 11 고3학평 변형

Day 28

MP3

811 **plunge** [plʌndʒ]
동 감소하다, 급락하다, 뛰어들다 명 낙하, 급락, 뛰어듦
plunge nearly 70% 거의 70% 감소하다

812 **perish** [périʃ]
동 죽다, 사라지다
perish in the fire 화재로 죽다

813 **recruit** [rikrúːt]
동 채용하다, 모집하다, 보충하다 명 신입회원, 신병
recruit the professional librarian 전문 사서를 채용하다

814 **purify** [pjú(ː)ərəfài]
동 정화하다, 깨끗이 하다 명 purity 순수성, 순도
purify water 물을 정화하다

815 **prevailing** [privéiliŋ]
형 우세한, 널리 퍼진 유 widespread 널리 보급된, 널리 퍼진
a prevailing view 우세한 견해 the prevailing disease 널리 퍼진 질병

816 **plausible** [plɔ́ːzəbl]
형 그럴듯한, 타당한
his plausible excuse 그의 그럴듯한 변명

817 **interval** [íntərvəl]
명 (두 사건 사이의) 간격, 중간 휴식 시간
at an interval of seven years 7년의 간격을 두고

818 **scorn** [skɔːrn]
동 경멸하다 명 경멸, 멸시
scorn the murderer 살인범을 경멸하다

819 **parameter** [pərǽmitər]
명 한도, 매개변수
set the parameters 한도를 정하다 within the parameters 한도 내에서

820 **acoustic** [əkúːstik]
형 청각의, 소리의
acoustic effects 청각 효과 an acoustic instrument 보청기

821 **nominate** [nάmənèit]
동 지명하다, 후보자로 추천하다, 임명하다 명 nominee 지명된 사람, 후보
nominate a candidate 후보자를 지명하다

822 **fragment** [frǽgmənt]
명 조각, 파편 동 조각나다, 부서지다
remove tiny fragments 아주 작은 파편을 제거하다

823 **accelerate** [əksélərèit]
동 속도를 늘리다, 가속화하다
accelerate the aging process 노화 과정을 가속화하다

824 **partial** [pάːrʃəl]
형 부분적인, 편파적인 반 impartial 공정한
partial consent 부분적인 동의

825 **swell** [swel]
동 붓다, 부풀다, 증가하다 명 부어오름, 증가, 팽창
begin to swell 부풀기 시작하다

Daily Test

| 월 일 |

A 우리말에 맞게 빈 칸에 알맞은 단어를 쓰세요.

1 We learn that trauma is survivable, so we don't ______________ too deeply following setbacks.
우리는 트라우마가 살아남을 수 있다고 배우기에, 우리는 그 후의 좌절에 너무 깊게 빠지지 않는다. 14 고3평가원 변형

2 Max joined an organization that ______________ volunteers to teach in low-income communities.
Max는 저소득층 주민들을 가르칠 봉사자를 모집하는 단체에 가입했다. 2015 수능 변형

3 Alex invented the new machine which is made to ______________ air and water.
Alex는 물과 공기를 정화하도록 만들어진 새 기계를 발명했다.

4 You can get slim by eating healthy foods at the right ______________ each day.
당신은 매일 건강한 음식을 적절한 간격에 먹음으로써 날씬해 질 수 있다. 06 고1평가원 변형

5 Some people ______________ tradition but that attitude is wrong.
몇몇 사람들은 전통을 경멸하지만 그런 태도 역시 잘못된 것일 수 있다.

6 According to the theory, television is basically an ______________ medium.
그 이론에 따르면, 텔레비전은 기본적으로 청각 매체이다. 2009 수능 변형

7 Sarah belongs to an organization that ______________ candidates and elects officers.
Sarah는 후보자를 지명하고 공무원을 뽑는 기관에 속해 있다. 06 고3학평 변형

8 The lamp shattered into a thousand ______________ after it was hit by the baseball.
그 등불은 야구공에 의해 깨진 후에 천여개의 조각으로 부서졌다.

9 If the elevator ______________ downward, the spring is less compressed and your weight reading is less.
엘리베이터가 아래쪽으로 빨라지면 거울 안의 용수철은 압력을 덜 받게 되어 당신의 체중 표시가 더 작아지게 된다. 08 고2평가원 변형

10 The snake started to ______________ up, hiss loudly, vibrate its tail, and bite.
뱀은 몸을 부풀리고, 크게 쉬익 소리를 내고, 그의 꼬리를 떨고, 물기 시작했다. 05 고3평가원 변형

Day 28

MP3

826 **populate** [pάpjəlèit]
동 살다, 거주하다, (장소를) 차지하고 있다
a densely populated city 인구밀도가 조밀한 도시

827 **overdue** [òuvərdjúː]
형 연체된, 늦어진
an overdue payment 연체된 지불

828 **manifest** [mǽnəfèst]
동 나타내다, 드러내다 형 분명한, 명백한
manifest absurdity 모순을 드러내다

829 **painkiller** [péinkìlər]
명 진통제
take a painkiller 진통제를 먹다 inject a painkiller 진통제를 주입하다

830 **lease** [liːs]
명 임대차 계약 동 임대하다 유 let 세를 주다
renew a lease 임대를 갱신하다 lease facilities 시설을 임대하다

831 **recur** [rikə́ːr]
동 재발하다, 되풀이되다 형 recurring 되풀이하여 발생하는
a recurring problem 되풀이되는 문제

832 **reside** [rizáid]
동 거주하다, 살다 명 resident 거주자, 주민
reside in a dormitory 기숙사에 살다

833 **roar** [rɔːr]
동 으르렁 거리다, 포효하다
The lion roars at tourists. 사자가 관광객들에게 으르렁 거리다.

834 **sphere** [sfiər]
명 구, 하늘, 창공, 영역(권)
the shape of a perfect sphere 완벽한 구의 모양

835 **compile** [kəmpáil]
동 편집하다, 편찬하다, 작성하다
compile a report 보고서를 편집하다

836 **refraction** [rifrǽkʃən]
명 굴절, 비뚤어짐, 왜곡
cause a refraction of light 빛의 굴절을 야기하다

837 **segregation** [sègrəgéiʃən]
명 분리, 차별
the strict gender segregation 엄격한 성 분리

838 **scheme** [skiːm]
명 계획, 제도, 책략 동 책략을 꾸미다, 계획하다
a dangerous scheme 위험한 계획

839 **surplus** [sə́ːrplʌs]
명 과잉, 잉여, 흑자 형 과잉의, 잉여의
surplus population 과잉 인구 surplus capital 잉여 자본

840 **effectual** [iféktʃuəl]
형 효과적인, 유효한
an effectual cure 효과적인 치료

Daily Test

| 월 일 |

A 우리말에 맞게 빈 칸에 알맞은 단어를 쓰세요.

1 The galaxies refer to the enormous star systems that ______________ our universe.
은하는 우리의 우주를 차지하고 있는 거대한 별 체계를 일컫는다.

2 We urge your company to implement strict regulations on ______________ for GM and non-GM crops.
우리는 유전적으로 조작된 농작물과 조작되지 않은 농작물에 대한 분리의 강력한 규제안을 만들어 시행할 것을 촉구한다. 09 고3학평 변형

3 Emotional eaters ______________ their problem in lots of different ways.
감정적으로 먹는 사람들은 다양한 많은 방법으로 그들의 문제를 드러낸다. 2012 수능 변형

4 Some don't believe in acupuncture's effect as a ______________.
몇몇 사람들은 진통제로서 침술의 효과를 믿지 않는다. 10 고2학평 변형

5 The same mistake ______________ over and over again.
같은 실수가 계속해서 되풀이 되었다.

6 Harry was scheduled to return to his hometown next week, having ______________ in London for 10 years.
Harry는 10년간 London에서 살다가 다음 주에 그의 고향으로 돌아갈 예정이었다.

7 Our ship was rising and falling among the ______________ waves.
우리 배는 포효하는 파도 사이에서 오르락 내리락 하는 중이었다. 09 고3학평 변형

8 Researchers investigated the ______________ of light through lenses to improve the development of glasses.
연구원들은 안경 개발을 개선하기 위해 렌즈를 통해 빛의 굴절을 조사했다. 09 고2평가원 변형

9 Wetlands are converted in favor of more profitable options such as dams or irrigation ______________.
습지는 댐이나 관개 시설과 같이 더 이득이 되는 것으로 전환된다. 11 고3학평 변형

10 Agricultural production, which developed fastest in regions of Asia, led to food ______________.
아시아 지역에서 가장 빠르게 성장한 농업 생산은 음식의 과잉을 만들어냈다.

A 우리말에 맞게 빈 칸에 알맞은 단어를 쓰시오.

1 ______________ labor 헛수고

2 ______________ a word 단어를 대문자로 시작하다

3 ______________ in the sunlight 햇빛 속에서 빛나다

4 ______________ personally in the situation 상황에 개인적으로 개입하다

5 her ______________ duty 그녀의 가장 중요한 의무

6 the ______________ disease 널리 퍼진 질병

7 ______________ the murderer 살인범을 경멸하다

8 inject a ______________ 진통제를 주입하다

9 the shape of a perfect ______________ 완벽한 구의 모양

10 ______________ capital 잉여 자본

B 영어에 맞게 빈 칸에 알맞은 우리말을 쓰시오.

1 go completely insane 완전히 ______________

2 doze in an armchair 안락의자에서 ______________

3 the fragrances of flowers 꽃 ______________

4 major in hygiene ______________을 전공하다

5 flush with anger 화가 나서 얼굴이 ______________

6 perish in the fire 화재로 ______________

7 within the parameters ______________ 내에서

8 begin to swell ______________ 시작하다

9 an overdue payment ______________ 지불

10 reside in a dormitory 기숙사에 ______________

C 다음 영어 풀이에 알맞은 어휘를 〈보기〉에서 고르시오.

보기	flourish	recur	flaw	plausible	reside

1 ______________ : seeming true, reasonable, or realistic

2 ______________ : to live in a particular place or area

3 ______________ : to grow or develop well; successful

4 ______________ : to happen or occur again

5 ______________ : a fault or weakness; a small problem with a thing

D 문맥에 맞게 다음 문장을 완성하시오.

1 We all have a tendency to look at •	• a that populate our universe.
2 Andrew felt something begin •	• b our own flaws with a magnifying glass.
3 Although the freezing wind pounds upon me, •	• c basically an acoustic medium.
4 According to the theory, television is •	• d to drip from his eyes.
5 The galaxies refer to the enormous star systems •	• e Allen felt flushed with warmth of the fire.

E 문장을 읽고 문맥에 적절한 단어를 고르시오.

1 Many people moved to this city, (lured/dozed) by good jobs and nice weather.

2 The two countries agreed to establish official (acoustic/diplomatic) relations.

3 The company is (flinging/recruiting) experienced software developers.

4 Greg's (inconsistent/hygiene) statements made people doubt his true intentions.

5 Lisa had a (hectic/effectual) day due to the large volume of current orders.

F 문장의 빈칸에 알맞은 단어를 〈보기〉에서 찾아 쓰시오. (필요하면 형태를 고치시오.)

보기 plunge compile accelerate diagnose manifest

1 Mischel did not simply point out the problem; he ______________ the reasons for it.
Mischel은 그 문제점을 지적하기만 한 것이 아니라 그 이유를 진단했다. 15 고3학평

2 We all shouted encouragingly as the other rafts ______________ into the river ahead of us.
다른 뗏목들이 우리 앞의 강물 속으로 뛰어들 때 우리 모두는 격려의 함성을 질렀다. 06 고2학평

3 The disease was ______________ in many different ways.
그 질병은 여러 다양한 방식으로 나타났다.

4 During the Post Classical Period, the pace and impact of international trade ______________.
고전 후기 시대에 국제 무역의 속도와 영향력이 가속화되었다. 12 고3학평 변형

5 The ecologist ______________ a large list of wild plants peculiar to the region.
그 생태학자는 그 지역 특유의 야생 식물 리스트를 작성했다.

G 다음 <보기> 중 두 문장에 공통으로 사용할 수 있는 어휘를 고르시오.

1 Brain researches show that some of our intelligence may indeed be ___________(e)d. 15 고2학평 변형
The new king ___________(e)d the throne at the age of only 19. 09 고3학평 변형

① perish ② inherit ③ populate ④ flush ⑤ intrude

2 The best way for learning new words is to repeat words at various ___________(e)s. 15 고2학평 변형
The reporter checks news websites at regular ___________(e)s to keep up to date.

① interval ② flaw ③ parameter ④ sphere ⑤ insulation

3 Each candidate for the award must be ___________(e)d by his or her homeroom teacher. 14 고3학평 변형
Only club members can ___________ a candidate for club president.

① linger ② inhale ③ glitter ④ capitalize ⑤ nominate

Study More

'-ify' : [동사에서] '~화하다', '~하게 하다' 의 뜻을 나타낸다.

- [simplify] 동 간소화 (단순화) 하다
  I think you need to **simplify** your life. 난 네가 생활을 좀 간소화 시킬 필요가 있다고 생각해.
- [intensify] 동 강화하다, 심해지다
  Teenage violence has **intensified** in the last few years.
  지난 몇 년간 10대들에 의한 폭력은 점점 심해졌다.

Day 29

MP3

841 **triumph** [tráiəmf]
명 큰 승리, 대성공 동 이기다, 성공하다
achieve a triumph 승리를 거두다 triumph over fate 운명을 이기다

842 **authorize** [ɔ́:θəràiz]
동 승인하다, 권한을 부여하다
authorize him to enter the room 그가 방에 들어오는 것을 허가하다

843 **tyrant** [táiərənt]
명 독재자, 폭군 명 tyranny 압제, 폭압
be ruled by a merciless tyrant 무자비한 독재자에 의해 통치 받다

844 **byproduct** [báipràdəkt]
명 부산물, 부작용
byproduct of coal-fired power plants 화력 발전소로부터 나온 부산물

845 **phenomenal** [finámənəl]
형 경이적인, 경탄스러운
a phenomenal success 경이로운 성공

846 **splinter** [splíntər]
명 파편, 조각 동 쪼개지다, 분리되다
break into splinters 산산조각이 나다 splinter the wood 나무를 쪼개다

847 **refute** [rifjú:t]
동 반박하다, 논박하다
refute his argument 그의 논쟁을 반박하다

848 **lament** [ləmént]
동 한탄하다, 애도하다 명 비탄, 한탄
lament the decline in moral standards 도덕적 기준 하락에 대해 한탄하다

849 **vomit** [vámit]
동 토하다, 게우다 유 throw up 토하다
vomit up supper 저녁 먹은 걸 토하다

850 **magnify** [mǽgnəfài]
동 확대하다, 과장하다 명 magnifier 확대경, 돋보기
magnify the picture 그림을 확대하다

851 **obstruct** [əbstrʌ́kt]
동 방해하다, 막다
obstruct a search 조사를 방해하다 obstruct the view 전망을 방해하다

852 **chick** [tʃik]
명 병아리
chicks in the garden 정원의 병아리들 a pea chick 공작새의 새끼

853 **nomad** [nóumæd]
명 유목민 형 nomadic 유목의, 방랑의
last nomads of Africa 아프리카의 마지막 유목민

854 **invariable** [invɛ́(:)əriəbl]
형 불변의, 일정한 명 변치않는 것, 상수
invariable element 불변의 요소

855 **designate** [dézignit]
동 지정하다, 지명하다 형 지명을 받은, 지명된
designate a non-smoking area 비흡연지역으로 지정하다

Daily Test

| 월 일 |

Ⓐ 우리말에 맞게 빈 칸에 알맞은 단어를 쓰세요.

1 People hope good almost always ______________ over evil.
사람들은 거의 항상 선이 악에게 승리하기를 희망한다. 05 고3학평 변형

2 E-mail has recently become an electronic ______________.
이메일은 최근에 전자매체 독재자가 되었다. 13 고1학평 변형

3 The decline in wine consumption in France is a ______________ of the emergence of the faster, more modern lifestyle.
프랑스의 와인 소비량 감소는 더 빠르고, 더 현대적인 생활방식의 등장의 부산물이다. 13 고3평가원 변형

4 Peter's new theory ______________ the Big Bang theory, stating that humans lived at the same time as dinosaurs.
Peter의 새 이론은 인류가 공룡과 동시대에 살았음을 언급하면서 빅뱅이론에 반박했다.

5 The symptoms of hemlock poisoning include ______________ and loss of muscular power.
독미나리 중독의 증상은 구토와 근력의 손실을 포함한다. 08 고2평가원 변형

6 My grandfather uses a ______________ glasses to read the tiny print.
할아버지는 작은 글씨를 보기 위해서 확대경을 사용한다.

7 Our view of the stream is ______________ by the trees.
그 개울의 경관이 나무들로 인해 막혔다.

8 ______________ can get out of their nest within three hours of hatching.
병아리는 부화 후 3시간 안에 그들의 둥지 밖으로 나올 수 있다. 15 고2학평 변형

9 The king ______________ the prince his sister to act for him while he was away.
왕은 왕자에게 그가 없는 동안 그를 대행할 권한을 주었다.

10 The square has been ______________ as a no-smoking area.
그 광장은 금연 구역으로 지정되어 있다.

Day 29

MP3

856 **entitle** [intáitl]
동 자격을 주다, 제목을 붙이다
entitled to a pension 연금 받을 자격을 주다

857 **versatile** [vəːrsətil]
형 다재 다능한, 다용도의, 다목적의
a versatile inventor 다재 다능한 발명가

858 **fusion** [fjúːʒən]
명 융해, 융합 동 fuse 융합되다, 융합시키다
the heat of fusion 융해열

859 **expire** [ikspáiər]
동 만기가 되다, 기한이 끝나다
The lease will expire next week. 다음 주에 임대 계약이 만기 될 것이다.

860 **incline** [inkláin]
동 기울다, 경향이 있다 명 경사(면)
incline to the right side 오른편으로 기울다

861 **startle** [stáːrtl]
동 깜짝 놀라게 하다 형 startling 아주 놀라운
be startled by his answer 그의 답에 깜짝 놀라다

862 **terrify** [térəfài]
동 무섭게 하다, 겁먹게하다 유 frighten 놀라게 하다, 섬뜩하게 하다
be terrified at the news 그 소식에 겁을 먹다

863 **zealous** [zéləs]
형 열심인, 열성적인
make zealous efforts 열심히 노력을 하다

864 **fed up with** [fed ʌp wið]
~에 싫증 난, ~에 질린
be fed up with domestic politics 국내 정치에 진저리가 나다

865 **unify** [júːnəfài]
동 통합(통일) 하다 유 unite 연합하다, 합치다
unify the region 지역을 통합하다

866 **recede** [risiːd]
동 물러나다, 감소하다
the receding tide 썰물 recede in importance 중요성이 감소하다

867 **pillar** [pílər]
명 기둥, (기둥 모양의) 기념비, 기념물
enter a nail in a pillar 기둥에 못을 박다 a pillar of fire 불기둥

868 **enlist** [inlíst]
동 참여하다, 입대하다, 징집하다
enlist in the military 군대에 입대하다

869 **unanimous** [juːnǽnəməs]
형 만장일치의, 이구동성의
unanimous consent 만장일치의 동의

870 **pirate** [páiərət]
명 해적 동 해적 행위를 하다, 약탈하다
a pirate ship 해적선

Daily Test

| 월 일 |

A 우리말에 맞게 빈 칸에 알맞은 단어를 쓰세요.

1 Thomas was one of the most ______________ soccer players in history.
Thomas는 역사상 가장 다재다능한 축구 선수 중 한 명이었다. 06 고3학평 변형

2 When you feel a strong emotion, you are ______________ to do something vigorously.
당신이 강한 감정을 느낄 때, 당신은 왕성하게 무언가를 하는 경향이 있다. 11 고3학평

3 The sound, unexpected and loud, ______________ the cow, so it began to run away.
예기치 못했던 커다란 그 소리에 소가 깜짝 놀랐고 소는 도망가기 시작했다. 14 고1학평 변형

4 The sound of birds ______________ into the distance.
새 소리는 차츰 멀어져갔다.

5 The British people were ______________ the inequality between the noblemen and the lower classes.
영국 사람들은 상류층과 낮은 계급 사이의 불평등에 진저리가 났다.

6 The Mongol Empire was not a ______________ state but a vast collection of territories held together by military force.
몽고 제국은 통합된 상태가 아니라 다양한 영토들의 모임이 군대에 의해 함께 합쳐진 상태였다. 07 고3평가원 변형

7 What waited for Lily in the new world was brick buildings with white ______________.
새로운 세계에서 Lily를 기다리고 있던 것은 흰 기둥이 있는 벽돌 건물이었다. 12 고3평가원 변형

8 To test the theory, we ______________ the help of ninety people to take part in a pilot program.
그 이론을 시험해보기 위해서, 우리는 예비 연구에 참여할 90명의 도움을 얻었다. 11 고2학평 변형

9 By a ______________ vote, Lucy was elected as class president.
만장일치의 투표로, Lucy는 학급 회장으로 당선되었다. 13 고3학평 변형

10 Sue was captivated by Peter's story about ______________, treasure and the sea.
Sue는 Peter의 해적, 보물, 그리고 바다에 대한 이야기에 사로잡혔다. 09 고3학평 변형

Day 30

MP3

871 **torture** [tɔ́:rtʃər]
명 고문 동 고문하다, 지독히 괴롭히다
expose torture 고문을 폭로하다

872 **dismay** [disméi]
명 실망, 경악 동 경악하게 만들다 유 frustration 좌절, 낙담
to one's dismay 놀랍게도 dismay at the news 소식에 경악하다

873 **procession** [prəséʃən]
명 행진, 행렬
a torchlight procession 횃불 행진 a festival procession 축제 행렬

874 **astronomical** [æ̀strənάmikəl]
형 천문학의, 천문학적인, 어마어마한
astronomical observation 천문학적 관찰

875 **undertake** [ʌ̀ndərtéik]
동 떠맡다, 착수하다, 약속하다
undertake a task 과제를 떠맡다

876 **in terms of** [in t3:rmz əv]
~면에서, ~에 관하여
in terms of cost 가격 면에서

877 **vow** [vau]
명 맹세, 서약 동 맹세하다, 다짐하다
break a vow 맹세를 어기다 vow eternal love 영원한 사랑을 다짐하다

878 **anecdote** [ǽnikdòut]
명 일화, 비사
a funny anecdote 즐거운 일화 tell an anecdote 일화를 말하다

879 **nonverbal** [nonvɜ:rbl]
형 말을 사용하지 않는, 말이 서투른
the nonverbal aspects of communication 의사소통의 비언어적 측면

880 **patriotic** [pèitriάtik]
형 애국적인 명 patriot 애국자
sing patriotic songs 애국적 노래를 부르다

881 **ignite** [ignáit]
동 불이 붙다, 점화하다 명 ignition 점화, 발화, (차량의) 점화 스위치
ignite passion 열정에 불을 붙이다

882 **preservative** [prizə́:rvətiv]
명 방부제
a food preservative 식품 방부제 add a preservative 방부제를 첨가하다

883 **circulate** [s3:rkjəleit]
동 순환하다, 순환시키다, (소문 등이) 유포되다 형 circulatory 혈액 순환의
circulate throughout the cells 세포를 통해 순환하다

884 **fume** [fju:m]
동 (화가 나서) 씩씩대다, 연기를 내뿜다 명 연기, 화, 노기
fume with indignation 분이 나서 씩씩대다

885 **captive** [kǽptiv]
형 포로가 된, 사로잡힌 명 포로, 사로잡힌 사람
captive animals 포획 동물 take captives 포로를 잡다

Daily Test

| 월 일 |

Ⓐ 우리말에 맞게 빈 칸에 알맞은 단어를 쓰세요.

1 During the war, millions of people were killed, ______________, and buried in areas throughout the countryside.
전쟁 동안에 수백 만의 사람들이 죽고, 고문당하고, 나라 전역에 묻혔다.

2 Sean was most ______________ when his publisher told him his first book would not be issued until January 1954.
Sean은 그의 첫 번째 책이 1954년 1월까지는 출판되지 않을 것을 그의 출판인에게 들었을 때 가장 실망했다. 08 고3학평 변형

3 In 2006, the International ______________ Union (IAU) held a meeting.
2006년에 국제 천문학 협회는 회의를 열었다.

4 I think that Jimmy can't ______________ such a big job.
난 Jimmy가 그렇게 큰 일을 떠맡을 수 없다고 생각한다. 04 고2평가원 변형

5 When scientists describe tool use by human beings, it is usually ______________ mechanical tools.
과학자들이 인간에 의한 도구 사용을 설명할 때 그것은 대개 기계적 도구라는 면에서이다. 15 고3학평 변형

6 Silently, I was under a ______________ to tell the truth.
조용히, 나는 진실만을 말할 것을 맹세했다. 13 고3평가원 변형

7 Chris told an interesting ______________ about his daughter.
Chris는 그의 딸에 대한 흥미로운 일화를 들려주었다.

8 We can listen to ______________ songs on national memorial day.
우리는 국가 기념일에 애국적인 노래들을 들을 수 있다.

9 Timothy's family was suffocated in their sleep by ______________ from a fire.
Timothy의 가족은 불에서 나오는 연기로 인해 자는 사이에 질식해서 죽었다.

10 A big crowd turned out to watch the funeral ______________ of Steve Jobs'.
Steve Jobs의 장례 행렬을 보기 위해 많은 군중들이 모습을 드러냈다.

Day 30

MP3

886 **groan** [groun]
동 신음하다, 괴로워하다 명 (고통으로 인한) 신음소리
die groaning 신음하면서 죽다

887 **counterattack** [káuntərətæ̀k]
명 역습, 반격 동 역습, 반격하다
a counterattack from the enemy 적군으로부터의 역습

888 **dusk** [dʌsk]
명 황혼, 땅거미 유 twilight 황혼, 땅거미
after dusk 해가 진 후에 last until dusk 해가 질 때까지 계속되다

889 **utterance** [ʌ́tərəns]
명 발언, 말씨 동 utter 말을 하다
a public utterance 공식 발언 a man of good utterance 달변가

890 **trim** [trim]
동 다듬다, 잘라내다
trim her hair 그녀의 머리를 다듬다 trim the leaves 잎을 잘라내다

891 **account** [əkáunt]
명 계좌, 장부, 설명
open a bank account 은행 계좌를 개설하다

892 **standardize** [stǽndərdàiz]
동 표준화하다
standardize the size 크기를 표준화하다

893 **subdue** [səbdjú:]
동 진압하다, (감정을) 가라 앉히다
subdue the rebels 반란자들을 진압하다

894 **censorship** [sénsərʃìp]
명 검열 동 censor 검열하다
press censorship 언론 검열

895 **majestic** [mədʒéstik]
형 장엄한, 위풍 당당한 유 magnificient 장엄한, 웅대한
a majestic view 장엄한 광경 his majestic manner 그의 장엄한 태도

896 **dictator** [díkteitər]
명 독재자 명 dictatorship 독재정부
a military dictator 군사 독재자

897 **overtake** [òuvərtéik]
동 추월하다, 앞지르다
overtake demand 수요를 앞지르다

898 **intimidate** [intímidèit]
동 겁을 주다, 위협하다
intimidate a boy into stealing 소년을 위협하여 도둑질을 시키다

899 **tactics** [tǽktiks]
명 전술, 전략
psychological tactics 심리적 전술

900 **unscrupulous** [ʌnskrú:pjələs]
형 부도덕한, 파렴치한
unscrupulous practices 부도덕한 관습

Daily Test

| 월 일 |

A 우리말에 맞게 빈 칸에 알맞은 단어를 쓰세요.

1 The wounded man ______________ in pain and asked for medicine.
부상당한 남자는 고통에 신음했고 약을 달라고 요청했다.

2 I think internet ______________ is a necessity for our children.
우리 아이들을 위해서라도 인터넷 검열은 필수라고 생각한다.

3 Jack is ______________ the bushes and Amy is moving chairs and tables.
Jack은 관목을 자르고 있고 Amy는 의자와 탁자를 옮기는 중이다.

4 Ever since my daughter's sixth birthday, I've put Saturdays' earnings into a savings ______________ for her.
내 딸의 6살 생일 이래로, 나는 토요일에 버는 돈을 그녀를 위해 예금 계좌에 넣어왔다. 15 고3학평 변형

5 Some ______________ backgrounds of religious images acted as a device to exclude the individuality of the artists.
일부 종교 이미지의 표준화된 배경은 예술가들의 독립성을 배재하는 장치의 역할을 했다. 11 고2학평 변형

6 The country was governed by a ______________, and people had no freedom of speech.
그 나라는 독재자에 의해 통치되었고, 사람들은 발언의 자유가 없었다.

7 Although my hometown was small city, it was surrounded by ______________ mountains.
내 고향은 작은 도시였음에도, 장엄한 산들로 둘러싸여 있었다.

8 Because China ______________ the U.S, the U.S will no longer be the strongest economic leader.
중국이 미국을 앞질렀기 때문에, 미국은 더 이상 가장 강력한 경제 선두주자가 아닐 것이다. 09 고2학평 변형

9 The general won many battles because of his determination and wise ______________.
그 장군은 그의 투지와 현명한 전술 때문에 많은 전투에서 승리했다.

10 Many people blamed her for using ______________ methods to win the competition.
많은 사람들은 그녀가 경기에서 이기기 위해 부도덕한 방법을 사용한 것에 대해 비난했다. 06 고2학평 변형

A 우리말에 맞게 빈 칸에 알맞은 단어를 쓰시오.

1 be ruled by a merciless ________________ 무자비한 독재자에 의해 통치 받다

2 ________________ the wood 나무를 쪼개다

3 ________________ the picture 그림을 확대하다

4 be ________________ by his answer 그의 답에 깜짝 놀라다

5 ________________ in the military 군대에 입대하다

6 expose ________________ 고문을 폭로하다

7 a festival ________________ 축제 행렬

8 ________________ eternal love 영원한 사랑을 다짐하다

9 die ________________ 신음하면서 죽다

10 ________________ the rebels 반란자들을 진압하다

B 영어에 맞게 빈 칸에 알맞은 우리말을 쓰시오.

1 a phenomenal success ________________ 성공

2 vomit up supper 저녁 먹은 걸 ________________

3 invariable element ________________ 요소

4 incline to the right side 오른편으로 ________________

5 enter a nail in a pillar ________________에 못을 박다

6 undertake a task 과제를 ________________

7 take captives ________________를 잡다

8 standardize the size 크기를 ________________

9 a military dictator 군사 ________________

10 unscrupulous practices ________________ 관습

C 다음 영어 풀이에 알맞은 어휘를 〈보기〉에서 고르시오.

보기 overtake unscrupulous anecdote unanimous patriotic

1 ______________ : agreed or supported by all people

2 ______________ : feeling or showing pride, love, or respect for your country

3 ______________ : to catch up with or to go past someone or something

4 ______________ : not honest or doing something illegal

5 ______________ : a short story telling about a funny or interesting event

D 문맥에 맞게 다음 문장을 완성하시오.

1 People hope good almost •	• a always triumphs over evil.
2 Chicks can get out of their nest •	• b and asked for medicine.
3 By a unanimous vote, •	• c Lucy was elected to class president.
4 Chris told an interesting •	• d within three hours of hatching.
5 The wounded man groaned in pain •	• e anecdote about his daughter.

E 문장을 읽고 문맥에 적절한 단어를 고르시오.

1 I am (caught/fed) up with his rude and careless behavior.

2 He is fully (entitled/inclined) to be the winner of this year's singing contest.

3 The Health Department (authorized/overtook) the import of the new medicine.

4 The politician's recent interview (dismayed/ignited) a new round of debates on immigration.

5 Bill, we need to renew our car insurance. It will (expire/subdue) next month.

F 문장의 빈칸에 알맞은 단어를 〈보기〉에서 찾아 쓰시오. (필요하면 형태를 고치시오.)

보기 refute trim versatile undertake recede

1 Didn't you say you were going to get your hair ______________ a little?
머리를 조금만 다듬는다고 하지 않았니? 10 고3학평

2 In the modern world, traditional local communities are ______________ in importance.
현대 세계에서는 전통적인 지역 사회의 중요성이 감소하고 있다.

3 Nobody would dare to ______________ such a difficult task.
누구도 그런 어려운 과제를 떠맡으려고 하지 않을 것이다.

4 Wesley is a ______________ football player. He played several different positions this season.
Wesley는 다재다능한 축구선수이다. 그는 이번 시즌에 여러 다른 포지션을 맡았다.

5 We have found enough evidence to ______________ his claim.
우리는 그의 주장을 반박 할 충분한 증거를 찾았다.

G 다음 〈보기〉 중 두 문장에 공통으로 사용할 수 있는 어휘를 고르시오.

1 I'd like to withdraw money from my ___________. 15 고3평가원
If you send money overseas, please write your bank ___________ number here. 13 고3학평 변형

① fusion ② pillar ③ account ④ utterance ⑤ pirate

2 Hand movements are used as a means of ___________ communication. 15 고3평가원
Facial expression are the most important form of ___________ messages.

① patriotic ② nonverbal ③ majestic ④ unscrupulous ⑤ phenomenal

3 The blood ___________(e)s around the human body, providing oxygen.
Refrigerators work better when the cold air can ___________ easily. 15 고3학평 변형

① circulate ② fume ③ standardize ④ magnify ⑤ obstruct

Study More

혼동하기 쉬운 단어 vow vs. bow

- [vow] 명 맹세, 서약
  He broke his marriage **vow**. 그는 그의 결혼 서약을 어겼다.
- [bow] 동 (허리를 굽혀) 절하다
  All the people **bowed** down before the queen. 모든 사람들이 여왕 앞에서 엎드려 절했다.

Index

Answer Key

정답 및 해설

Answer Key

Day 01

Daily Test 1 P. 09

A
1 immediate
2 remains
3 majority
4 alternatives
5 definition
6 determined
7 annual
8 context
9 shift
10 evolution

Daily Test 2 P. 11

A
1 client
2 devices
3 vast
4 numerous
5 ensure
6 monitored
7 agricultural
8 occasionally
9 primitive
10 vocabulary

Day 02

Daily Test 1 P. 13

A
1 influence
2 Domestic
3 trends
4 council
5 definitely
6 isolated
7 mere
8 density
9 regard
10 ecosystems

Daily Test 2 P. 15

A
1 motivation
2 philosophy
3 initial
4 permanent
5 solids
6 civilization
7 distinct
8 distribution
9 core
10 relevant

Review Test 01

Day 01 + Day 02 P. 16

A
1 experienced
2 definition
3 junk
4 intense
5 agricultural
6 influence
7 fiber
8 density
9 initial
10 civilization

B
1 즉각적
2 이전
3 의뢰인
4 수많은
5 극심한
6 이사회
7 단순한
8 동기
9 탄탄한
10 핵심

C
1 previous
2 permanent
3 domestic
4 initial
5 massive

D
1 d
2 a
3 b
4 e
5 c

E
1 majority
2 domestic
3 on the contrary
4 account
5 regard

해석
1. 그 지역 거주자들의 대다수가 Kevin에게 투표했다.
2. 서울에서 제주도까지 많은 국내선이 있다.
3. John은 이탈리아 음식을 좋아한다. 반대로, Eric은 프랑스 음식을 선호한다.
4. 당신은 어제 회의에 불참한 것에 대해 설명해야 한다.
5. 우리는 지금 상황을 두 번째 기회로 여겨야 한다.

F

1 consumption
2 annual
3 monitor
4 permanent
5 endangered

G

1 ⑤ capable
2 ② influence
3 ③ shift

해석

1. 때때로 아이들은 그들이 할 수 있는 것 이상을 원한다.
 1960년대에 오직 인간이 이성적인 생각을 할 수 있다는 것이 확립되었다.
2. 비버들은 자연 법칙에 따라 풍경을 바꿈으로써 그들의 영향력을 행사한다.
 인지에 영향을 주는 다른 요소는 문맥이다.
3. 사고 방식의 한가지 중요한 변화와 함께, 나의 태도 전반이 바뀌었다.
 작년과 달리, 올해는 대중의 의견에 약간의 변화가 있는 것처럼 보인다.

Day 03

Daily Test 1 P. 21

A

1 alerts
2 extraordinary
3 Isolation
4 estimated
5 welfare
6 accuracy
7 avalanches
8 Countless
9 tune
10 Fatigue

Daily Test 2 P. 23

A

1 relief
2 via
3 astronomy
4 circular
5 defend
6 interpret
7 contemporary
8 phase
9 predator
10 bias

Day 04

Daily Test 1 P. 25

A

1 dilemma
2 extensive
3 reference
4 cliffs
5 somewhat
6 component
7 diminish
8 assignments
9 confusion
10 eliminate

Daily Test 2 P. 27

A

1 Admission
2 sophisticated
3 trigger
4 certificate
5 innocent
6 passive
7 pottery
8 precise
9 prehistoric
10 matures

Review Test 02

Day 03 + Day 04 P. 28

A

1 alert
2 extraordinary
3 accuracy
4 grasp
5 phase
6 cliff
7 diminish
8 admission
9 certificate
10 prehistoric

B

1 추정
2 많은
3 해석하다
4 포식자들
5 확인하다
6 딜레마
7 혼란
8 제거하다
9 방아쇠
10 무고한

C

1 alert
2 prior
3 estimate
4 eliminate
5 innocent

D

1 b
2 e
3 c
4 a
5 d

E

1 subtle
2 Prior
3 somewhat
4 split
5 countless

해석

1. 나는 정확하게 그것들이 무엇인지 말할 순 없지만 그 두 그림 간에 미묘한 차이가 있다.
2. 집에 가기 전에 우리는 교실을 치워야 한다.
3. 난 이 시계의 가격이 다소 비싸다고 생각한다.
4. 우리는 사과가 하나만 있어서 나는 사과를 두 조각으로 나눴다.
5. 인간의 몸은 수많은 세포들로 이루어져있다.

F

1 temporary
2 sophisticated
3 abounds
4 extensive
5 contemporary

G

1 ④ relief
2 ① precise
3 ② enhance

해석

1. 남자와 다르게, 여자들은 자신들의 하루 동안 있었던 문제들에 대해 얘기함으로써 안도감을 찾고 싶어 한다.
경호원은 안도의 한숨을 쉬었다.
2. 특별한 비행기는 은하의 정확한 관찰을 위해 아주 성능이 좋은 망원경을 가지고 있다.
그 식당의 정확한 위치는 지도에서 찾을 수 있다.
3. 규칙적인 신문 읽기는 당신의 일반 상식을 강화시켜줄 수도 있다.
음악은 우리 감정에 작용한다. 예를 들어, 음악은 우리의 기분을 조성하거나 강화시킨다.

Day 05

Daily Test 1 P. 33

A

1 correlation
2 induce
3 substances
4 diversity
5 stable
6 bonds
7 Anthropologists
8 tuition
9 intent
10 circulation

Daily Test 2 P. 35

A

1 apparent
2 assist
3 era
4 abundant
5 adequate
6 draft
7 expedition
8 commerce
9 entry
10 earning

Day 06

Daily Test 1 P. 37

A

1 ambiguous
2 guilty
3 offspring
4 compensation
5 diabetes
6 medication
7 devastating
8 magnetic
9 bargain
10 genuine

Daily Test 2 P. 39

A

1 biodiversity
2 dominated
3 enterprise
4 expressive
5 ultimate
6 real estate
7 assistance
8 cereal
9 inefficient
10 equilibrium

Review Test 03

Day 05 + Day 06 P. 40

A

1 correlation
2 diversity
3 bond
4 apparent
5 draft
6 guilty

7 diabetes
8 bargain
9 expressive
10 assistance

B
1 유도하다
2 뚜렷한
3 쉽게
4 탐험
5 가입
6 후손
7 파괴적인
8 천식
9 생물의 다양성
10 수평

C
1 stable
2 prominent
3 bond
4 adequate
4 abundant

D
1 b
2 c
3 a
4 e
5 d

E
1 stable
2 dislike
3 sake
4 substituted
5 prominent

해석

1. 우리는 과일과 곡식을 자라게 하기 위해 안정적인 물의 공급이 필요합니다.
2. 그는 다른 사람들의 얘기를 듣지 않는다. 그것이 내가 그를 싫어하는 이유이다.
3. Justin은 그의 건강을 위해서 식습관을 바꿨다.
4. 그 미식 축구 매니저는 부상당한 선수를 신참 선수와 교체시켰다.
5. 유명한 정치인과 예술가를 포함해서 많은 저명한 사람들이 그 회의에 참석했다.

F
1 abundant
2 enthusiastic
3 adequate
4 dominate
5 circulation

G
1 ② stunned
2 ④ ultimate
3 ⑤ evaluate

해석

1. 비탄으로 망연자실해서 그는 울었다. 엄마는 그의 무례한 태도에 망연자실 했다.
2. 서투른 의사소통이 당신 아이디어의 궁극적인 성공을 망치지 않게 하세요. 궁극적인 힘은 당신이 원하는 대로 사람들이 하게끔 만드는 힘이다.
3. 교사 위원회는 각각의 참가자들을 평가할 것이고 우승자를 결정할 것이다. 나는 사람들의 외모나 소유물로 그들을 평가하지 않는다.

Day 07

Daily Test 1 P. 45

A
1 indifferent
2 wages
3 federal
4 transported
5 hardship
6 intake
7 modest
8 inexpensive
9 intermediate
10 favorable

Daily Test 2 P. 47

A
1 expansion
2 column
3 curriculum
4 flesh
5 exceed
6 wilderness
7 breakthrough
8 foraged
9 substantial
10 overnight

Day 08

Daily Test 1 P. 49

A
1 inappropriate
2 accustomed
3 domain
4 update
5 exclusive
6 sacrifice
7 contagious
8 immense
9 defensive
10 Potters

Daily Test 2 P. 51

A
1 retail
2 latitude

3 amateur's
4 pests
5 Antibiotics
6 volcanic
7 solely
8 controversy
9 assembly
10 distress

Review Test 04

Day 07 + Day 08 P. 52

A
1 indifferent
2 hardship
3 input
4 usage
5 substantial
6 rank
7 dawn
8 exclusive
9 retail
10 antibiotic

B
1 임금
2 섭취
3 중립
4 교육과정
5 찾다
6 희생하다
7 방어용
8 방패
9 위도
10 오두막

C
1 update
2 controversy
3 hardship
4 forage
5 ridiculous

D
1 a
2 e
3 b
4 d
5 c

E
1 intake
2 urgent
3 update
4 inappropriate
5 accustomed

해석
1. 균형 잡힌 영양 섭취량을 유지하는 것은 당신의 건강에 필수적이다.
2. 우리는 시간이 많이 없어요. 가장 급한 일을 먼저 합시다.
3. 나는 오늘 밤에 컴퓨터 시스템을 최신 버전으로 업데이트 할 거에요.
4. 이 영화에 폭력적인 장면이 많기 때문에 아이들에게 부적절하다.
5. 너는 곧 새로운 학급 친구들과 공부하는 데 익숙해 질 것이다.

F
1 contagious
2 precipitation
3 identification
4 breakthrough
5 controversy

G
1 ③ urgent
2 ② exceed
3 ① distress

해석
1. 급한 용무가 Justin이 그 회의에 참석하지 못하게 만들었다.
나는 내 목표에 근접하기 위한 변화가 절실함을 느끼기 시작했다.
2. 당신의 이미지 파일의 크기는 100 megabyte를 초과해서는 안 됩니다.
놀랍게도, 그 결과는 내 기대를 상회했다.
3. 우리가 건전한 한계를 설정하지 못할 때, 괴로움은 우리 관계에 나타날 수 있다.
그 마을 사람들은 최근의 태풍 피해 때문에 고통에 빠졌다.

Day 09

Daily Test 1 P. 57

A
1 facilitate
2 ignorance
3 traced
4 impatient
5 reception
6 subsequent
7 circumstance
8 vigorous
9 transmit
10 exceptional

Daily Test 2 P. 59

A
1 Globalization
2 voluntary
3 reinforce
4 humiliated
5 farewell
6 equator
7 recite
8 flock
9 chaos
10 worthwhile

Day 10

Daily Test 1 P. 61

A
1 deeds
2 sensation
3 checkups
4 biography
5 stung
6 sewage
7 nursery
8 brochure
9 ongoing
10 criminals

Daily Test 2 P. 63

A
1 proceed
2 exploit
3 intuitive
4 blade
5 occupying
6 transition
7 outbreak
8 barns
9 notable
10 disturbing

Review Test 05

Day 09 + Day 10 P. 64

A
1 ignorance
2 hemisphere
3 symbolic
4 voluntary
5 humiliate
6 negotiate
7 magnitude
8 exploit
9 intuitive
10 transition

B
1 촉진시키다
2 동등한
3 감사
4 송별회
5 혼란
6 행동
7 하수
8 습지대
9 날
10 충격적인

C
1 ongoing
2 transmit
3 sting
4 occupy
5 deed

D
1 c
2 a
3 d
4 b
5 e

E
1 ongoing
2 reception
3 subsequent
4 flock
5 trace

해석
1. 그 사건에 대한 조사는 여전히 진행 중이다.
2. 결혼식 피로연은 Olympia Bar and Grill에서 열릴 거에요.
3. 남아있는 이슈들은 다음 회의에서 토론 될 것입니다.
4. 한 떼의 새들이 산 너머로 날아가는 중이다.
5. 손님들은 흔적 없이 그 집을 떠났다.

F
1 reinforced
2 abuse
3 comprehension
4 outbreak
5 sting

G
1 ② transmit
2 ① dumped
3 ③ exceptional

해석
1. 지난 수업에서, 우리는 특정한 질병을 옮길 수 있는 곤충에 대해 배웠다.
내 딸은 어떻게 발전소가 우리 집으로 전기를 전달하는지 궁금해 하고 있다.
2. 약 20억 톤의 과일과 채소가 전 세계에서 매년 버려진다.
그들은 쓰레기 매립지에 버려진 낡은 신발들을 재활용한다.
3. 대개, 뛰어난 성취는 각고의 노력으로 귀결된다.
그 투수는 그의 뛰어난 커브 볼로 유명했다.

Day 11

Daily Test 1 P. 69

A
1 outfit
2 mentor
3 optimal
4 diameter
5 dignity

6 longevity
7 minimal
8 imperfect
9 exerts
10 irrigation

Daily Test 2 P. 71

A
1 dietary
2 nasty
3 equality
4 disguise
5 keen
6 hierarchical
7 donors
8 insufficient
9 converted
10 renowned

Day 12

Daily Test 1 P. 73

A
1 pedestrian
2 reservoirs
3 absurd
4 outraged
5 swayed
6 loomed
7 contradicted
8 supervised
9 aesthetic
10 activate

Daily Test 2 P. 75

A
1 advocates
2 sustainable
3 cosmetic
4 plentiful
5 tense
6 regulations
7 synthetic
8 spiritual
9 legacy
10 sorrow

Review Test 06

Day 11 + Day 12 P. 76

A
1 outfit
2 elastic
3 longevity
4 foster
5 cube
6 pedestrian
7 absurd
8 aesthetic
9 cosmetic
10 synthetic

B
1 최적
2 불충분한
3 암시하다
4 식사
5 성급한
6 축적
7 격분
8 부정하다
9 정신적
10 유산

C
1 sustainable
2 trivial
3 disguise
4 contradict
5 mentor

D
1 a
2 e
3 c
4 b
5 d

E
1 decisive
2 impractical
3 minimal
4 tense
5 plentiful

해석

1. 우리는 현재의 어려움을 극복하기 위해 단호한 조치를 취했다.
2. 이 차가 좋아 보임에도 불구하고, 이것은 실제 생활에서는 비실용적이다.
3. 우리 예산이 빠듯했기 때문에, 최소한의 금액으로 여행을 해야 한다.
4. Gerald는 그 회의의 긴장감 있는 분위기를 완화시키려 노력했다.
5. 대부분의 식물은 풍부한 햇빛 없이는 살 수 없다.

F
1 irrigation
2 sustainable
3 regulations
4 converted
5 advent

G
1 ② keen
2 ④ competent
3 ④ illustrate

해석

1. Adrian이 항상 아버지의 충고를 받아

들이기를 원한 것은 아니었다.
그의 어린 시절부터 Alvin은 날카로운 모형 제작자였다.

2. Brian은 능숙한 일꾼이고 그의 일을 매우 잘 해내왔다.
수 년의 연습 후에, 그는 지금 대중 앞에서 말하는 것에 자신감을 느낀다.

3. 그의 새 소설에서, 작가는 신뢰가 얼마나 허약해질 수 있는지 설명하기를 원한다.
현실을 따라 하는 대신에, 일부 화가들은 그들의 예술 안에서 사회적 상황을 그려내길 원한다.

Day 13

Daily Test 1 P. 81

A
1 lottery
2 punched
3 Persuasion
4 fertile
5 manipulate
6 layouts
7 incorporated
8 intact
9 evergreen
10 inborn

Daily Test 2 P. 83

A
1 manuscript
2 discrimination
3 microscope
4 Radioactive
5 assured
6 rejected
7 optimism
8 presumably
9 unwilling
10 spacious

Day 14

Daily Test 1 P. 85

A
1 dual
2 cherished
3 furious
4 mourned
5 boundary
6 withstand
7 abrupt
8 timber
9 weeds
10 undergo

Daily Test 2 P. 87

A
1 faraway
2 competitor
3 decay
4 stubborn
5 starvation
6 extracted
7 epidemic
8 coordination
9 amnesia
10 longitude

Review Test 07

Day 13 + Day 14 P. 88

A
1 metropolitan
2 fertile
3 manuscript
4 responsive
5 rotation
6 furious
7 deceased
8 timber
9 ecology
10 starvation

B
1 복권
2 배치
3 온전히
4 차별
5 순전한
6 이중
7 자발적인
8 잡초
9 썩고 있는
10 조종하다

C
1 fertile
2 revive
3 epidemic
4 abrupt
5 withstand

D
1 b
2 a
3 c
4 e
5 d

E
1 revived
2 stubborn
3 extract
4 duration
5 lessen

해석
1. 그 유명한 노래는 다음 세대에 의해 다시 제작되었다.
2. 그가 매우 완강하기 때문에 쉽게 설득당하지 않을 거에요.
3. 이 기계는 오렌지에서 주스를 추출하는 것을 도와준다.

4. 그 기념식의 소요시간은 약 2시간 정도 일 거에요.
5. 우리는 낭비되는 종이의 양을 줄이려고 노력하는 중이다.

F
1 rejected
2 manipulate
3 epidemics
4 suppress
5 Cherish

G
1 ① thrive
2 ② assure
3 ⑤ undergo

해석
1. 이 연못 물 속에서, 작은 유기체들은 잘 자란다.
자작나무는 스웨덴과 러시아와 같이 추운 나라에서 잘 자라는 나무다.
2. Nasrudin은 그가 더 이상 실수를 하지 않겠다고 그에게 장담했다.
위원회는 우리에게 동등한 기회를 장담했다.
3. 자동차 산업은 현재 위대한 기술적 발전을 겪고 있는 중이다.
그 의사는 내 아버지께 그가 무릎 수술을 받아야 한다고 말했다.

Day 15

Daily Test 1 P. 93

A
1 prompts
2 hostile
3 restless
4 relevance
5 regain
6 malnutrition
7 parasite
8 retreat
9 leopards
10 inadequate

Daily Test 2 P. 95

A
1 intuition
2 gorgeous
3 assert
4 outlook
5 penetrate
6 irrational
7 mammal
8 implemented
9 surgeon
10 compromise

Day 16

Daily Test 1 P. 97

A
1 egocentric
2 agony
3 swarming
4 choke
5 Textiles
6 warriors
7 womb
8 cuddle
9 texture
10 tenant

Daily Test 2 P. 99

A
1 ultraviolet
2 burial
3 abolish
4 adhere
5 Compulsive
6 beforehand
7 childish
8 collaborate
9 intersection
10 dim

Review Test 08

Day 15 + Day 16 P. 100

A
1 hostile
2 malnutrition
3 retreat
4 intuition
5 irrational
6 egocentric
7 textiles
8 cuddle
9 burial
10 affirmative

B
1 가만히 못 있는
2 기하학
3 부도덕한
4 포유동물
5 녹
6 떼
7 무인
8 질식해
9 고수하다
10 유치한

C
1 abolish
2 probe
3 consent
4 hostile
5 prompt

D

1 b
2 d
3 a
4 e
5 c

E

1 penetrated
2 outlook
3 abolished
4 relevance
5 beforehand

해석

1. 밝은 햇살이 어두운 방 안을 뚫고 들어왔다.
2. 컴퓨터 제조업자들은 내년에 대해 긍정적인 전망을 갖고 있다.
3. 오래되고 불공정한 규제들이 마침내 폐지되었다.
4. 네 에세이는 오늘 수업의 주제와 거의 관련이 없구나.
5. 만약 당신이 그 회의에 참여하고 싶다면, 그 전에 우리에게 연락하세요.

F

1 infinite
2 parasite
3 probe
4 compromising
5 intersection

G

1 ⑤ anticipate
2 ① regain
3 ② suspend

해석

1. 그는 아무도 예상하지 않았던 도전을 마주했다.
우리는 소풍 날에 그런 나쁜 날씨는 기대하지 않았어요.
2. 대개의 경우 고객들을 잃기는 쉽지만 다시 얻는 것은 힘들다.
그는 자신감을 되찾았고 새로운 친구들을 많이 사귀었다.
3. 우리는 겨울 동안 이 수업들을 중단해야만 했다.
두 선수는 팀 규칙을 어겼기 때문에 팀에서부터 출전 정지를 당했다.

Day 17

Daily Test 1 P. 105

A

1 prism
2 prestigious
3 dilute
4 episode
5 injured
6 evoke
7 diagnosis
8 dummy's
9 nurture
10 implication

Daily Test 2 P. 107

A

1 erodes
2 hinder
3 dreaded
4 enriched
5 intellect
6 discern
7 racism
8 imposed
9 atomic
10 pleading

Day 18

Daily Test 1 P. 109

A

1 shiver
2 artifacts
3 armor
4 Simplifying
5 upcoming
6 strands
7 sprout
8 obliged
9 soothe
10 tolerate

Daily Test 2 P. 111

A

1 transplant
2 particles
3 successive
4 superb
5 Soaring
6 shrines
7 Yeast
8 vanished
9 radical
10 humanitarian

Review Test 09

Day 17 + Day 18 P. 112

A

1 prestigious
2 evoke
3 conservative
4 ambition
5 racism
6 hinge

7 sprout
8 acupuncture
9 particle
10 shrine

B
1 희석된
2 할당하다
3 키우다
4 지적 능력
5 품위 있는
6 갑옷
7 진정시키다
8 날아오르다
9 자제하다
10 왜곡하다

C
1 prestigious
2 luxurious
3 bankrupt
4 dichotomy
5 discern

D
1 c
2 a
3 e
4 d
5 b

E
1 diploma
2 dread
3 pleaded
4 radical
5 shivering

해석

1. 내년에 Cindy는 대학을 졸업해서 학위를 받을 예정이다.
2. 내 딸들은 치과에 가는 것을 두려워한다.
3. 그 소년은 동물원에 데려다 달라고 아버지께 애원했다.
4. 우리가 필요한 것은 급진적 변화가 아니라 점차적인 변화이다.
5. 그녀는 찬 바람 때문에 떨고 있었다.

F
1 upcoming
2 tolerate
3 superb
4 impose
5 soothe

G
1 ② injure
2 ④ simplify
3 ④ successive

해석

1. 나는 너무 부상이 너무 심해서 수영을 할수도 수면 위로 나오지 못했다.
어떤 경우에는, 애완동물이 야생동물에 의해 부상을 당하거나 죽임을 당한다.
2. 나는 사람들을 관리하는 일을 단순화 시키기 위해 이 일을 시작했다.
연구에 의하면 우리가 우리의 가장 잘 부합하는 방식으로 현실을 단순화 시킬 필요가 있다는 것을 보여준다.
3. 우리는 어떤 경험을 연속적으로 할 때, 빠르게 이에 적응하기 시작한다
그의 고된 연습은 그가 3년 연속 세계 체스 챔피언이 되게 했다.

Day 19

Daily Test 1 P. 117

A
1 flames
2 glaciers
3 Epics
4 inhabit
5 diaper
6 graze
7 Indigenous
8 eternal
9 coarse
10 doses

Daily Test 2 P. 119

A
1 copyright
2 cuisine
3 evaporate
4 inhabit
5 congestion
6 handshakes
7 fleeing
8 connectivity
9 lump
10 overhear

Day 20

Daily Test 1 P. 121

A
1 pavement
2 multitask
3 renew
4 provision
5 prescribe
6 livelihood
7 mortgage
8 primate
9 remedy
10 precaution

Daily Test 2 P. 123

A
1 inquiry
2 radiated

3 irresponsible
4 mutations
5 irritates
6 pledged
7 quoted
8 linguistic
9 qualified
10 clusters

Review Test 10

Day 19 + Day 20 P. 124

A
1 bureaucracy
2 diaper
3 chronic
4 discard
5 flee
6 pavement
7 pessimistic
8 prescribe
9 overloaded
10 omission

B
1 서사시
2 영원한
3 밀착하다
4 거주하다
5 시체
6 앞서다
7 담보
8 경계
9 순진한
10 약속하다

C
1 evaporate
2 clarify
3 lump
4 decent
5 flee

D
1 e
2 b
3 d
4 c
5 a

E
1 overheard
2 irritated
3 indigenous
4 congestion
5 murmured

해석
1. 그 소년은 그의 학업에 대해 부모님이 말하는 것을 엿들었다.
2. Craig는 그의 어린 남동생이 끝없이 질문을 하는 것에 짜증이 났다.
3. 연구원들은 아마존 우림의 고유한 문화에 대해 조사했다.
4. 우리는 심각한 교통 체증 때문에 늦었다.
5. 그 남자는 무언가 중얼거렸지만, 우리는 이해할 수 없었다.

F
1 livelihoods
2 primates
3 quote
4 radiate
5 linguistic

G
1 ⑤ qualified
2 ② inquiry
3 ④ remedy

해석
1. 잡지 'Times'는 자격을 갖춘 학생 기자를 찾는 중입니다.
가장 힘든 부분은 자질이 있는 연구원을 찾는 것이었어요. 당신은 누구라도 찾았나요?
2. 그럼에도 불구하고, 과학적 조사는 대개 일련의 논리적 단계를 수반하지 않는다.
연구원들은 새로운 감염성 질병의 원인에 대해 조사를 착수했다.
3. 당신의 등 통증에 얼음을 사용하는 것은 단지 일시적 치료법입니다. 당신은 병원에 가는 게 좋을 거예요.
규칙적이고 가벼운 운동은 당신의 수면 문제에 있어 훌륭한 자연 치유법일 거예요.

Day 21

Daily Test 1 P. 129

A
1 panels
2 envision
3 dine
4 deception
5 tame
6 swamp
7 viewpoints
8 stabilize
9 awaiting
10 simultaneously

Daily Test 2 P. 131

A
1 uncover
2 vapor
3 footprints
4 surpassing
5 repetitive
6 vacant
7 superficial
8 weave
9 supplements
10 Clutching

Day 22

Daily Test 1 P. 133

A

1 blisters
2 counterparts
3 contend
4 Appliance
5 auction
6 bless
7 conceals
8 baggage
9 continual
10 attic

Daily Test 2 P. 135

A

1 aristocracy
2 carbohydrates
3 corruption
4 bruise
5 contemplate
6 blurred
7 confronted
8 comprise
9 broaden
10 condense

Review Test 11

Day 21 + Day 22 P. 136

A

1 panels
2 accommodation
3 await
4 vapor
5 vacant
6 blisters
7 appliance
8 baggage
9 categorize
10 bribe

B

1 속임수
2 안정시키다
3 발자국
4 열망
5 엮다
6 부정적인
7 사과의
8 청사진
9 타박상을 입은
10 넓히다

C

1 envision
2 simultaneously
3 conceal
4 swamp
5 vacant

D

1 d
2 b
3 e
4 a
5 c

E

1 stabilize
2 amended
3 compelled
4 ventilate
5 ample

해석

1. 정부는 통화를 안정화 하기 위해 노력했다.
2. 개인의 사생활 보호법은 몇 차례 수정되었다.
3. 내 의지와 반대로, 나는 그 전체 과정을 다시 수행하도록 강요 받았다.
4. Sue는 그녀의 차를 환기 시키기 위해 창문을 돌려 내렸다.
5. 서두를 필요 없어요. 우리는 회의를 준비하기 위한 많은 시간이 있습니다.

F

1 dimensions
2 comprised
3 concealed
4 contemplating
5 simultaneously

G

1 ① surpass
2 ② astonish
3 ⑤ uncover

해석

1. 이는 28년간 뛰어넘지 못한 엄청난 기록이었다.
그 호텔의 훌륭한 시설과 분위기는 우리의 기대를 뛰어넘었다.
2. 깜짝 놀란 대표는 놀라서 그곳에 서 있었다.
우리는 모두 그 소년의 놀라운 암기력을 보고 놀랐다.
3. 석기, 동물의 뼈, 화살촉과 다른 공예품은 그 마을에서 발견되었다.
과학의 정수는 정확한 정보 분석을 기반으로 한 자연의 유형과 규칙성을 발견한다.

Day 23

Daily Test 1 P. 141

A

1 idiom
2 eradicate
3 frail 4 furnished

5 fortress
6 hospitality
7 drastic
8 inflated
9 crave
10 empowered

Daily Test 2 P. 143

A
1 deplete
2 fermentation
3 dictates
4 enclosing
5 futile
6 counterproductive
7 dip
8 harnesses
9 cozy
10 locomotive

Day 24

Daily Test 1 P. 145

A
1 reformed
2 indulge
3 itches
4 provoked
5 protests
6 sin
7 refugees
8 omit
9 patron
10 refinement

Daily Test 2 P. 147

A
1 proficient
2 persevered
3 originated
4 integrated
5 shave
6 mocking
7 pondered
8 dispute
9 inject
10 prosperous

Review Test 12

Day 23 + Day 24 P. 148

A
1 idioms
2 fortress
3 fermentation
4 divine
5 cozy
6 reform
7 provoke
8 refugee
9 shaving
10 mock

B
1 퇴치하다
2 미성숙한
3 갈망하다
4 내쉬다
5 받아쓰게 하다
6 가려운
7 산문
8 소수
9 심사 숙고하다
10 주사하다

C
1 protest
2 eradicate
3 exhale
4 seize
5 reform

D
1 b
2 a
3 d
4 e
5 c

E
1 improper
2 eligible
3 furnished
4 drastic
5 proficient

해석

1. 그 보고서의 가장 심각한 문제는 통계적 정보의 부적절한 사용이다.
2. 우리는 Randy가 학생 회장이 될 자격이 있다고 생각한다.
3. 그 집은 고풍스러운 소파와 탁자가 구비되어 있었다.
4. 지방 정부는 불필요한 지출을 줄이기 위한 극적 조치들을 취하는 중이다.
5. 이 학교의 지원자들은 3개 국어 이상에 능숙해야 한다.

F
1 integrate
2 originated
3 dispense
4 futile
5 harness

G

1 ② immature
2 ④ refinement
3 ③ protest

해석

1. 내가 어렸을 때, 내가 경험 했던 유일한 사랑은 미성숙하고, 이기적인 사랑이었다. 나는 해로운 결과들을 가져오는 미숙한 판단의 가능성들을 제한 하기 위한 좀 더 엄격한 법안을 강하게 주장한다.
2. 과학적 이론은 재정의와 개선의 과정을 겪으면서 발전한다. 기름의 원래 형태는 그것이 차와 기계에 사용되기 전에 몇 차례의 정재 과정을 거쳐야 한다.
3. 나는 우리가 틀린 것에 반해 항의하지 말아야 한다는 것은 아니다. 많은 사람들이 자동차에 대한 부과세에 반대하여 항의했다.

Day 25

Daily Test 1 P. 153

A

1 thrusting
2 statesman
3 beams
4 tempts
5 wipe
6 stance
7 wicked
8 submerged
9 skull
10 landslides

Daily Test 2 P. 155

A

1 eluded
2 utmost
3 surrender
4 adolescents
5 subscribed
6 brand-new
7 weeping
8 accused
9 veteran
10 devastated

Day 26

Daily Test 1 P. 157

A

1 commemorate
2 delegate
3 confessed
4 Archeology
5 darts
6 cognition
7 blush
8 confidential
9 betrayed
10 Comply

Daily Test 2 P. 159

A

1 barometer
2 consecutive
3 chattering
4 anonymous
5 cripple
6 cemetery
7 deepen
8 brisk
9 creek
10 constraints

Review Test 13

Day 25 + Day 26 P. 160

A

1 surgical
2 wipe
3 broker
4 exclaimed
5 weep
6 cognition
7 archeology
8 blush
9 anonymous
10 brisk

B

1 자존심
2 두개골
3 항복하다
4 옷
5 일 중독자
6 불러일으키다
7 화살
8 수다
9 깊게 하다
10 결정적

C

1 brisk
2 surrender
3 anonymous
4 subscribe
5 submerge

D

1 c
2 e
3 d
4 b
5 a

E

1 terminated
2 subscribing
3 confidential
4 afflicted
5 abnormal

해석

1. 그 야구팀은 결국 그 선수와 계약을 끝냈다.
2. 그는 많은 스포츠 잡지를 구독하는 중이다.
3. 이 정보는 매우 중요하다. 그래서 이것은 비밀로 유지되어야 한다.
4. 이 학교의 많은 아이들은 감염성 질병에 시달리고 있다.
5. 그의 개는 비정상적인 행동을 보이기 시작했다.

F

1 tribute
2 enlightened
3 constraint
4 alleviate
5 devastated

G

1 ① accuse
2 ③ confess
3 ⑤ tempt

해석

1. 그 남자는 쇼핑객들로부터 돈을 훔쳐서 기소 당했다.
배심원은 기소된 사람이 유죄인지 아닌지 결정한다.
2. 그 소년들은 자신들이 교실 창문을 깼다고 고백했다.
그는 부모님께 자신의 비행들을 고백하고 사과했다.
3. 우리는 종종 다른 것들을 생각함으로써 듣고 있는 것을 방해하려는 유혹에 시달린다.
Jamie의 친구들은 그에게 바이올린 수업을 빠지고 대신 영화를 보러 가자고 꼬드겼다.

Day 27

Daily Test 1

P. 165

A

1 flaws
2 drip
3 hectic
4 insane
5 elevate
6 insulation
7 inherit
8 dozed
9 linger
10 fragrances

Daily Test 2

P. 167

A

1 inconsistent
2 Glittering
3 inhale
4 frontiers
5 diagnosed
6 fling
7 flourish
8 flushed
9 homesick
10 spectators

Day 28

Daily Test 1

P. 169

A

1 plunge
2 recruits
3 purify
4 intervals
5 scorn
6 acoustic
7 nominates
8 fragments
9 accelerates
10 swell

Daily Test 2

P. 171

A

1 populate
2 segregation
3 manifest
4 painkiller
5 recurred
6 resided
7 roaring
8 refraction
9 schemes
10 surpluses

Review Test 14

Day 27 + Day 28

P. 172

A

1 fruitless
2 capitalize
3 glitter
4 intervene
5 foremost
6 prevailing
7 scorn
8 painkiller
9 sphere
10 surplus

B

1 미치다
2 졸다

3 향기
4 위생학
5 빨개지다
6 죽다
7 한도
8 부풀기
9 연체된
10 살다

C
1 plausible
2 reside
3 flourish
4 recur
5 flaw

D
1 b
2 d
3 e
4 c
5 a

E
1 lured
2 diplomatic
3 recruiting
4 inconsistent
5 hectic

해석

1. 많은 사람들이 좋은 직업과 날씨에 마음이 끌려 그 도시로 이사했다.
2. 그 두 나라는 공식적인 외교 관계를 구축하는 데 동의했다.
3. 그 회사는 경력직 소프트웨어 개발자를 모집하는 중이다.
4. Greg의 일관성 없는 진술은 사람들이 그의 진짜 의도를 의심하게 했다.
5. Lisa는 현재 엄청난 양의 업무량 때문에 빡빡한 하루를 보냈다.

F
1 diagnosed
2 plunged
3 manifested
4 accelerated
5 compiled

G
1 ② inherit
2 ① interval
3 ⑤ nominate

해석

1. 뇌 연구가들은 우리의 지능 중 일부는 사실 유전적으로 물려받는 것임을 보여줬다.
새로운 왕은 고작 19살의 나이로 왕위를 물려 받았다.
2. 새로운 단어를 학습하는 최선의 방법은 다양한 간격으로 단어를 반복하는 것이다.
그 기자는 최신 정보를 유지하기 위해 규칙적인 간격으로 웹사이트를 확인했다.
3. 그 시상식의 참여자 각각은 그들의 담임 선생님에 의해 추천을 받아야 한다.
오직 동아리 멤버들만이 동아리 회장 후보를 추천할 수 있다.

Day 29

Daily Test 1 P. 177

A
1 triumphs
2 tyrant
3 byproduct
4 refuted
5 vomiting
6 magnifying
7 obstructed
8 chicks
9 authorized
10 designated

Daily Test 2 P. 179

A
1 versatile
2 inclined
3 startled
4 receding
5 fed up with
6 unified
7 pillars
8 enlisted
9 unanimous
10 pirates

Day 30

Daily Test 1 P. 181

A
1 tortured
2 dismayed
3 Astronomical
4 undertake
5 in terms of
6 vow
7 anecdote
8 patriotic
9 fumes
10 procession

Daily Test 2 P. 183

A
1 groaned
2 censorship
3 trimming
4 account

5 standardized
6 dictator
7 majestic
8 overtook
9 tactics
10 unscrupulous

Review Test 15

Day 29 + Day 30 P. 184

A
1 tyrant
2 splinter
3 magnify
4 startled
5 enlist
6 torture
7 procession
8 vow
9 groaning
10 subdue

B
1 경이로운
2 토하다
3 불변의
4 기울다
5 기둥
6 떠맡다
7 포로
8 표준화하다
9 독재자
10 부도덕한

C
1 unanimous
2 patriotic
3 overtake
4 unscrupulous
5 anecdote

D
1 a
2 d
3 c
4 e
5 b

E
1 fed
2 entitled
3 authorized
4 ignited
5 expire

해석

1. 나는 그의 무례하고 부주의한 행동에 질렸다.
2. 그는 올해의 노래자랑 우승자가 될 자격이 충분히 있다.
3. 보건부는 신약의 수입을 허가했다.
4. 그 정치인의 최근 인터뷰는 이민에 대한 새로운 토론의 불씨를 붙였다.
5. Bill, 우리는 우리의 자동차 보험을 갱신해야 해요. 그것은 다음달에 만료될 거에요.

F
1 trimmed
2 receding
3 undertake
4 versatile
5 refute

G
1 ③ account
2 ② nonverbal
3 ① circulate

해석

1. 제 계좌에서 돈을 인출하고 싶어요. 만약 해외로 돈을 보낸다면, 여기에 계좌 번호를 적으세요.
2. 손동작은 비언어적 의사소통의 수단으로 사용된다. 표정은 비언어적 메시지의 가장 중요한 형태이다.
3. 혈액은 산소를 생산하면서 사람의 몸을 순환한다. 냉장고는 찬 공기가 쉽게 순환 할 때 더 잘 작동한다.

WORD MAX 5 5300

Workbook

WorldCom Edu

Workbook

WORD MAX 5 5300

WorldCom Edu

Workbook

Day 01

| 월 일 |

영어 단어에 해당하는 한국어 뜻을 함께 적으세요.

consumption	소비(량)	consumption	소비(량)
experienced	경력이 있는, 능숙한		
immediate	즉각적인, 직접적인		
remains	유적, 유해		
majority	대다수, 과반수		
previous	이전의, 앞선		
alternative	대안; 대체의		
definition	정의		
determined	단호한, 결심한		
annual	연간의		
context	문맥, 맥락, 전후사정		
shift	이동하다; 이동		
contrary	반대되는		
evolution	진화		
besides	~외에도, 게다가		
junk	쓰레기, 쓸모없는 물건		
client	의뢰인, 고객		
device	장치, 기기		
vast	광대한, 방대한		
numerous	수많은		
ensure	보장하다, 반드시 ~하게 하다		
monitor	감시하다, 관찰하다		
intense	격렬한, 극심한		
fellow	동료		
agricultural	농업의, 농사의		
massive	엄청난, 거대한, 극심한		
interact	소통하다, 상호작용하다		
occasionally	가끔		
primitive	원시의, 초기의		
vocabulary	어휘, 용어		

다음 단어에 해당하는 영어 단어 또는 우리말을 쓰세요.

O____개 X____개

영어	한국어
consumption	
agricultural	
alternative	
annual	
besides	
client	
context	
contrary	
definition	
determined	
device	
ensure	
evolution	
experienced	
fellow	
immediate	
intense	
interact	
junk	
majority	
massive	
monitor	
numerous	
occasionally	
previous	
primitive	
remains	
shift	
vast	
vocabulary	

한국어	영어
형 광대한, 방대한	
명 소비(량)	
형 원시의, 초기의	
명 쓰레기, 쓸모없는 물건	
명 장치, 기기	
명 의뢰인, 고객	
형 즉각적인, 직접적인	
명 어휘, 용어	
형 수많은	
형 경력이 있는, 능숙한	
부 가끔	
동 보장하다, 반드시 ~하게 하다	
명 유적, 유해	
형 격렬한, 극심한	
동 감시하다, 관찰하다	
명 대다수, 과반수	
형 이전의, 앞선	
명 정의	
명 동료	
명 대안 형 대체의	
동 이동하다 명 이동	
명 문맥, 맥락, 전후사정	
부 ~외에도, 게다가	
형 단호한, 결심한	
형 연간의	
형 농업의, 농사의	
형 엄청난, 거대한, 극심한	
형 반대되는	
명 진화	
동 소통하다, 상호작용하다	

Workbook

Day 02

| 월 일 |

영어 단어에 해당하는 한국어 뜻을 함께 적으세요.

account for	차지하다, 설명하다	account for	차지하다, 설명하다
capable	유능한, ~할 수 있는		
influence	영향; 영향을 미치다		
domestic	국내의, 가정 내의		
trend	추세, 경향		
council	의회, 이사회, 협의회		
definitely	분명히, 틀림없이		
endangered	멸종 위기에 처한, 위험에 처한		
fiber	섬유(질)		
isolated	고립된, 외딴, 격리된		
mere	단순한, (한낱) ~에 불과한		
density	밀도, 농도		
regard	~으로 여기다, 간주하다		
burden	짐, 부담		
ecosystem	생태계		
motivation	자극, 유도, 동기(부여)		
executive	(기업, 조직의) 경영 간부 (이사, 중역)		
philosophy	철학, 인생관		
strict	엄격한, 엄밀한		
initial	처음의, 초기의		
observation	관찰, 관측		
permanent	영구적인, 종신의		
solid	고체; 고체의, 단단한		
civilization	문명, 문명사회		
distinct	뚜렷한, 분명한, 별개의		
distribution	분배, 분포, 배급		
core	핵심, 핵		
protein	단백질		
refrigerator	냉장고		
relevant	관련 있는		

다음 단어에 해당하는 영어 단어 또는 우리말을 쓰세요. ○____개 ×____개

영어	한국어
account for	
burden	
capable	
civilization	
core	
council	
definitely	
density	
distinct	
distribution	
domestic	
ecosystem	
endangered	
executive	
fiber	
influence	
initial	
isolated	
mere	
motivation	
observation	
permanent	
philosophy	
protein	
refrigerator	
regard	
relevant	
solid	
strict	
trend	

한국어	영어
명 자극, 유도, 동기(부여)	
형 뚜렷한, 분명한, 별개의	
명 (기업, 조직의) 경영 간부 (이사, 중역)	
형 유능한, ~할 수 있는	
명 철학, 인생관	
명 영향 동 영향을 미치다	
명 문명, 문명사회	
형 영구적인, 종신의	
형 엄격한, 엄밀한	
형 국내의, 가정 내의	
명 관찰, 관측	
명 고체 형 고체의, 단단한	
형 처음의, 초기의	
동 차지하다, 설명하다	
명 생태계	
명 의회, 이사회, 협의회	
명 분배, 분포, 배급	
명 추세, 경향	
명 핵심, 핵	
명 섬유(질)	
명 짐, 부담	
부 분명히, 틀림없이	
명 단백질	
형 고립된, 외딴, 격리된	
형 멸종 위기에 처한, 위험에 처한 명 섬유(질)	
명 냉장고	
명 밀도, 농도	
형 단순한, (한낱) ~에 불과한	
형 관련 있는	
동 ~으로 여기다, 간주하다	

Day 03

| 월 일 |

영어 단어에 해당하는 한국어 뜻을 함께 적으세요.

alert	경계하는; 알리다	alert	빈틈 없는; 알리다
extraordinary	뛰어난, 비상한, 기이한		
isolation	고립, 분리, 격리		
prior	이전의, 사전의		
subtle	미묘한		
temporary	일시적인, 임시의		
estimate	추정(치), 견적; 추산하다		
welfare	복지, 후생		
accuracy	정확도, 정확		
avalanche	눈사태		
countless	무수한, 수많은		
debt	빚, 부채		
excess	지나침, 초과		
tune	곡조; 조율하다		
fatigue	피로, 피곤		
statistics	통계(학)		
relief	안도, 경감, 구호품, 위안		
via	~을 경유하여, 거쳐		
astronomy	천문학		
circular	원형의, 순환적인		
defend	방어하다, 지키다, 변호하다		
enhance	~을 높이다, 향상시키다		
grasp	꽉 잡다, 이해하다		
interpret	해석하다		
contemporary	현대의, 동시대의		
phase	단계		
predator	포식자, 천적		
confirm	확인하다, 확정하다		
recognition	인식, 인정, 승인		
bias	편견, 치우침		

다음 단어에 해당하는 영어 단어 또는 우리말을 쓰세요. ○____개 ×____개

영어	한국어
accuracy	
alert	
astronomy	
avalanche	
bias	
circular	
confirm	
contemporary	
countless	
debt	
defend	
enhance	
estimate	
excess	
extraordinary	
fatigue	
grasp	
interpret	
isolation	
phase	
predator	
prior	
recognition	
relief	
statistics	
subtle	
temporary	
tune	
via	
welfare	

한국어	영어
명 통계(학)	
형 뛰어난, 비상한, 기이한	
명 지나침, 초과	
명 천문학	
전 ~을 경유하여, 거쳐	
형 경계하는 동 알리다	
명 안도, 경감, 구호품, 위반	
명 고립, 분리, 격리	
형 일시적인, 임시의	
형 원형의, 순환적인	
명 추정(치), 견적 동 추산하다	
형 미묘한	
명 빚, 부채	
동 방어하다, 지키다, 변호하다	
형 이전의, 사전의	
형 무수한, 수많은	
동 ~을 높이다, 향상시키다	
명 눈사태	
명 복지, 후생	
명 피로, 피곤	
명 정확도, 정확	
동 해석하다	
동 꽉 잡다, 이해하다	
명 곡조 동 조율하다	
명 포식자, 천적	
명 단계	
형 현대의, 동시대의	
동 확인하다, 확정하다	
명 인식, 인정, 승인	
명 편견, 치우침	

Day 04

| 월 일 |

영어 단어에 해당하는 한국어 뜻을 함께 적으세요.

be derived from	~에서 유래되다	be derived from	~에서 유래되다
dilemma	딜레마		
extensive	광범위한, 대규모의		
reference	참조, 언급, 추천서		
cliff	낭떠러지, 절벽		
glance	힐끗 보다, 흘끗 봄, 번득임		
somewhat	다소, 어느 정도		
component	요소, 부품		
diminish	줄어들다, 감소하다		
abound	풍부하다, 많이 있다		
assignment	숙제, 임무, 배정, 배치		
confusion	혼란		
corporation	기업, 회사		
eliminate	제거하다, 삭제하다, 탈락시키다		
self-esteem	자존감, 자부심		
admission	입학, 입장		
slang	속어, 은어		
sophisticated	세련된, 정교한, 복잡한		
trigger	유발하다; 방아쇠		
certificate	증서, 수료증		
disorder	혼란, 무질서, 장애		
innocent	무고한, 순수한		
mechanism	기계장치 구조, 체계		
passive	수동적인		
pottery	도자기		
precise	정확한, 정밀한		
prehistoric	선사 시대의		
split	나누다, 쪼개다, 분열시키다		
breed	새끼를 낳다, 사육하다		
mature	성숙한, 숙성된		

다음 단어에 해당하는 영어 단어 또는 우리말을 쓰세요.

O____개 X____개

영어	한국어
abound	
admission	
assignment	
be derived from	
breed	
certificate	
cliff	
component	
confusion	
corporation	
dilemma	
diminish	
disorder	
eliminate	
extensive	
glance	
innocent	
mature	
mechanism	
passive	
pottery	
precise	
prehistoric	
reference	
self-esteem	
slang	
somewhat	
sophisticated	
split	
trigger	

한국어	영어
형 성숙한, 숙성된	
명 입학, 입장	
명 딜레마	
명 증서, 수료증	
~에서 유래되다	
동 유발하다 명 방아쇠	
명 자존감, 자부심	
동 새끼를 낳다, 사육하다	
명 속어, 은어	
형 광범위한, 대규모의	
형 세련된, 정교한, 복잡한	
명 혼란, 무질서, 장애	
동 힐끗 보다, 흘끗 봄, 번득임	
형 무고한, 순수한	
명 참조, 언급, 추천서	
명 기계장치 구조, 체계	
명 요소, 부품	
명 낭떠러지, 절벽	
형 수동적인	
동 풍부하다, 많이 있다	
명 도자기	
부 다소, 어느 정도	
동 제거하다, 삭제하다, 탈락시키다	
명 숙제, 임무, 배정, 배치	
명 기업, 회사	
동 줄어들다, 감소하다	
형 선사 시대의	
형 정확한, 정밀한	
명 혼란	
동 나누다, 쪼개다, 분열시키다	

Day 05

| 월 일 |

영어 단어에 해당하는 한국어 뜻을 함께 적으세요.

correlation	연관성, 상관관계	correlation	연관성
induce	유도하다, 유발하다		
substance	물질, 실제, 요지		
diversity	다양성		
stable	안정적인		
strain	부담, 압박, (근육 등의) 접질림		
prominent	유명한, 두드러진		
bond	유대, 끈		
noticeable	뚜렷한, 현저한		
satisfy	만족시키다, 충족시키다		
dislike	싫어하다; 반감, 싫음		
anthropologist	인류학자		
tuition	수업, 교습		
intent	의도, 의향		
circulation	순환, 유통, 판매부수		
readily	손쉽게, 순조롭게		
apparent	분명한, 명백한		
assist	돕다, 지원하다, 조력, 원조		
era	시대, 연대		
sake	이익, 동기		
abundant	풍부한, 넘쳐나는		
evaluate	평가하다, 검토하다		
adequate	적당한, 충분한		
draft	초안, 밑그림, 선발, 징집		
expedition	탐험(대), 원정, 짧은 여행		
commerce	상업, 무역		
stack	더미; 쌓다, 포개다		
entry	입장, 가입, 참가		
earning	소득, 획득		
enthusiastic	열렬한, 열광적인		

다음 단어에 해당하는 영어 단어 또는 우리말을 쓰세요.

O___개 X___개

영어	한국어
abundant	
adequate	
anthropologist	
apparent	
assist	
bond	
circulation	
commerce	
correlation	
dislike	
diversity	
draft	
earning	
enthusiastic	
entry	
era	
evaluate	
expedition	
induce	
intent	
noticeable	
prominent	
readily	
sake	
satisfy	
stable	
stack	
strain	
substance	
tuition	

한국어	영어
명 연관성, 상관관계	
명 소득, 획득	
형 뚜렷한, 현저한	
형 열렬한, 열광적인	
명 다양성	
명 더미 동 쌓다, 포개다	
동 유도하다, 유발하다	
명 입장, 가입, 참가	
명 유대, 끈	
형 분명한, 명백한	
명 물질, 실체, 요지	
동 만족시키다, 충족시키다	
부 손쉽게, 순조롭게	
명 부담, 압박, (근육 등의) 접질림	
명 상업, 무역	
형 유명한, 두드러진	
동 돕다, 지원하다 명 조력, 원조	
명 인류학자	
명 시대, 연대	
형 안정적인	
동 싫어하다 명 반감, 싫음	
형 풍부한, 넘쳐나는	
명 이익, 동기	
명 순환, 유통, 판매부수	
명 초안, 밑그림, 선발, 징집	
명 의도, 의향	
동 평가하다, 검토하다	
형 적당한, 충분한	
명 수업, 교습	
명 탐험(대), 원정, 짧은 여행	

Workbook

Day 06

| 월 일 |

영어 단어에 해당하는 한국어 뜻을 함께 적으세요.

ambiguous	애매모호한	ambiguous	애매모호한
crude	대충의, 미가공의		
guilty	유죄의, 죄책감을 느끼는		
Celsius	섭씨의		
stun	기절시키다		
offspring	자식, 자손		
compensation	보상, 보상금		
diabetes	당뇨병		
medication	약(물)		
polish	닦다, 광을 내다		
devastating	파괴적인, 충격적인, 치명적인		
magnetic	자기의, 자석같은, 매력있는		
bargain	흥정하다; 흥정		
asthma	천식		
genuine	진짜의, 진품의		
lever	지레, 지렛대		
biodiversity	생물의 다양성		
dominate	~을 지배하다		
enterprise	기업, 회사, 사업(운영)		
expressive	(생각, 표정을) 나타내는		
horizontal	수평의, 가로의		
ultimate	궁극적인, 최후의, 근본적인		
real estate	부동산, 토지, 팔 집		
assistance	도움, 지원, 원조		
substitute	대체하다; 대체품, 교체선수		
cereal	곡물, 시리얼		
recess	휴식, (의회 등의) 휴회기간		
inefficient	비효율적인, 비능률적인		
spectacular	장관을 이루는, 멋진, 극적인		
equilibrium	균형, 평정		

다음 단어에 해당하는 영어 단어 또는 우리말을 쓰세요. O____개 X____개

영어	한국어
ambiguous	
assistance	
asthma	
bargain	
biodiversity	
Celsius	
cereal	
compensation	
crude	
devastating	
diabetes	
dominate	
enterprise	
equilibrium	
expressive	
genuine	
guilty	
horizontal	
inefficient	
lever	
magnetic	
medication	
offspring	
polish	
real estate	
recess	
spectacular	
stun	
substitute	
ultimate	

한국어	영어
형 대충의, 미가공의	
명 생물의 다양성	
형 애매모호한	
형 궁극적인, 최후의, 근본적인	
명 지레, 지렛대	
형 유죄의, 죄책감을 느끼는	
형 수평의, 가로의	
동 ~을 지배하다	
명 보상, 보상금	
명 기업, 회사, 사업(운영)	
동 기절시키다	
형 섭씨의	
형 (생각, 표정을) 나타내는	
형 자기의, 자석같은, 매력있는	
명 당뇨병	
명 자식, 자손	
명 부동산, 토지, 팔 집	
명 약(물)	
동 대체하다 명 대체품, 교체선수	
동 닦다, 광을 내다	
명 도움, 지원, 원조	
형 파괴적인, 충격적인, 치명적인	
형 비효율적인, 비능률적인	
동 흥정하다 명 흥정	
명 휴식, (의회 등의) 휴회기간	
명 곡물, 시리얼	
명 천식	
형 진짜의, 진품의	
명 균형, 평정	
형 장관을 이루는, 멋진	

Workbook

Day 07

| 월 일 |

영어 단어에 해당하는 한국어 뜻을 함께 적으세요.

friction	마찰, 알력, 불화	friction	마찰
indifferent	무관심한, 중요하지 않은		
allegory	우화, 풍자		
transport	수송, 이동 수단; 수송하다, 이동시키다		
identification	신원 확인, 신분증, 식별		
federal	연방의, 연방 정부의		
wage	임금, 급료		
hardship	고난, 고충, 곤란		
guarantee	보장하다, (품질을) 보증하다		
intake	섭취, 흡입, 채용, 수입		
modest	적절한, 겸손한		
inexpensive	비싸지 않은, 값이 싼		
intermediate	중간의		
neutral	중립의, 중립국의, 중성의		
favorable	유리한, 호의적인, 양호한		
urgent	긴급한, 시급한		
expansion	확대, 팽창		
grant	승인하다, 허락하다		
column	기둥, 열, 세로줄		
curriculum	교육과정, 이수과정		
input	투입, 입력, 조언		
flesh	살, 고기		
exceed	넘다, 초과하다		
usage	사용(량), (단어의) 용법, 어법		
wilderness	황야, 황무지		
breakthrough	돌파구, (난관의) 타개		
forage	먹이를 찾다; 먹이, 사료		
substantial	상당한, 실질적인, 본질적인		
overnight	밤새도록, 밤 사이에		
lifelong	평생의, 일생 동안의		

다음 단어에 해당하는 영어 단어 또는 우리말을 쓰세요.

○___개 ×___개

영어	한국어
friction	
breakthrough	
column	
curriculum	
exceed	
expansion	
favorable	
federal	
flesh	
forage	
grant	
guarantee	
hardship	
identification	
indifferent	
inexpensive	
input	
intake	
intermediate	
lifelong	
allegory	
modest	
neutral	
overnight	
substantial	
transport	
urgent	
usage	
wage	
wilderness	

한국어	영어
형 밤새도록, 밤 사이에	
형 긴급한, 시급한	
명 마찰, 알력, 불화	
형 상당한, 실질적인, 본질적인	
형 유리한, 호의적인, 양호한	
명 기둥, 열, 세로줄	
형 중립의, 중립국의, 중성의	
명 확대, 팽창	
형 연방의, 연방 정부의	
명 돌파구, (난관의) 타개	
형 무관심한, 중요하지 않은	
동 먹이를 찾다 명 먹이, 사료	
명 임금, 급료	
동 승인하다, 허락하다	
명 신원 확인, 신분증, 식별	
명 투입, 입력, 조언	
명 우화, 풍자	
명 교육과정, 이수과정	
명 사용(량), (단어의) 용법, 어법	
명 수송, 이동 수단 동 수송하다, 이동시키다	
형 중간의	
명 살, 고기	
명 섭취, 흡입, 채용, 수입	
동 보장하다, (품질을) 보증하다	
형 비싸지 않은, 값이 싼	
명 고난, 고충, 곤란	
동 넘다, 초과하다	
형 적절한, 겸손한	
명 황야, 황무지	
형 평생의, 일생 동안의	

Day 08

| 월 일 |

영어 단어에 해당하는 한국어 뜻을 함께 적으세요.

rank	계층, 계급	rank	계층, 계급
frost	서리, 성에		
ridiculous	말도 안 되는, 웃기는		
dawn	새벽, 시작		
inappropriate	부적절한		
accustomed	익숙한, 평소의		
domain	영역, 범위		
update	업데이트하다, 가장 최근의 정보를 알려주다		
exclusive	독점적인, 배타적인		
sacrifice	희생하다; 희생, 제물		
contagious	전염되는, 옮기 쉬운		
immense	굉장한, 막대한, 한없는		
defensive	방어의, 방어적인, 수비적인		
potter	도예가		
shield	방패, 보호막, 보호장치		
hesitation	주저, 망설임		
retail	소매		
latitude	위도		
amateur	비전문가; 전문이 아닌, 아마추어인		
pest	해충, 기생충		
antibiotic	항생제; 항생의		
cottage	오두막, 별장		
volcanic	화산의		
loan	대출(금), 대여		
solely	오로지, 단지		
controversy	논란, 논쟁		
assembly	의회, 조립		
fatal	치명적인		
distress	고통, 고뇌; 괴롭히다		
precipitation	강수(량)		

다음 단어에 해당하는 영어 단어 또는 우리말을 쓰세요.

O____개 X____개

영어	한국어
accustomed	
amateur	
antibiotic	
assembly	
contagious	
controversy	
cottage	
dawn	
defensive	
distress	
domain	
exclusive	
fatal	
frost	
hesitation	
immense	
inappropriate	
latitude	
loan	
pest	
potter	
precipitation	
rank	
retail	
ridiculous	
sacrifice	
shield	
solely	
update	
volcanic	

한국어	영어
형 굉장한, 막대한, 한없는	
명 위도	
형 익숙한, 평소의	
명 소매	
형 부적절한	
형 말도 안 되는, 웃기는	
명 주저, 망설임	
명 서리, 성에	
명 항생제 형 항생의	
명 영역, 범위	
형 전염되는, 옮기 쉬운	
형 화산의	
명 새벽, 시작	
명 해충, 기생충	
명 계층, 계급	
형 오로지, 단지	
명 비전문가 형 전문이 아닌, 아마추어인	
동 업데이트하다, 가장 최근의 정보를 알려주다	
명 오두막, 별장	
형 독점적인, 배타적인	
동 희생하다 명 희생, 제물	
명 대출(금), 대여	
명 강수(량)	
형 방어의, 방어적인, 수비적인	
명 논란, 논쟁	
명 방패, 보호막, 보호장치	
명 의회, 조립	
명 도예가	
명 고통, 고뇌 동 괴롭히다	
형 치명적인	

Workbook

Day 09

| 월 일 |

영어 단어에 해당하는 한국어 뜻을 함께 적으세요.

facilitate	용이하게 하다, 촉진시키다	facilitate	용이하게 하다, 촉진시키다
ignorance	무지, 무식		
sacred	신성한, 성스러운		
trace	쫓다; 자취		
competent	유능한, 능숙한, 만족할만한		
equivalent	동등한, 맞먹는		
hemisphere	반구		
impatient	참을성 없는, 조급한		
reception	수신, 환영 연회, 접수처		
subsequent	그 후의, 차후의		
circumstance	환경, 상황		
symbolic	상징적인		
vigorous	활발한, 격렬한		
transmit	전달하다, 전송하다, 전염시키다		
exceptional	뛰어난, 아주 훌륭한		
globalization	세계화		
voluntary	자발적인		
gratitude	감사, 고마움		
autograph	사인; 자필의		
dump	(쓰레기 등을) 버리다; 쓰레기 더미		
reinforce	강화하다, 보강하다		
humiliate	창피를 주다, 모욕하다		
abuse	남용; 남용하다		
farewell	작별		
equator	적도		
recite	낭독하다, 열거하다		
flock	떼, 무리; 떼지어 가다		
chaos	혼란, 카오스		
vessel	(대형) 선박, 혈관		
worthwhile	가치 있는		

다음 단어에 해당하는 영어 단어 또는 우리말을 쓰세요.

O____개 X____개

영어	한국어
abuse	
autograph	
chaos	
circumstance	
competent	
dump	
equator	
equivalent	
exceptional	
facilitate	
farewell	
flock	
globalization	
gratitude	
hemisphere	
humiliate	
ignorance	
impatient	
reception	
recite	
reinforce	
sacred	
subsequent	
symbolic	
trace	
transmit	
vessel	
vigorous	
voluntary	
worthwhile	

한국어	영어
명 세계화	
명 (대형) 선박, 혈관	
형 뛰어난, 아주 훌륭한	
형 가치 있는	
동 용이하게 하다, 촉진시키다	
명 떼, 무리 동 떼지어 가다	
형 유능한, 능숙한, 만족할만한	
동 전달하다, 전송하다, 전염시키다	
명 무지, 무식	
동 쫓다 명 자취	
형 자발적인	
형 신성한, 성스러운	
동 창피를 주다, 모욕하다	
형 활발한, 격렬한	
명 감사, 고마움	
형 동등한, 맞먹는	
동 낭독하다, 열거하다	
명 사인 형 자필의	
형 참을성 없는, 조급한	
동 강화하다, 보강하다	
동 (쓰레기 등을) 버리다 명 쓰레기 더미	
명 반구	
형 그 후의, 차후의	
명 남용 동 남용하다	
명 수신, 환영 연회, 접수처	
명 적도	
형 상징적인	
명 작별	
명 환경, 상황	
명 혼란, 카오스	

Workbook

Day 10

| 월 일 |

영어 단어에 해당하는 한국어 뜻을 함께 적으세요.

deed	행위, 행동	deed	행위, 행동
negotiate	협상하다		
sensation	감각, 느낌		
checkup	점검, 건강검진, 시험		
biography	전기, 자서전		
sting	쏘다; (곤충 등의) 침, 가시		
sewage	하수, 오물		
spouse	배우자		
magnitude	규모, 중요성		
nursery	탁아소, 아기 방		
terrain	지형, 지역		
audition	(가수, 배우 등의) 오디션; 오디션을 보다		
brochure	(안내, 광고용) 책자		
ongoing	계속 진행 중인		
criminal	범죄의; 범인		
proceed	진행하다, 나아가다		
coward	겁쟁이, 비겁한 사람		
exploit	(부당하게) 이용하다, 착취하다		
desperation	자포자기, 필사적임		
cabin	객실, 선실, 오두막집		
comprehension	이해(력)		
intuitive	직관력 있는, 직감에 의한		
blade	(칼, 도구 등의) 날		
stiff	뻣뻣한, 빡빡한, 경직된		
occupy	차지하다, 점령하다		
transition	인수, 이동, 변천		
outbreak	발생, 발발		
barn	곳간, 마구간		
notable	주목할 만한, 눈에 띄는		
disturbing	충격적인, 불안감을 주는		

다음 단어에 해당하는 영어 단어 또는 우리말을 쓰세요.

O____개 X____개

영어	한국어
barn	
biography	
blade	
brochure	
cabin	
checkup	
comprehension	
coward	
criminal	
deed	
desperation	
disturbing	
exploit	
audition	
intuitive	
magnitude	
negotiate	
notable	
nursery	
occupy	
ongoing	
outbreak	
proceed	
sensation	
sewage	
spouse	
stiff	
sting	
terrain	
transition	

한국어	영어
명 겁쟁이, 비겁한 사람	
형 계속 진행 중인	
동 진행하다, 나아가다	
명 (안내, 광고용) 책자	
명 전기, 자서전	
동 (부당하게) 이용하다, 착취하다	
동 협상하다	
명 감각, 느낌	
명 이해(력)	
명 지형, 지역	
명 자포자기, 필사적임	
명 객실, 선실, 오두막집	
명 점검, 건강검진, 시험	
명 행위, 행동	
형 충격적인, 불안감을 주는	
형 직관력 있는, 직감에 의한	
동 쏘다 명 (곤충 등의) 침, 가시	
명 (칼, 도구 등의) 날	
형 범죄의 명 범인	
명 배우자	
명 하수, 오물	
형 뻣뻣한, 뻑뻑한, 경직된	
동 차지하다, 점령하다	
명 규모, 중요성	
명 인수, 이동, 변천	
명 탁아소, 아기 방	
명 발생, 발발	
명 (가수, 배우 등의) 오디션 동 오디션을 보다	
명 곳간, 마구간	
형 주목할 만한, 눈에 띄는	

Workbook

Day 11 | 월 일 |

영어 단어에 해당하는 한국어 뜻을 함께 적으세요.

impractical	터무니없는, 비현실적인	impractical	터무니없는, 비현실적인
outfit	의상, 복장, 용품		
mentor	스승, 조언자		
optimal	최적의, 최상의		
elastic	탄력 있는, 신축적인		
diameter	지름, 직경, 배율		
dignity	존엄, 위엄, 품위, 자존감		
longevity	장수, 수명		
illustrate	설명하다, 삽화를 넣다		
minimal	최소의		
imperfect	불완전한, 불충분한		
exert	(권력, 영향력을) 행사하다, 가하다		
editorial	편집의; 사설		
imply	암시하다, 함축하다		
irrigation	관개, 물대기		
foster	조성하다, 위탁 양육하다		
dietary	음식의, 식이요법의		
nasty	더러운, 형편없는		
equality	평등, 동등		
disguise	변장하다, 위장하다		
keen	간절히 하고 싶어하는, 예민한		
cube	정육면체		
hasty	서두른, 성급한, 경솔한		
hierarchical	계급(계층)에 따른		
donor	기부자, 기증자		
insufficient	불충분한, 부족한		
impulsive	충동적인, 감정에 끌린		
endeavor	노력, 시도; 노력하다		
convert	전환하다, 바꾸다		
renowned	유명한, 명성 있는		

다음 단어에 해당하는 영어 단어 또는 우리말을 쓰세요. ○___개 ×___개

영어	한국어
convert	
cube	
diameter	
dietary	
dignity	
disguise	
donor	
editorial	
elastic	
endeavor	
equality	
exert	
foster	
hasty	
hierarchical	
illustrate	
imperfect	
imply	
impractical	
impulsive	
insufficient	
irrigation	
keen	
longevity	
mentor	
minimal	
nasty	
optimal	
outfit	
renowned	

한국어	영어
형 터무니없는, 비현실적인	
동 조성하다, 위탁 양육하다	
형 불충분한	
명 의상, 복장, 용품	
형 음식의, 식이요법의	
형 최적의, 최상의	
명 스승, 조언자	
명 관개, 물대기	
동 변장하다, 위장하다	
명 장수, 수명	
형 더러운, 형편없는	
명 지름, 직경, 배율	
명 평등, 동등	
명 존엄, 위엄, 품위, 자존감	
형 서두른, 성급한, 경솔한	
동 설명하다, 삽화를 넣다	
형 탄력 있는, 신축적인	
형 계급(계층)에 따른	
형 최소의	
형 불충분한, 부족한	
명 정육면체	
동 (권력, 영향력을) 행사하다, 가하다	
형 간절히 하고 싶어하는, 예민한	
형 편집의 명 사설	
동 암시하다, 함축하다	
동 전환하다, 바꾸다	
명 기부자, 기증자	
명 노력, 시도 동 노력하다	
형 충동적인, 감정에 끌린	
형 유명한, 명성 있는	

Workbook

Day 12

| 월 일 |

영어 단어에 해당하는 한국어 뜻을 함께 적으세요.

pedestrian	보행자; 보행의	pedestrian	보행자; 보행의
reservoir	저수지, 저장소		
trivial	사소한, 하찮은		
retain	유지하다, 간직하다		
absurd	터무니없는, 황당한		
outrage	격분, 격노, (수동태로) 격분하게 만들다		
sway	흔들다, 흔들리다		
decisive	결정적인, 단호한		
aesthetic	심미적, 미학의		
stall	가판대; 멈추게 하다		
contradict	부정하다, 모순되다		
supervise	감독하다, 지휘하다		
loom	어렴풋이 나타나다		
appreciation	감상, 감사		
activate	작동시키다, 활성화시키다		
advocate	지지하다, 옹호하다; 옹호자		
sustainable	(환경 등과 관련해서) 지속 가능한		
cosmetic	화장품; 성형의, 겉치레에 불과한		
reciprocal	상호간의		
plentiful	풍부한, 많은		
advent	도래, 출현		
tense	긴박한, 긴장한, 팽팽한		
regulation	규정, 규제		
health care	의료 서비스		
synthetic	인공의, 합성의		
spiritual	정신의		
perceptual	지각의, 지각에 의한		
honorable	존경할 만한, 고결한		
legacy	유산, 업적		
sorrow	슬픔, 비애		

다음 단어에 해당하는 영어 단어 또는 우리말을 쓰세요. O____개 X____개

영어	한국어	한국어	영어
absurd		명 유산, 업적	
activate		명 보행자 형 보행의	
advent		형 풍부한, 많은	
advocate		동 유지하다, 간직하다	
aesthetic		명 가판대 동 멈추게 하다	
appreciation		형 사소한, 하찮은	
contradict		명 저수지, 저장소	
cosmetic		명 격분, 격노, 동 (수동태로) 격분하게 만들다	
decisive		동 지지하다, 옹호하다 명 옹호자	
health care		형 터무니없는, 황당한	
honorable		명 화장품 형 성형의	
legacy		형 상호간의	
loom		동 흔들다, 흔들리다	
outrage		형 지각의, 지각에 의한	
pedestrian		형 결정적인, 단호한	
perceptual		형 (환경 등과 관련해서) 지속 가능한	
plentiful		형 심미적, 미학의	
reciprocal		명 도래, 출현	
regulation		동 작동시키다, 활성화시키다	
reservoir		명 규정, 규제	
retain		형 긴박한, 긴장한, 팽팽한	
sorrow		명 감상, 감사	
spiritual		동 어렴풋이 나타나다	
stall		명 의료 서비스	
supervise		동 감독하다, 지휘하다	
sustainable		형 인공의, 합성의	
sway		동 부정하다, 모순되다	
synthetic		형 정신의	
tense		명 슬픔, 비애	
trivial		형 존경할 만한, 고결한	

Workbook

Day 13

| 월 일 |

영어 단어에 해당하는 한국어 뜻을 함께 적으세요.

metropolitan	대도시의, 수도권의	metropolitan	대도시의, 수도권의
lottery	복권, 제비 뽑기		
punch	주먹으로 치다, 때리다		
prolonged	오래 계속되는, 장기적인		
persuasion	설득		
duration	지속, 기간		
fertile	(땅, 토양 등이) 비옥한		
manipulate	조정하다, 조작하다		
layout	배치, (출판물의) 지면배정		
glimpse	언뜻 보다, 잠깐 보다		
intact	손상되지 않은, 온전한		
evergreen	상록수		
incorporate	(일부러) 포함하다, 합병하다		
inborn	타고난, 선천적인		
revive	되살아나다, 회복하다, 다시 제작하다		
platform	승강장, 플랫폼, 연단, 강단		
manuscript	원고, 필사본, 사본		
discrimination	차별		
microscope	현미경		
radioactive	방사능의		
assure	장담하다, 보장하다, 확인하다		
responsive	즉각 반응하는, 민감한		
reject	거부하다		
optimism	낙관론, 낙관적 생각		
sheer	순전히, 완전히		
lessen	줄이다, 완화하다		
rotation	회전, 순환		
presumably	아마(도)		
unwilling	꺼리는, 싫어하는, 본의 아닌		
spacious	넓은, 널찍한		

다음 단어에 해당하는 영어 단어 또는 우리말을 쓰세요.

O____개 X____개

영어	한국어
assure	
discrimination	
duration	
evergreen	
fertile	
glimpse	
inborn	
incorporate	
intact	
layout	
lessen	
lottery	
manipulate	
manuscript	
metropolitan	
microscope	
optimism	
persuasion	
platform	
presumably	
prolonged	
punch	
radioactive	
reject	
responsive	
revive	
rotation	
sheer	
spacious	
unwilling	

한국어	영어
명 원고, 필사본, 사본	
형 대도시의, 수도권의	
명 승강장, 플랫폼, 연단, 강단	
형 꺼리는, 싫어하는	
동 되살아나다, 회복하다, 다시 제작하다	
명 현미경	
동 주먹으로 치다, 때리다	
명 복권, 제비뽑기	
명 설득	
명 차별	
형 오래 계속되는, 장기적인	
명 회전, 순환	
동 조정하다, 조작하다	
동 줄이다, 완화하다	
형 (땅, 토양 등이) 비옥한	
형 방사능의	
명 지속, 기간	
동 거부하다	
형 손상되지 않은, 온전한	
동 언뜻 보다, 잠깐 보다	
동 장담하다, 보장하다	
명 배치, (출판물의) 지면배정	
형 즉각 반응하는, 민감한	
명 상록수	
형 타고난, 선천적인	
동 (일부러) 포함하다, 합병하다	
부 아마(도)	
명 낙관론, 낙관적 생각	
형 순전히, 완전히	
형 넓은, 널찍한	

Day 14

| 월 일 |

영어 단어에 해당하는 한국어 뜻을 함께 적으세요.

flap	펄럭이다, 퍼덕거리다	flap	펄럭이다
dual	두 부분으로 된, 이중의		
cherish	소중히 여기다, 아끼다		
furious	몹시 화가 난, 맹렬한		
mourn	애도하다, 슬퍼하다		
spontaneous	자발적인, 즉흥적인		
deceased	사망한		
boundary	경계, 영역		
withstand	견디다, 이겨내다		
abrupt	갑작스러운, 퉁명스러운		
timber	목재, 수목, 삼림(지)		
thrive	번창하다, 잘 해내다		
deliberate	고의의, 의도적인		
weed	잡초, 수초		
undergo	겪다, 경험하다, 견디다		
faraway	먼, 멀리 떨어진		
competitor	경쟁자		
ecology	생태(학)		
withdraw	철회하다, 물러나다		
decay	부패; 썩다, 부패하다		
stubborn	완강한, 고질적인		
starvation	기아, 굶주림		
willingness	의향, 기꺼이 하기		
extract	추출하다, 발췌하다		
epidemic	유행병		
steer	조종하다, 돌리다		
coordination	조직, 합동		
amnesia	기억상실(증)		
suppress	억압하다, 진압하다		
longitude	경도		

다음 단어에 해당하는 영어 단어 또는 우리말을 쓰세요.

O____개 X____개

영어	한국어
abrupt	
amnesia	
boundary	
cherish	
competitor	
coordination	
decay	
deceased	
deliberate	
dual	
ecology	
epidemic	
extract	
faraway	
flap	
furious	
longitude	
mourn	
spontaneous	
starvation	
steer	
stubborn	
suppress	
thrive	
timber	
undergo	
weed	
willingness	
withdraw	
withstand	

한국어	영어
동 펄럭이다, 퍼덕거리다	
명 조직, 합동	
동 조종하다, 돌리다	
명 기억상실(증)	
명 유행병	
형 두 부분으로 된, 이중의	
동 소중히 여기다, 아끼다	
동 억압하다, 진압하다	
동 추출하다, 발췌하다	
명 경도	
명 경계, 영역	
동 번창하다, 잘 해내다	
형 먼, 멀리 떨어진	
형 사망한	
명 목재, 수목, 삼림(지)	
동 견디다, 이겨내다	
명 경쟁자	
형 자발적인, 즉흥적인	
명 생태(학)	
동 철회하다, 물러나다	
형 몹시 화가 난, 맹렬한	
형 갑작스러운, 퉁명스러운	
명 부패 동 썩다, 부패하다	
동 애도하다, 슬퍼하다	
형 고의의, 의도적인	
형 완강한, 고질적인	
동 겪다, 경험하다, 견디다	
명 기아, 굶주림	
명 잡초, 수초	
명 의향, 기꺼이 하기	

Day 15

| 월 일 |

영어 단어에 해당하는 한국어 뜻을 함께 적으세요.

prompt	신속한, 즉각적인; 촉발하다	prompt	신속한, 즉각적인; 촉발하다
hostile	적대적인, 불리한		
restless	가만히 못 있는, 불안한		
reckless	무모한, 부주의한		
morality	도덕(성)		
relevance	관련(성), 적절(성), 타당(성)		
regain	되찾다, 회복하다		
probe	조사하다, 수사하다, 살피다		
malnutrition	영양실조		
parasite	기생충, 기생 동물		
geometric	기하학의, 기하학적인		
retreat	물러서다; 후퇴		
leopard	표범		
inadequate	부적절한, 불충분한		
segment	부분, 분절, 조각; 나누다		
intuition	직관(력)		
gorgeous	아주 멋진, 화려한, 굉장한		
assert	주장하다, 단언하다		
outlook	관점, 전망, 견해		
penetrate	관통하다, 뚫고 들어가다		
immoral	부도덕한, 비도덕적인		
leak	(액체, 기체가) 새다; 새는 곳		
infinite	무한한, 무한정의		
irrational	비이성적인		
mammal	포유동물		
implement	실행하다; 기구, 도구		
surgeon	외과의사		
rust	녹; 녹슬다, 부식하다		
compromise	타협하다, 손상하다; 타협		
suspend	중지하다, 유예하다, 매달다		

다음 단어에 해당하는 영어 단어 또는 우리말을 쓰세요.

O____개 X____개

영어	한국어
assert	
compromise	
geometric	
gorgeous	
hostile	
immoral	
implement	
inadequate	
infinite	
intuition	
irrational	
leak	
leopard	
malnutrition	
mammal	
morality	
outlook	
parasite	
penetrate	
probe	
prompt	
reckless	
regain	
relevance	
restless	
retreat	
rust	
segment	
surgeon	
suspend	

한국어	영어
형 아주 멋진, 화려한, 굉장한	
명 직관(력)	
형 신속한, 즉각적인 동 촉발하다	
동 중지하다, 유예하다, 매달다	
명 관련(성), 적절(성), 타당(성)	
형 적대적인, 불리한	
명 녹 동 녹슬다, 부식하다	
형 가만히 못 있는, 불안한	
동 주장하다, 단언하다	
형 비이성적인	
형 무모한, 부주의한	
동 관통하다, 뚫고 들어가다	
형 기하학의, 기하학적인	
명 도덕(성)	
명 관점, 전망, 견해	
명 기생충, 기생동물	
동 물러서다 명 후퇴	
동 되찾다, 회복하다	
형 부도덕한, 비도덕적인	
동 조사하다, 수사하다, 살피다	
동 (액체, 기체가) 새다 명 새는 곳	
명 영양실조	
형 무한한, 무한정의	
형 부적절한, 불충분한	
명 포유동물	
명 표범	
동 타협하다, 손상하다 명 타협	
동 실행하다 명 기구, 도구	
명 부분, 분절, 조각 동 나누다	
명 외과의사	

Workbook

Day 16

| 월 일 |

영어 단어에 해당하는 한국어 뜻을 함께 적으세요.

egocentric	자기 중심적인, 이기적인	egocentric	자기 중심적인, 이기적인
patch	헝겊 조각; 헝겊 조각을 대다		
anticipate	예측하다, 기대하다		
proclaim	선포하다, 선언하다, 칭송하다		
swarm	떼 ; 떼를 지어 다니다		
conflicting	상반되는, 모순되는		
textile	직물, 옷감		
agony	(극도의) 고민, 고통, 격정		
warrior	용사, 전사		
womb	자궁		
cuddle	껴안다; 껴안기, 포옹		
texture	질감		
choke	질식시키다, 막다, 숨이 막히다		
credible	믿을 수 있는		
tenant	세입자, 임차인		
ultraviolet	자외선		
ally	동맹, 연합; 편들다, 지지하다		
burial	매장, 장례식		
unrealistic	비현실적인, 비사실적인		
abolish	(법률, 제도 등을) 폐지하다		
adhere	들러붙다, 고수하다		
compulsive	강박적인, 조절이 힘든		
beforehand	미리, 사전에		
affirmative	긍정의 ; 긍정의 대답		
childish	유치한, 어린애같은		
consent	동의하다; 동의		
collaborate	협력하다, 공동으로 작업하다		
absent-minded	멍한, 얼빠진		
intersection	교차로, 교차점		
dim	어두운; ~을 어둑하게 하다		

다음 단어에 해당하는 영어 단어 또는 우리말을 쓰세요.

O____개 X____개

영어	한국어
abolish	
absent-minded	
adhere	
affirmative	
agony	
ally	
anticipate	
beforehand	
burial	
childish	
choke	
collaborate	
compulsive	
conflicting	
consent	
credible	
cuddle	
dim	
egocentric	
intersection	
patch	
proclaim	
swarm	
tenant	
textile	
texture	
ultraviolet	
unrealistic	
warrior	
womb	

한국어	영어
[명] 헝겊 조각 [동] 헝겊 조각을 대다	
[명] 동맹, 연합 [동] 편들다, 지지하다	
[부] 미리, 사전에	
[형] 자기 중심적인, 이기적인	
[명] 자외선	
[명] 매장, 장례식	
[동] 예측하다, 기대하다	
[형] 강박적인, 조절이 힘든	
[명] 용사, 전사	
[동] 선포하다, 선언하다	
[형] 비현실적인, 비사실적인	
[명] 떼 [동] 떼를 지어 다니다	
[명] 질감	
[형] 상반되는, 모순되는	
[동] 들러붙다, 고수하다	
[명] 직물, 옷감	
[명] (극도의) 고민, 고통, 격정	
[동] (법률, 제도 등을) 폐지하다	
[형] 긍정의 [명] 긍정의 대답	
[명] 자궁	
[동] 껴안다 [명] 껴안기, 포옹	
[형] 유치한, 어린애같은	
[동] 동의하다 [명] 동의	
[형] 믿을 수 있는	
[동] 협력하다, 공동으로 작업하다	
[동] 질식시키다, 막다	
[형] 멍한, 얼빠진	
[명] 교차로, 교차점	
[명] 세입자, 임차인	
[형] 어두운 [동] ~을 어둡게 하다	

Workbook

Day 17 | 월 일 |

영어 단어에 해당하는 한국어 뜻을 함께 적으세요.

diploma	졸업장, 학위	diploma	졸업장, 학위
prism	프리즘, 분광기		
prestigious	명성 있는, 일류의		
dilute	희석하다, 묽게하다		
episode	사건, 에피소드		
injure	다치게 하다, 손상시키다		
evoke	불러 일으키다, 환기시키다		
luxurious	호화로운, 고급의		
allocate	할당하다, 배치하다		
diagnosis	진단		
porch	현관		
dummy	인체 모형, 견본; 모조의		
nurture	양육하다, 키우다; 양육, 육성		
dormitory	기숙사		
implication	영향, 함축		
erode	침식 시키다, 약화 시키다		
conservative	보수적인		
hinder	방해하다, 훼방하다		
dread	몹시 무서워하다, 두려워하다		
enrich	부유하게 하다, 풍성하게 하다		
intellect	지성, 지적 능력		
ambition	야망, 포부		
discern	식별하다, 분간하다		
marble	대리석, 구슬		
racism	인종 차별(주의)		
impose	부과하다, 도입하다, 강요하다		
gracious	품위 있는, 자애로운		
revenge	보복, 복수		
atomic	원자의, 원자력의, 핵무기의		
plead	애원하다, 호소하다		

다음 단어에 해당하는 영어 단어 또는 우리말을 쓰세요.

O____개 X____개

영어	한국어
allocate	
ambition	
atomic	
conservative	
diagnosis	
dilute	
diploma	
discern	
dormitory	
dread	
dummy	
enrich	
episode	
erode	
evoke	
gracious	
hinder	
implication	
impose	
injure	
intellect	
luxurious	
marble	
nurture	
plead	
porch	
prestigious	
prism	
racism	
revenge	

한국어	영어
명 졸업장, 학위	
동 애원하다, 호소하다	
형 명성 있는, 일류의	
동 방해하다, 훼방하다	
명 프리즘, 분광기	
동 침식 시키다, 약화 시키다	
명 영향, 함축	
동 희석하다, 묽게하다	
형 보수적인	
명 사건, 에피소드	
명 야망, 포부	
동 불러 일으키다, 환기시키다	
형 원자의, 원자력의, 핵무기의	
동 다치게 하다, 손상시키다	
동 몹시 무서워하다, 두려워하다	
형 호화로운, 고급의	
동 부유하게 하다, 풍성하게 하다	
동 할당하다, 배치하다	
명 지성, 지적 능력	
명 진단	
명 기숙사	
동 식별하다, 분간하다	
명 현관	
동 양육하다, 키우다 명 양육	
명 대리석, 구슬	
명 인체 모형, 견본 형 모조의	
형 품위 있는, 자애로운	
동 부과하다, 도입하다	
명 인종 차별(주의)	
명 보복, 복수	

Workbook

Day 18

| 월 일 |

영어 단어에 해당하는 한국어 뜻을 함께 적으세요.

hinge	경첩; ~여하에 달려있다	hinge	경첩
shiver	(추위, 두려움, 흥분 등으로) 떨다; 전율		
artifact	인공물, 인공 유물		
armor	갑옷, 장갑, 방호구		
simplify	간소화하다, 단순화하다		
upcoming	다가오는, 곧 있을		
strand	가닥; 오도가도 못하게 하다		
sprout	싹; 싹이 나기 시작하다		
oblige	의무적으로 ~하게 하다		
soothe	진정시키다, 달래다, 누그러뜨리다		
dichotomy	양분, 이분법		
reassure	안심시키다, 힘을 북돋우다		
acupuncture	침술		
tolerate	참다, 견디다, 용인하다		
bankrupt	파산한		
transplant	이식하다; 이식		
particle	입자, 티끌, (문서 등의) 항목		
sympathetic	동정적인, 동조하는, 호감이 가는		
successive	연속적인, 연이은		
superb	최고의, 최상의		
recession	불경기, 불황		
soar	(가치, 물가 등이) 치솟다		
wreck	난파선; 망가뜨리다		
shrine	성지, 사당		
yeast	효모균, 이스트		
vanish	사라지다, 없어지다		
radical	급진적인		
refrain	삼가다, 자제하다		
humanitarian	인도주의적인		
distort	왜곡하다, 비틀다		

다음 단어에 해당하는 영어 단어 또는 우리말을 쓰세요.

O____개 X____개

영어	한국어
acupuncture	
armor	
artifact	
bankrupt	
dichotomy	
distort	
hinge	
humanitarian	
oblige	
particle	
radical	
reassure	
recession	
refrain	
shiver	
shrine	
simplify	
soar	
soothe	
sprout	
strand	
successive	
superb	
sympathetic	
tolerate	
transplant	
upcoming	
vanish	
wreck	
yeast	

한국어	영어
명 경첩 동 ~여하에 달려있다	
명 입자, 티끌, (문서 등의) 항목	
동 왜곡하다, 비틀다	
동 떨다 명 전율	
형 동정적인, 동조하는, 호감이 가는	
동 이식하다 명 이식	
명 인공물, 인공 유물	
형 인도주의적인	
명 갑옷, 장갑, 방호구	
형 연속적인, 연이은	
형 최고의, 최상의	
동 간소화하다, 단순화하다	
명 불경기, 불황	
형 다가오는, 곧 있을	
명 싹 동 싹이 나기 시작하다	
동 (가치, 물가 등이) 치솟다	
명 가닥 동 오도가도 못하게 하다	
동 의무적으로 ~하게 하다	
명 난파선 동 망가뜨리다	
동 참다, 견디다, 용인하다	
명 침술	
명 성지, 사당	
동 진정시키다, 달래다	
명 효모균, 이스트	
명 양분, 이분법	
동 안심시키다, 힘을 북돋우다	
동 사라지다, 없어지다	
형 파산한	
형 급진적인	
동 삼가다, 자제하다	

Day 19

| 월 일 |

영어 단어에 해당하는 한국어 뜻을 함께 적으세요.

flame	불꽃, 화염	flame	불꽃, 화염
bureaucracy	관료(제)		
doom	죽음, 파멸; ~을 운명짓다		
glacier	빙하		
epic	서사시, 장편 서사 영화		
commentary	해설, 논평, 주석		
clarify	명백히 하다, 분명히 하다		
diaper	기저귀		
complementary	상호 보완적인		
graze	풀을 뜯다, 방목하다		
indigenous	고유의, 토착의		
chronic	(병, 질환 등이) 만성의		
eternal	영원한, 끊임없는		
coarse	(피부, 천 등이) 거친, 굵은		
dose	(약의) 복용량 (투여량)		
cling	꼭 붙잡다, 매달리다		
copyright	저작권; 저작권을 얻다		
cuisine	요리, 요리법		
curb	억제하다, 제한하다		
discard	버리다, 폐기하다		
evaporate	증발하다, 증발시키다		
inhabit	거주하다, 서식하다		
congestion	(교통 등의) 혼잡, 밀집, 정체		
handshake	악수		
connectivity	연결(성)		
flee	도망치다, 달아나다		
decent	제대로 된, 품위 있는		
corpse	시체, 송장		
lump	덩어리, 혹		
overhear	우연히 듣다, 엿듣다		

다음 단어에 해당하는 영어 단어 또는 우리말을 쓰세요. O____개 X____개

영어	한국어
bureaucracy	
chronic	
clarify	
cling	
coarse	
commentary	
complementary	
congestion	
connectivity	
copyright	
corpse	
cuisine	
curb	
decent	
diaper	
discard	
doom	
dose	
epic	
eternal	
evaporate	
flame	
flee	
glacier	
graze	
handshake	
indigenous	
inhabit	
lump	
overhear	

한국어	영어
명 덩어리, 혹	
명 저작권 동 저작권을 얻다	
명 시체, 송장	
명 빙하	
동 꼭 붙잡다, 매달리다	
명 요리, 요리법	
명 죽음, 파멸 동 ~을 운명짓다	
동 우연히 듣다, 엿듣다	
명 불꽃, 화염	
동 억제하다, 제한하다	
명 관료(제)	
동 버리다, 폐기하다	
명 (교통 등의) 혼잡, 밀집, 정체	
명 서사시, 장편 서사 영화	
동 증발하다, 증발시키다	
명 해설, 논평, 주석	
동 거주하다, 서식하다	
동 명백히 하다, 분명히 하다	
명 악수	
명 기저귀	
형 상호 보완적인	
명 연결(성)	
형 고유의, 토착의	
동 풀을 뜯다, 방목하다	
명 (약의) 복용량 (투여량)	
형 (병, 질환 등이) 만성의	
형 제대로 된, 품위 있는	
형 영원한, 끊임없는	
동 도망치다, 달아나다	
형 (피부, 천 등이) 거친, 굵은	

Workbook

Day 20

| 월 일 |

영어 단어에 해당하는 한국어 뜻을 함께 적으세요.

pavement	인도, 보도, 포장도로	pavement	포장도로
multitask	다중 작업 처리를 하다		
precede	앞서다, 선행하다		
renew	재개하다, 갱신하다		
morale	사기, 의욕		
pessimistic	비관적인		
provision	(법률 등의) 조항, 규정		
prescribe	처방을 내리다, 처방전을 쓰다		
livelihood	생계, 생계수단		
mortgage	저당, 담보대출		
primate	영장류		
oval	계란형의, 타원형의		
remedy	치료(약), 해결책		
precaution	예방(책), 조심, 경계		
ornament	장식(품)		
inquiry	조사, 수사, 연구, 탐구		
radiate	내뿜다, (사방으로) 퍼지다		
irresponsible	무책임한, 책임감이 없는		
overload	과적하다; 과부하		
naive	순진한, 고지식한, 속기 쉬운		
meteorite	운석, 유성체		
mutation	돌연변이, 변화		
irritate	거슬리게 하다, 몹시 짜증내다		
pledge	약속, 맹세; 약속하다		
quote	인용하다, 예를 들다		
linguistic	언어의, 언어적인		
murmur	중얼거리다, 속삭이다		
qualified	자격이 있는		
cluster	떼를 지어 모이다 ; 무리, 떼		
omission	생략, 누락		

다음 단어에 해당하는 영어 단어 또는 우리말을 쓰세요.

O____개 X____개

영어	한국어
cluster	
inquiry	
irresponsible	
irritate	
linguistic	
livelihood	
meteorite	
morale	
mortgage	
multitask	
murmur	
mutation	
naive	
omission	
ornament	
oval	
overload	
pavement	
pessimistic	
pledge	
precaution	
precede	
prescribe	
primate	
provision	
qualified	
quote	
radiate	
remedy	
renew	

한국어	영어
동 내뿜다, (사방으로) 퍼지다	
명 조사, 수사, 연구, 탐구	
명 인도, 보도, 포장도로	
명 생략, 누락	
동 다중 작업 처리를 하다	
형 무책임한, 책임감이 없는	
동 과적하다 명 과부하	
동 앞서다, 선행하다	
명 돌연변이, 변화	
동 재개하다, 갱신하다	
명 장식(품)	
형 순진한, 고지식한, 속기 쉬운	
명 치료(약), 해결책	
명 운석, 유성체	
명 예방(책), 조심, 경계	
명 사기, 의욕	
동 인용하다, 예를 들다	
명 (법률 등의) 조항, 규정	
동 거슬리게 하다, 몹시 짜증내다	
형 비관적인	
명 저당, 담보대출	
명 약속, 맹세 동 약속하다	
동 처방을 내리다, 처방전을 쓰다	
동 중얼거리다, 속삭이다	
명 생계, 생계수단	
형 언어의, 언어적인	
형 자격이 있는	
명 영장류	
형 계란형의, 타원형의	
동 떼를 지어 다니다 명 무리, 떼	

Day 21

| 월 일 |

영어 단어에 해당하는 한국어 뜻을 함께 적으세요.

panel	(사각형) 판, 조각, 토론단	panel	판, 위원단
subordinate	종속된, 부차적인		
envision	마음속에 그리다, 상상하다		
dine	식사를 하다, 만찬을 들다		
deception	속임, 사기		
accommodation	숙소, 거처, 수용, 화해, 조정		
tame	길들이다; 길들여진		
swamp	늪; 늪에 빠지다		
viewpoint	관점, 견해, 시각		
stabilize	안정시키다, 안정되다		
await	~을 기다리다		
astonish	깜짝 놀라게 하다		
simultaneously	동시에		
interchange	(생각, 정보 등의)교환		
amend	개정하다, 수정하다		
archery	활쏘기, 궁술		
enchant	황홀하게 만들다		
uncover	밝히다, 발견하다		
vapor	증기, 증발 기체		
footprint	발자국, (무엇이) 차지하는 공간		
surpass	능가하다, 뛰어넘다		
repetitive	반복적인, 반복되는		
vacant	(객실, 방 등이) 비어 있는, 공석인		
craving	갈망, 열망		
superficial	피상적인, 얄팍한, 깊이 없는		
dimension	치수, 차원		
weave	짜다, 엮다		
supplement	보충(추가)물; 보완하다		
ventilate	환기하다, 통풍시키다		
clutch	움켜잡다; 움켜쥠		

다음 단어에 해당하는 영어 단어 또는 우리말을 쓰세요. ○____개 ✕____개

영어	한국어
accommodation	
amend	
archery	
astonish	
await	
clutch	
craving	
deception	
dimension	
dine	
enchant	
envision	
footprint	
interchange	
panel	
repetitive	
simultaneously	
stabilize	
subordinate	
superficial	
supplement	
surpass	
swamp	
tame	
uncover	
vacant	
vapor	
ventilate	
viewpoint	
weave	

한국어	영어
명 발자국, (무엇이) 차지하는 공간	
동 밝히다, 발견하다	
동 황홀하게 만들다	
명 (사각형) 판, 조각, 토론단	
명 증기, 증발 기체	
동 식사를 하다, 만찬을 들다	
명 활쏘기, 궁술	
형 반복적인, 반복되는	
동 마음속에 그리다, 상상하다	
동 능가하다, 뛰어넘다	
형 종속된, 부차적인	
명 속임, 사기	
형 (객실, 방 등이) 비어 있는, 공석인	
동 ~을 기다리다	
동 깜짝 놀라게 하다	
명 갈망, 열망	
명 숙소, 거처, 수용, 화해, 조정	
형 피상적인, 얄팍한, 깊이 없는	
동 안정시키다, 안정되다	
동 길들이다 형 길들여진	
명 치수, 차원	
명 늪 동 늪에 빠지다	
동 짜다, 엮다	
명 관점, 견해, 시각	
명 보충(추가)물 동 보완하다	
부 동시에	
동 움켜잡다 명 움켜쥠	
명 (생각, 정보 등의) 교환	
동 환기하다, 통풍시키다	
동 개정하다, 수정하다	

Day 22

| 월 일 |

영어 단어에 해당하는 한국어 뜻을 함께 적으세요.

adorable	사랑스러운, 귀여운	adorable	사랑스러운
blister	물집; 물집이 생기게 하다		
counterpart	상대, 상대역, 등가물, 복사본		
contend	싸우다, 주장하다, 논쟁하다		
adverse	부정적인, 불리한		
appliance	(가정용)기기, 적용, 응용		
auction	경매; 경매로 팔다		
bless	축복하다, 은혜를 베풀다		
apologetic	사과하는, 미안해하는, 변명의		
conceal	숨기다, 감추다		
baggage	짐, 수화물		
continual	끊임없는, 거듭되는, 빈번한		
ample	풍부한, 넓은, 충분한		
attic	다락방		
compel	강요하다, 강제하다		
blueprint	청사진, 계획		
aristocracy	귀족(제)		
carbohydrate	탄수화물		
beware	조심하다, 경계하다		
bruise	타박상을 입히다; 멍, 상처		
contemplate	고려하다, 심사 숙고하다		
blur	흐리게 하다; 흐릿함		
corruption	부패, 타락		
categorize	분류하다, ~의 범주에 넣다		
confront	직면하다, 맞서다		
comprise	포함하다, ~을 구성하다, 차지하다		
broaden	넓히다, 확장하다		
bribe	뇌물; 뇌물을 주다		
condense	농축하다, 응축하다, 응축되다		
creep	기다, 살금살금 움직이다		

다음 단어에 해당하는 영어 단어 또는 우리말을 쓰세요.

O____개 X____개

영어	한국어
adorable	
adverse	
ample	
apologetic	
appliance	
aristocracy	
attic	
auction	
baggage	
beware	
bless	
blister	
blueprint	
blur	
bribe	
broaden	
bruise	
carbohydrate	
categorize	
compel	
comprise	
conceal	
condense	
confront	
contemplate	
contend	
continual	
corruption	
counterpart	
creep	

한국어	영어
형 사랑스러운, 귀여운	
명 청사진, 계획	
명 물집 동 물집이 생기게 하다	
동 기다, 살금살금 움직이다	
동 농축하다, 응축하다, 응축되다	
명 탄수화물	
명 귀족(제)	
동 숨기다, 감추다	
명 뇌물 동 뇌물을 주다	
동 싸우다, 주장하다, 논쟁하다	
동 조심하다, 경계하다	
동 흐리게 하다 명 흐릿함	
명 상대, 상대역, 등가물, 복사본	
동 분류하다, ~의 범주에 넣다	
동 타박상을 입히다 명 멍, 상처	
형 부정적인, 불리한	
명 (가정용) 기기, 적용, 응용	
동 고려하다, 심사 숙고하다	
명 경매 동 경매로 팔다	
명 부패, 타락	
동 축복하다, 은혜를 베풀다	
동 강요하다, 강제하다	
형 사과하는, 미안해하는, 변명의	
동 넓히다, 확장하다	
형 끊임없는, 거듭되는, 빈번한	
명 짐, 수화물	
동 직면하다, 맞서다	
명 다락방	
형 풍부한, 넓은, 충분한	
동 포함하다, ~을 구성하다, 차지하다	

Workbook

Day 23

| 월 일 |

영어 단어에 해당하는 한국어 뜻을 함께 적으세요.

idiom	관용구, 숙어	idiom	관용구, 숙어
improper	부적절한, 잘못된		
eradicate	근절(퇴치)하다, 뿌리뽑다		
frail	허약한, 노쇠한		
furnish	(가구를) 비치하다, 제공하다		
immature	미숙한, 미완성의		
fortress	요새		
hospitality	환대, 후대		
dispense	나누어주다, 베풀다, 없애다		
drastic	과감한, 극단적인		
escort	호위대(원); 호위하다		
geometry	기하학, 기하학적 구조		
inflate	부풀리다, 부풀다, 가격이 오르다		
crave	갈망하다, 열망하다		
empower	권한(권리)을 주다		
exhale	(숨 등을) 내쉬다, 내뿜다		
deplete	고갈시키다, 격감시키다		
fermentation	발효		
glare	노려보다, 쏘아보다		
embassy	대사관		
dictate	받아쓰게 하다, 좌우하다, ~에 영향을 주다		
exterior	외부의, 옥외의		
divine	신성한		
enclose	동봉하다, 둘러싸다		
futile	헛된, 소용없는		
counterproductive	역효과를 낳는, 비생산적인		
dip	살짝 담그다, 적시다		
harness	이용하다, 마구를 채우다; 마구		
cozy	아늑한, 안락한		
locomotive	기관차, 견인차; 기관차의		

다음 단어에 해당하는 영어 단어 또는 우리말을 쓰세요.

O____개 X____개

영어	한국어
counterproductive	
cozy	
crave	
deplete	
dictate	
dip	
dispense	
divine	
drastic	
embassy	
empower	
enclose	
eradicate	
escort	
exhale	
exterior	
fermentation	
fortress	
frail	
furnish	
futile	
geometry	
glare	
harness	
hospitality	
idiom	
immature	
improper	
inflate	
locomotive	

한국어	영어
동 고갈시키다, 격감시키다	
명 관용구, 숙어	
형 미숙한, 미완성의	
동 (숨 등을) 내쉬다, 내뿜다	
형 부적절한, 잘못된	
동 노려보다, 쏘아보다	
동 (가구를) 비치하다, 제공하다	
명 발효	
동 근절(퇴치)하다, 뿌리뽑다	
명 대사관	
형 허약한, 노쇠한	
형 외부의, 옥외의	
형 과감한, 극단적인	
동 받아쓰게 하다, 좌우하다, ~에 영향을 주다	
명 기관차, 견인차 형 기관차의	
동 나누어주다, 베풀다, 없애다	
동 이용하다, 마구를 채우다 명 마구	
명 요새	
명 환대, 후대	
동 권한(권리)을 주다	
명 호위대(원) 동 호위하다	
형 헛된, 소용없는	
명 기하학, 기하학적 구조	
형 신성한	
동 부풀리다, 부풀다, 가격이 오르다	
형 역효과를 낳는, 비생산적인	
동 동봉하다, 둘러싸다	
동 갈망하다, 열망하다	
동 살짝 담그다, 적시다	
형 아늑한, 안락한	

Workbook

Day 24

| 월 일 |

영어 단어에 해당하는 한국어 뜻을 함께 적으세요.

eligible	자격이 있는, 권한이 있는	eligible	자격이 있는, 권한이 있는
reform	개혁하다; 개혁		
indulge	빠지다, 탐닉하다		
itch	가렵다; 가려움, 욕망		
provoke	자극하다, 유발하다		
meditate	명상하다, 묵상하다, 숙고하다		
sin	죄, 죄악		
prose	산문(체)		
minority	소수		
refugee	난민, 망명자		
patriotism	애국심		
omit	빠뜨리다, 제외하다		
patron	후원자, 보호자, 단골손님		
refinement	정제, 제련, 개선		
protest	항의하다; 시위, 항의		
erect	똑바로 선; 똑바로 세우다		
persevere	인내하며 계속하다		
seize	붙잡다, 움켜잡다, 체포하다		
proficient	능숙한, 숙달한		
originate	비롯하다, 유래하다		
integrate	통합하다, 합병하다		
shave	면도하다; 면도		
lodge	오두막		
ponder	심사 숙고하다		
prophecy	예언		
mock	가짜의, 모의의; 놀리다, 무시하다		
dispute	분쟁하다, 반박하다; 분쟁		
inject	주사하다, 주입하다		
prosperous	번영하는, 번창하는		
supreme	최고의, 최대의		

다음 단어에 해당하는 영어 단어 또는 우리말을 쓰세요.

O____개 X____개

영어	한국어
dispute	
eligible	
erect	
indulge	
inject	
integrate	
itch	
lodge	
meditate	
minority	
mock	
omit	
originate	
patriotism	
patron	
persevere	
ponder	
proficient	
prophecy	
prose	
prosperous	
protest	
provoke	
refinement	
reform	
refugee	
seize	
shave	
sin	
supreme	

한국어	영어
동 인내하며 계속하다	
명 소수	
형 똑바로 선 동 똑바로 세우다	
형 능숙한, 숙달한	
명 산문(체)	
형 자격이 있는, 권한이 있는	
명 죄, 죄악	
동 붙잡다, 움켜잡다, 체포하다	
동 개혁하다 명 개혁	
동 면도하다 명 면도	
동 명상하다, 묵상하다, 숙고하다	
동 비롯하다, 유래하다	
동 통합하다, 합병하다	
동 빠지다, 탐닉하다	
형 최고의, 최대의	
동 자극하다, 유발하다	
명 오두막	
동 가렵다 명 가려움, 욕망	
형 번영하는, 번창하는	
동 항의하다 명 시위, 항의	
동 심사 숙고하다	
명 난민, 망명자	
명 예언	
명 애국심	
형 가짜의 동 놀리다, 무시하다	
동 빠뜨리다, 제외하다	
동 분쟁하다, 반박하다 명 분쟁	
명 정제, 제련, 개선	
명 후원자, 보호자, 단골손님	
동 주사하다, 주입하다	

Workbook

Day 25

| 월 일 |

영어 단어에 해당하는 한국어 뜻을 함께 적으세요.

thrust	찔러 넣다, 밀다	thrust	찔러 넣다, 밀다
statesman	정치인		
stance	입장, 자세		
tribute	감사의 표시, 경의, 헌사, 공물		
surgical	외과의, 수술의		
beam	광선, 빛, 기둥; 활짝 웃다		
tempt	유혹하다, 꾀다, 자극하다		
afflict	괴롭히다, 가하다		
wipe	닦다, 없애다, 지우다		
terminate	끝내다, 끝나다		
ego	자아, 자존심		
wicked	못된, 사악한, 장난기있는		
submerge	잠수하다		
skull	두개골		
landslide	산사태, 압도적인 승리		
abnormal	비정상적인		
elude	(교묘히) 피하다, 빠져나가다		
utmost	최고의, 극도의		
broker	중개인; (협상 등을) 중개하다		
surrender	항복하다, 넘겨주다; 항복, 굴복		
adolescent	청소년; 사춘기의, 청춘의		
subscribe	구독하다		
brand-new	신품의, 아주 새로운		
exclaim	소리치다, 외치다		
garment	의복, 옷		
workaholic	일 중독자; 일에 중독된		
weep	울다, 눈물을 흘리다		
accuse	고발하다, 혐의를 제기하다		
veteran	전문가, 참전용사		
devastate	완전히 파괴하다, 엄청난 충격을 주다		

다음 단어에 해당하는 영어 단어 또는 우리말을 쓰세요.

O____개 X____개

영어	한국어
abnormal	
accuse	
adolescent	
afflict	
beam	
brand-new	
broker	
devastate	
ego	
elude	
exclaim	
garment	
landslide	
skull	
stance	
statesman	
submerge	
subscribe	
surgical	
surrender	
tempt	
terminate	
thrust	
tribute	
utmost	
veteran	
weep	
wicked	
wipe	
workaholic	

한국어	영어
동 (교묘히) 피하다, 빠져나가다	
동 찔러 넣다, 밀다	
형 비정상적인	
명 중개인 동 (협상등을) 중개하다	
명 두개골	
형 최고의, 극도의	
명 산사태, 압도적인 승리	
명 청소년 형 사춘기의, 청춘의	
형 못된, 사악한, 장난기있는	
동 항복하다, 넘겨주다 명 항복	
명 정치인	
동 잠수하다	
동 완전히 파괴하다, 엄청난 충격을 주다	
명 감사의 표시, 경의, 헌사, 공물	
형 외과의, 수술의	
동 구독하다	
동 소리치다, 외치다	
명 입장, 자세	
형 신품의, 아주 새로운	
동 끝내다, 끝나다	
명 의복, 옷	
동 유혹하다, 꾀다, 자극하다	
명 전문가, 참전용사	
명 광선, 빛, 기둥 동 활짝웃다	
동 닦다, 없애다, 지우다	
명 일 중독자 형 일에 중독된	
동 괴롭히다, 가하다	
동 울다, 눈물을 흘리다	
명 자아, 자존심	
동 고발하다, 혐의를 제기하다	

Day 26

| 월 일 |

영어 단어에 해당하는 한국어 뜻을 함께 적으세요.

commemorate	기념하다, 축하하다	commemorate	기념하다
delegate	대표(자); 위임하다, 파견하다		
depiction	묘사, 서술		
cognition	인식, 인지		
confess	자백하다, 고백하다		
arouse	불러일으키다, 깨우다		
cathedral	대성당		
archeology	고고학		
chunk	큰 덩어리, 상당히 많은 양		
dart	가늘고 짧은 화살; 돌진하다		
alleviate	완화하다, 경감하다		
blush	얼굴이 붉어지다; 얼굴이 붉어짐		
confidential	기밀의, 비밀의		
betray	배신하다, 저버리다, 누설하다		
comply	따르다, 순응하다, 준수하다		
barometer	기압계, (여론, 상황 등의) 지표		
blunder	(어리석은) 실수; (어리석은) 실수를 하다		
assassin	암살자		
chatter	수다를 떨다; 수다		
consecutive	연속되는, 연속적인		
constitution	헌법, 구조, 조직, 관행		
anonymous	익명인, 작자 미상의		
cripple	불구로 만들다, 무력하게 만들다		
cemetery	묘지		
deepen	~을 깊게하다, 악화되다		
brisk	빠른, 활발한		
creek	작은 만, 개울, 시내		
conclusive	결정적인, 명확한		
constraint	제약, 제한, 통제		
enlighten	계몽하다, 깨우침을 주다		

다음 단어에 해당하는 영어 단어 또는 우리말을 쓰세요. O____개 X____개

영어	한국어
alleviate	
anonymous	
archeology	
arouse	
assassin	
barometer	
betray	
blunder	
blush	
brisk	
cathedral	
cemetery	
chatter	
chunk	
cognition	
commemorate	
comply	
conclusive	
confess	
confidential	
consecutive	
constitution	
constraint	
creek	
cripple	
dart	
deepen	
delegate	
depiction	
enlighten	

한국어	영어
명 제약, 제한, 통제	
동 기념하다, 축하하다	
형 연속되는, 연속적인	
동 계몽하다, 깨우침을 주다	
동 수다를 떨다 명 수다	
명 대표(자) 동 위임하다, 파견하다	
명 기압계, (여론, 상황 등의) 지표	
형 결정적인, 명확한	
명 암살자	
명 (어리석은) 실수 동 (어리석은) 실수를 하다	
명 묘사, 서술	
동 ~을 깊게하다, 악화되다	
명 헌법, 구조, 조직, 관행	
명 인식, 인지	
동 자백하다, 고백하다	
명 묘지	
형 익명인, 작자 미상의	
명 고고학	
동 불러일으키다, 깨우다	
명 큰 덩어리, 상당히 많은 양	
동 불구로 만들다, 무력하게 만들다	
명 대성당	
형 빠른, 활발한	
동 얼굴이 붉어지다 명 얼굴이 붉어짐	
동 완화하다, 경감하다	
형 기밀의, 비밀의	
명 가늘고 짧은 화살	
명 작은 만, 개울, 시내	
동 따르다, 준수하다	
동 배신하다, 저버리다	

Workbook

Day 27

| 월 일 |

영어 단어에 해당하는 한국어 뜻을 함께 적으세요.

flaw	(사물의) 결함, 결점	flaw	(사물의) 결함, 결점
intrude	침해하다, 방해하다		
drip	(방울 등이) 뚝뚝 떨어지다		
hectic	정신 없이 바쁜, 빡빡한		
insane	미친, 정신 이상의		
elevate	들어올리다, 승격시키다		
fruitless	성과 없는, 보람 없는		
lure	유혹하다, 꾀다; 유혹, 매력		
insulation	절연체, 절연처리, 격리, 고립		
capitalize	대문자로 쓰다, 자본화하다		
inherit	상속하다, 물려받다		
doze	깜빡 잠이 들다, 졸다		
intelligible	(쉽게) 이해할 수 있는		
linger	오래 머물다, 오래 끌다		
fragrance	향기, 향, 향수		
inconsistent	일치하지 않는, 일관성 없는		
glitter	반짝반짝 빛나다, 번들거리다		
inhale	들이마시다		
intervene	개입하다, 끼어들다		
frontier	국경, 변경, 한계		
hygiene	위생, 위생학		
diagnose	진단하다, 밝혀내다		
fling	(거칠게) 내던지다; 내던지기		
flourish	번성하다, 번창하다, 잘 자라다		
flush	붉어지다; 홍조		
homesick	향수에 잠긴, 향수병의		
diplomatic	외교의		
foremost	가장 중요한, 선두의		
spectator	관중, 구경꾼, 목격자		
cannon	대포, 기관포; 대포를 쏘다		

다음 단어에 해당하는 영어 단어 또는 우리말을 쓰세요.

O____개 X____개

영어	한국어
cannon	
capitalize	
diagnose	
diplomatic	
doze	
drip	
elevate	
flaw	
fling	
flourish	
flush	
foremost	
fragrance	
frontier	
fruitless	
glitter	
hectic	
homesick	
hygiene	
inconsistent	
inhale	
inherit	
insane	
insulation	
intelligible	
intervene	
intrude	
linger	
lure	
spectator	

한국어	영어
동 반짝반짝 빛나다	
형 일치하지 않는, 일관성 없는	
명 대포, 기관포 동 대포를 쏘다	
동 침해하다, 방해하다	
명 관중, 구경꾼, 목격자	
명 (사물의) 결함, 결점	
동 들이마시다	
동 개입하다, 끼어들다	
형 정신 없이 바쁜, 빡빡한	
형 가장 중요한, 선두의	
동 (방울 등이) 뚝뚝 떨어지다	
형 미친, 정신 이상의	
명 국경, 변경, 한계	
명 위생, 위생학	
동 들어올리다, 승격시키다	
동 진단하다, 밝혀내다	
형 성과 없는, 보람 없는	
동 (거칠게) 내던지다	
동 상속하다, 물려받다	
동 유혹하다, 꾀다 명 유혹, 매력	
명 향기, 향, 향수	
명 절연체, 절연처리, 격리, 고립	
동 번성하다, 번창하다, 잘 자라다	
동 대문자로 쓰다, 자본화하다	
동 오래 머물다, 오래끌다	
동 붉어지다 명 홍조	
형 (쉽게) 이해할 수 있는	
동 깜빡 잠이 들다, 졸다	
형 외교의	
형 향수에 잠긴, 향수병의	

Workbook

Day 28

| 월 일 |

영어 단어에 해당하는 한국어 뜻을 함께 적으세요.

plunge	감소하다, 뛰어들다; 낙하	plunge	감소하다, 뛰어들다
perish	죽다, 사라지다		
recruit	채용하다, 모집하다; 신입회원		
purify	정화하다, 깨끗이 하다		
prevailing	우세한, 널리 퍼진		
plausible	그럴듯한, 타당한		
interval	(두 사건 사이의) 간격, 중간 휴식시간		
scorn	경멸하다; 경멸, 멸시		
parameter	한도, 매개 변수		
acoustic	청각의, 소리의		
nominate	지명하다, 후보자로 추천하다		
fragment	조각, 파편; 조각나다		
accelerate	속도를 늘리다, 가속화하다		
partial	부분적인, 편파적인		
swell	붓다, 부풀다, 증가하다		
populate	살다, 거주하다, (장소를) 차지하고 있다		
overdue	연체된, 늦어진		
manifest	나타내다, 드러내다		
painkiller	진통제		
lease	임대; 임대하다		
recur	재발하다, 되풀이되다		
reside	거주하다, 살다		
roar	으르렁 거리다, 포효하다		
sphere	구, 하늘, 창공, 영역(권)		
compile	편집하다, 편찬하다, 작성하다		
refraction	굴절, 비뚤어짐, 왜곡		
segregation	분리, 차별		
scheme	계획, 제도; 책략을 꾸미다		
surplus	과잉, 잉여, 흑자; 과잉의		
effectual	효과적인, 유효한		

다음 단어에 해당하는 영어 단어 또는 우리말을 쓰세요.

O____개 X____개

영어	한국어
accelerate	
acoustic	
compile	
effectual	
fragment	
interval	
lease	
manifest	
nominate	
overdue	
painkiller	
parameter	
partial	
perish	
plausible	
plunge	
populate	
prevailing	
purify	
recruit	
recur	
refraction	
reside	
roar	
scheme	
scorn	
segregation	
sphere	
surplus	
swell	

한국어	영어
동 나타내다, 드러내다	
동 감소하다, 뛰어들다 명 낙하	
형 연체된, 늦어진	
동 지명하다, 후보자로 추천하다	
동 살다, 거주하다	
동 죽다, 사라지다	
명 진통제	
동 살다, 거주하다, (장소를) 차지하고 있다	
동 채용하다, 모집하다	
명 임대 동 임대하다	
동 재발하다, 되풀이되다	
동 정화하다, 깨끗이 하다	
형 효과적인, 유효한	
형 우세한, 널리 퍼진	
명 구, 하늘, 창공, 영역(권)	
동 으르렁 거리다, 포효하다	
명 (두 사건 사이의) 간격, 중간 휴식시간	
형 그럴듯한, 타당한	
형 청각의, 소리의	
명 분리, 차별	
동 경멸하다 명 경멸, 멸시	
동 편집하다, 편찬하다, 작성하다	
명 한도, 매개변수	
동 붓다, 부풀다, 증가하다	
명 조각, 파편 동 조각나다	
명 굴절, 비뚤어짐, 왜곡	
동 속도를 늘리다, 가속화하다	
명 계획, 제도 동 책략을 꾸미다	
형 부분적인, 편파적인	
명 과잉, 잉여, 흑자 형 과잉의	

Workbook

Day 29

| 월 일 |

영어 단어에 해당하는 한국어 뜻을 함께 적으세요.

triumph	승리; 이기다, 성공하다	triumph	승리; 이기다
authorize	승인하다, 권한을 부여하다		
tyrant	독재자, 폭군		
byproduct	부산물, 부작용		
phenomenal	경이적인, 경탄스러운		
splinter	파편, 조각; 쪼개지다, 분리되다		
refute	반박하다, 논박하다		
lament	한탄하다, 애도하다; 비탄		
vomit	토하다, 게우다		
magnify	확대하다, 과장하다		
obstruct	방해하다, 막다		
chick	병아리		
nomad	유목민		
invariable	불변의, 일정한		
designate	지정하다, 지명하다; 지명된		
entitle	자격을 주다, 제목을 붙이다		
versatile	다재 다능한, 다용도의, 다목적의		
fusion	융해, 융합		
expire	만기가 되다, 기한이 끝나다		
incline	기울다, 경향이 있다; 경사(면)		
startle	깜짝 놀라게 하다		
terrify	무섭게 하다, 겁먹게 하다		
zealous	열심인, 열성적인		
fed up with	~에 싫증난, ~에 질린		
unify	통합(통일) 하다		
recede	물러나다, 감소하다		
pillar	기둥, (기둥 모양의) 기념비		
enlist	참여하다, 입대하다, 징집하다		
unanimous	만장일치의, 이구동성의		
pirate	해적; 해적 행위를 하다, 약탈하다		

다음 단어에 해당하는 영어 단어 또는 우리말을 쓰세요.

O____개 X____개

영어	한국어
authorize	
byproduct	
chick	
designate	
enlist	
entitle	
expire	
fed up with	
fusion	
incline	
invariable	
lament	
magnify	
nomad	
obstruct	
phenomenal	
pillar	
pirate	
recede	
refute	
splinter	
startle	
terrify	
triumph	
tyrant	
unanimous	
unify	
versatile	
vomit	
zealous	

한국어	영어
동 만기가 되다, 기한이 끝나다	
명 독재자, 폭군	
명 융해, 융합	
동 승인하다, 권한을 부여하다	
명 해적 동 해적 행위를 하다, 약탈하다	
동 자격을 주다, 제목을 붙이다	
동 지정하다, 지명하다 형 지명된	
형 다재 다능한, 다용도의, 다목적의	
명 승리 동 이기다, 성공하다	
동 참여하다, 입대하다, 징집하다	
명 부산물, 부작용	
동 기울다, 경향이 있다	
~에 싫증난, ~에 질린	
형 경이적인, 경탄스러운	
명 파편, 조각 동 쪼개지다	
형 열심인, 열성적인	
형 불변의, 일정한	
동 한탄하다, 애도하다 명 비탄	
동 통합(통일) 하다	
동 반박하다, 논박하다	
명 유목민	
동 깜짝 놀라게 하다	
동 토하다, 게우다	
명 병아리	
동 확대하다, 과장하다	
동 무섭게 하다, 겁먹게 하다	
동 방해하다, 막다	
형 만장일치의, 이구동성의	
동 물러나다, 감소하다	
명 기둥, (기둥 모양의) 기념비	

Day 30

| 월 일 |

영어 단어에 해당하는 한국어 뜻을 함께 적으세요.

torture	고문; 고문하다, 지독히 괴롭히다	torture	고문
dismay	실망, 경악; 경악하게 만들다		
procession	행진, 행렬		
astronomical	천문학의, 천문학적인, 어마어마한		
undertake	떠맡다, 착수하다, 약속하다		
in terms of	~면에서, ~에 관하여		
vow	맹세; 맹세하다, 다짐하다		
anecdote	일화, 비사		
nonverbal	말을 사용하지 않는, 말이 서투른		
patriotic	애국적인		
ignite	불이 붙다, 점화하다		
preservative	방부제		
circulate	순환하다, (소문 등이) 유포되다		
fume	(화가 나서) 씩씩대다; 연기, 화		
captive	포로가 된; 포로		
groan	신음하다, 괴로워하다		
counterattack	역습, 반격; 역습, 반격하다		
dusk	황혼, 땅거미		
utterance	발언, 말씨		
trim	다듬다, 잘라내다		
account	계좌, 장부, 설명		
standardize	표준화하다		
subdue	진압하다, (감정을) 가라앉히다		
censorship	검열		
majestic	장엄한, 위풍당당한		
dictator	독재자		
overtake	추월하다, 앞지르다		
intimidate	겁을 주다, 위협하다		
tactics	전술, 전략		
unscrupulous	부도덕한, 파렴치한		

다음 단어에 해당하는 영어 단어 또는 우리말을 쓰세요.

○___개 ×___개

영어	한국어
account	
anecdote	
astronomical	
captive	
censorship	
counterattack	
dictator	
dismay	
dusk	
fume	
groan	
ignite	
in terms of	
circulate	
intimidate	
majestic	
nonverbal	
overtake	
patriotic	
preservative	
procession	
standardize	
subdue	
tactics	
torture	
trim	
undertake	
unscrupulous	
utterance	
vow	

한국어	영어
명 역습, 반격 동 역습, 반격하다	
명 고문 동 고문하다, 지독히 괴롭히다	
동 신음하다, 괴로워하다	
명 실망, 경악 동 경악하게 만들다	
명 발언, 말씨	
명 황혼, 땅거미	
명 행진, 행렬	
동 다듬다, 잘라내다	
형 천문학의, 천문학적인, 어마어마한	
형 포로가 된 명 포로	
동 표준화하다	
명 계좌, 장부, 설명	
동 떠맡다, 착수하다, 약속하다	
명 검열	
명 맹세 동 맹세하다, 다짐하다	
~면에서, ~에 관하여	
동 진압하다, (감정을) 가라앉히다	
명 일화, 비사	
형 장엄한, 위풍당당한	
명 방부제	
명 독재자	
형 말을 사용하지 않는, 말이 서투른	
동 추월하다, 앞지르다	
동 불이 붙다, 점화하다	
동 겁을 주다, 위협하다	
형 애국적인	
명 전술, 전략	
동 (화가 나서)씩씩대다 명 연기, 화	
동 순환하다, (소문 등이) 유포되다	
형 부도덕한, 파렴치한	